Dedication

To Alex, for your unfailing support
for each of my projects.

DIY Watercolor Jungle

Easy watercolor painting techniques
for tropical foliage and flowers

Marie Boudon

DAVID & CHARLES

www.davidandcharles.com

Contents

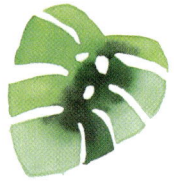

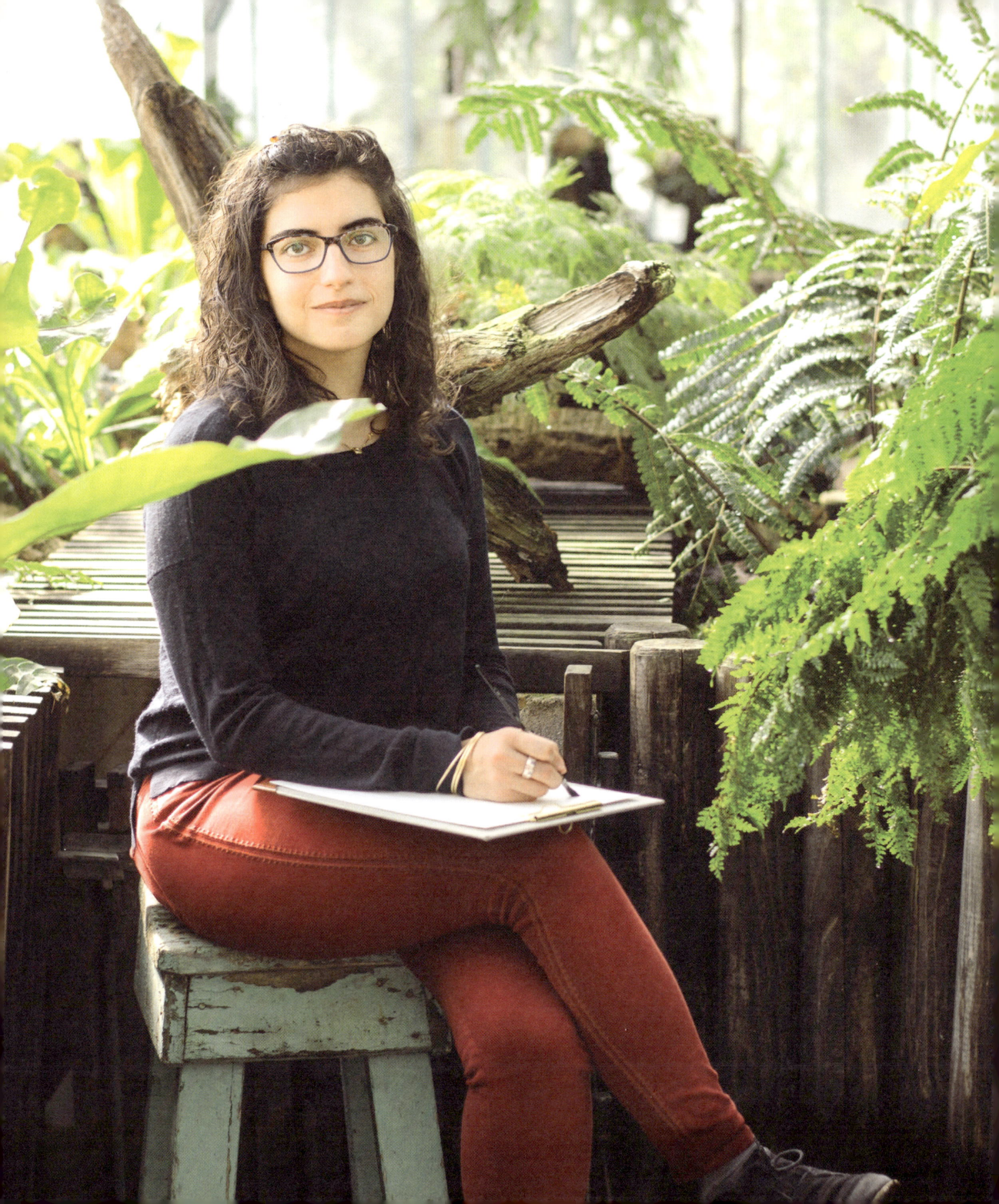

Foreword

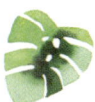

Want to find a relaxing, creative moment for yourself in your busy everyday life? Then watercolor painting is made for you. I'm delighted that more and more people are discovering a simple, fun and colorful way of tackling this medium. If you're not already, then you're soon going to find yourself hooked on watching the pigments and water merge together, believe me!

I've loved exploring the vivid colors and unusual shapes of tropical plants for this new work. Despite rather complex terminology at times, I've broken down each action as much as possible to help you paint in a spontaneous manner, without need of a pencil or being able to draw.

Gain confidence through the first chapter on the basic techniques that you will go on to use constantly. From majestic palm trees to the little missionary plant in your living room, in the chapters that follow, you'll paint perfect compositions for a card or poster. I will also explain my method for composition and framing, as well as ideas for how you can progress to a more advanced stage and put together your own jungle creations.

I hope you'll have as much fun as me with these luxurious plants. I can't wait to see your creations, so tag me on Instagram, using the hashtag #jungleaquarellemarie. See you soon.

Marie

Follow me :

Website - tribulationsdemarie.com
Instagram - @tribulationsdemarie
Email - contact@tribulationsdemarie.com

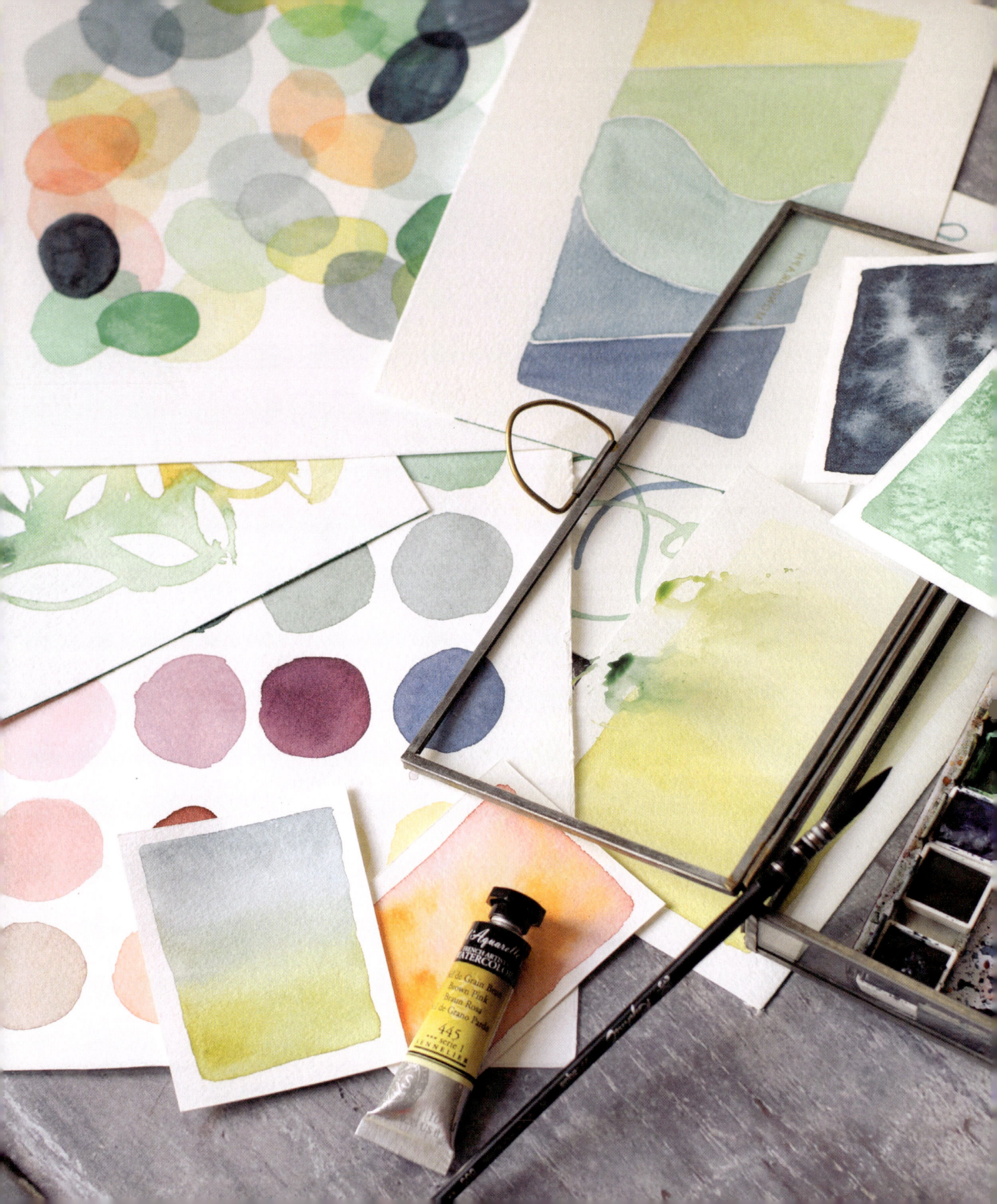

CHAPTER 01

Basic techniques

TO PRODUCE THE PAINTINGS IN THIS BOOK, YOU'RE GOING TO NEED ALL THE TECHNIQUES SHOWN IN THIS CHAPTER. I USED A SET OF SENNELIER "LA PETITE AQUARELLE" WATERCOLORS TO SHOW YOU THAT A BEGINNERS' KIT IS ENOUGH FOR YOU TO GET GREAT RESULTS. ALSO DISCOVER MY COMPLETE METHOD FOR PUTTING TOGETHER A COMPOSITION FROM START TO FINISH.

ESSENTIAL
materials

TO GET YOU STARTED, A SMALL BUDGET IS ENOUGH TO ASSEMBLE A GOOD QUALITY KIT THAT IS EASY TO WORK WITH AND STORE, ODOR-FREE AND NON-STAINING.

As watercolor paints are water-based, you will not need to use as much actual paint as you would, for example, with gouache, which means your kit is sure to last a long time. I recommend you buy equipment from the aquarelleetpinceaux.com website, which is my favorite store. You can easily find links to the following suggestions on my website at tribulationsdemarie.com.

A SET OF TWELVE HALF-PANS

There are two qualities of watercolor paints, available in two formats.

Quality : fine or extra-fine

It doesn't really matter which brand you choose. The main difference is the pigment concentration and quality of binding agents in the paint. For beginners, fine quality is sufficient and cheaper. I recommend the set of twelve fine colors in the Sennelier "La Petite Aquarelle" range (see opposite). The selection of colors is very interesting, particularly the pink, which is not found much in other similar sets. You can easily add pans to the center of the box in the space designed for this purpose, and this range does not contain any products of animal origin.

Format : pans or tubes

To start with, I recommend you use pans. This is the same paint as in a tube, but compressed into a small cube. If you are a beginner, this format will prevent you using watercolor like gouache, without stopping you from loading up your brush with pigment if you so wish.

A PAINTBRUSH

I recommend getting a single brush known as a pointed wash brush or mop brush, which holds water well. It lets you cover large areas fast, make expressive marks, but also add very fine details. To get started, choose a number 3/0 brush from the Raphael 805 range. This easy-to-handle brush has synthetic fibers and is the one used throughout this book.

There are two reasons why I do not recommend you use a brush with a built-in reservoir that holds a little water. While it may be ideal for adding little watercolor touches to a sketch when out and about, the quality of the brush is markedly inferior to that of a traditional brush. In addition, a reservoir brush requires you to combine two movements: pressing down to get the water to come out while tracing a stroke at the same time. For the type of painting explored in this book, you will get better results with a standard brush such as the one suggested above.

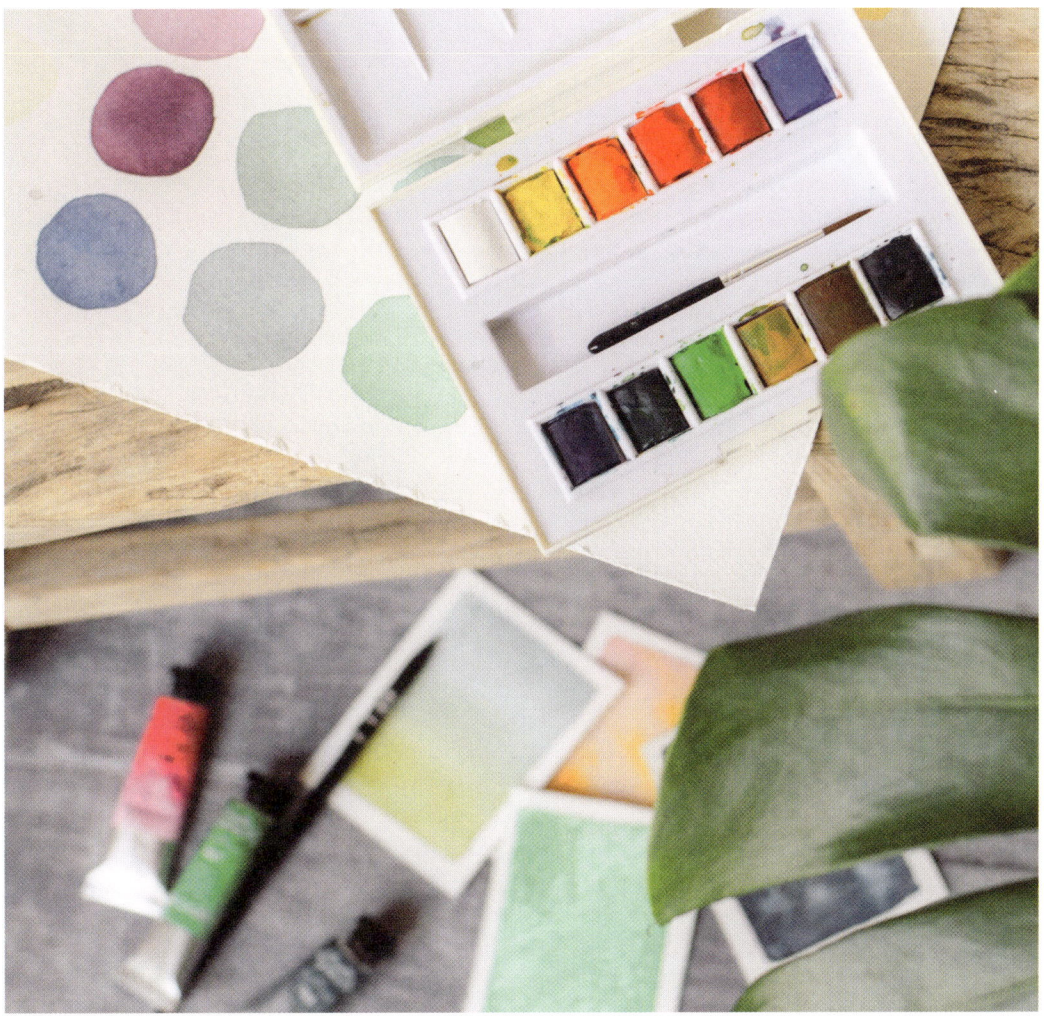

To take care of your brush, you just need to rinse it in clear water then squeeze it out gently on a clean cloth once you've finished your painting session. Ideally, you should hang it upside down so the water does not soak into the wood and risk cracking it. In practice, I leave it to dry horizontally on the cloth. When you rinse it in the jar, try not to scrape the bottom, do not leave it standing in water and do not try to remove the metal band, or ferrule, attaching the fibers to the handle.

PAPER

Watercolor paper is thick, so as to absorb water well. The standard weight, or "grammage", is 300 gsm (grams per square meter) [or 140 lb - pounds per ream]. You will have various characteristics to choose from in this range. Here are my recommendations as a guide.

Composition : cotton or cellulose fibers

Cellulose paper is more affordable than cotton paper and is perfect for beginners. However, as cotton fibers are longer, they dry more slowly than cellulose paper, making it easier to work "in the wet".

Format : loose sheet, pad or book

The most economical is the large format loose sheet. I personally buy 56 x 76cm (22 x 30in) sheets, then cut as I please. I do not recommend you buy a book as that can hold you up if you spoil a page. A pad is a good alternative as it is easy to tidy away and often gummed on one or more sides to prevent the paper getting crinkled. I recommend A4 (8¼ x 11½in) format at least - don't be afraid to go large. I first began with a postcard-sized format and it was when I increased the size of my paper that I noticed real progress.

Texture : fine, satin or rough grain

For the type of painting shown in this book, the paper texture I recommend is fine grain. This is a grain somewhere between satin grain (smooth) and rough grain, which is also known as torchon grain (coarsely textured). You generally only use the front of a sheet. The texture of the back is not the same quality, but you may use it for doing rough drafts. With some top-of-the-range paper made from 100% cotton, such as the Sennelier paper used for this book, there is less difference in quality between the two sides.

Recommended papers

Ideal for beginners:
• Hahnemühle Harmony A4 (8¼ x 11½in) pad (cellulose)
• Hahnemühle Moulin du Coq Le Rouge 24 x 32cm (9½ x 12½in) 100-page pad (cellulose)

Getting more advanced:
• Sennelier 30 x 30cm (12 x 12in) pad (cotton)
• Saunders Waterford extra-white 56 x 76cm (22 x 30in) sheets (cotton)
• Fabriano Artistico extra-white 56 x 76cm (22 x 30in) sheets (cotton)

OTHER ACCESSORIES

You then just need a water jar and cloth and you're ready to start! If you don't have a mixing palette, use a white plate.

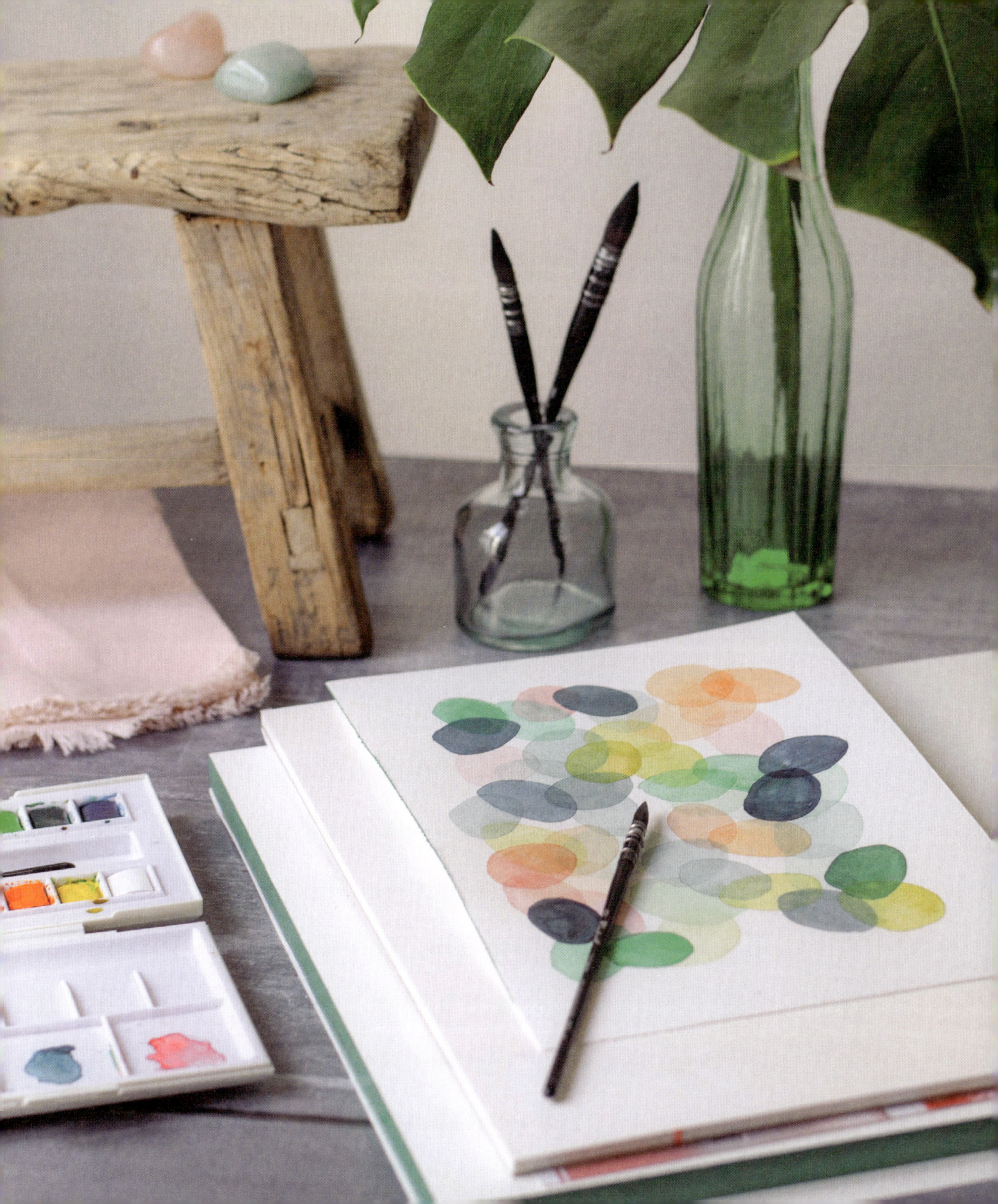

EXTRA-FINE

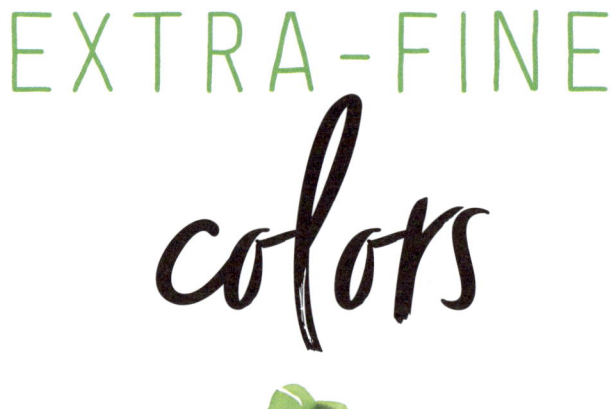

colors

IF YOU ALREADY HAVE SOME EXPERIENCE OF WATERCOLOR PAINTING OR WANT TO USE THE BEST QUALITY AVAILABLE, HERE ARE MY FAVORITE COLORS IN THE SENNELIER EXTRA-FINE RANGE FOR THE JUNGLE THEME.

Naturally, once you've made thorough use of your small fine watercolor palette, you will have your own favorites but will also want more colors. I recommend you then supplement or replace empty pans with extra-fine quality watercolors. The colors are smoother, more luminous and more pigmented. Personally, I like buying my favorite mixes instead of remaking them, so I can paint faster. I opt for the tube format because it is more economical. I fill a paint pan then let it dry at least overnight, so my brush does not pick up too much paint. On page 23, I explain how to obtain some of these colors and the mixes referred to most frequently in this book, made using the Sennelier "La Petite Aquarelle" kit.

  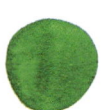  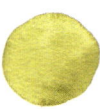 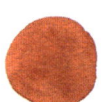 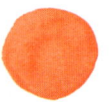 

Greenish Umber   Emerald Green   Hooker's Green   Olive Green   Brown Green   Alizarin Crimson   French Vermilion   Burnt Sienna

 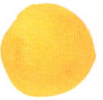 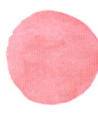 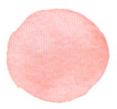 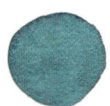 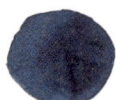 

Red Orange   Indian Yellow   Opera Rose   Carmine   Phthalo-cyanine Turquoise   Indigo   Raw Sepia

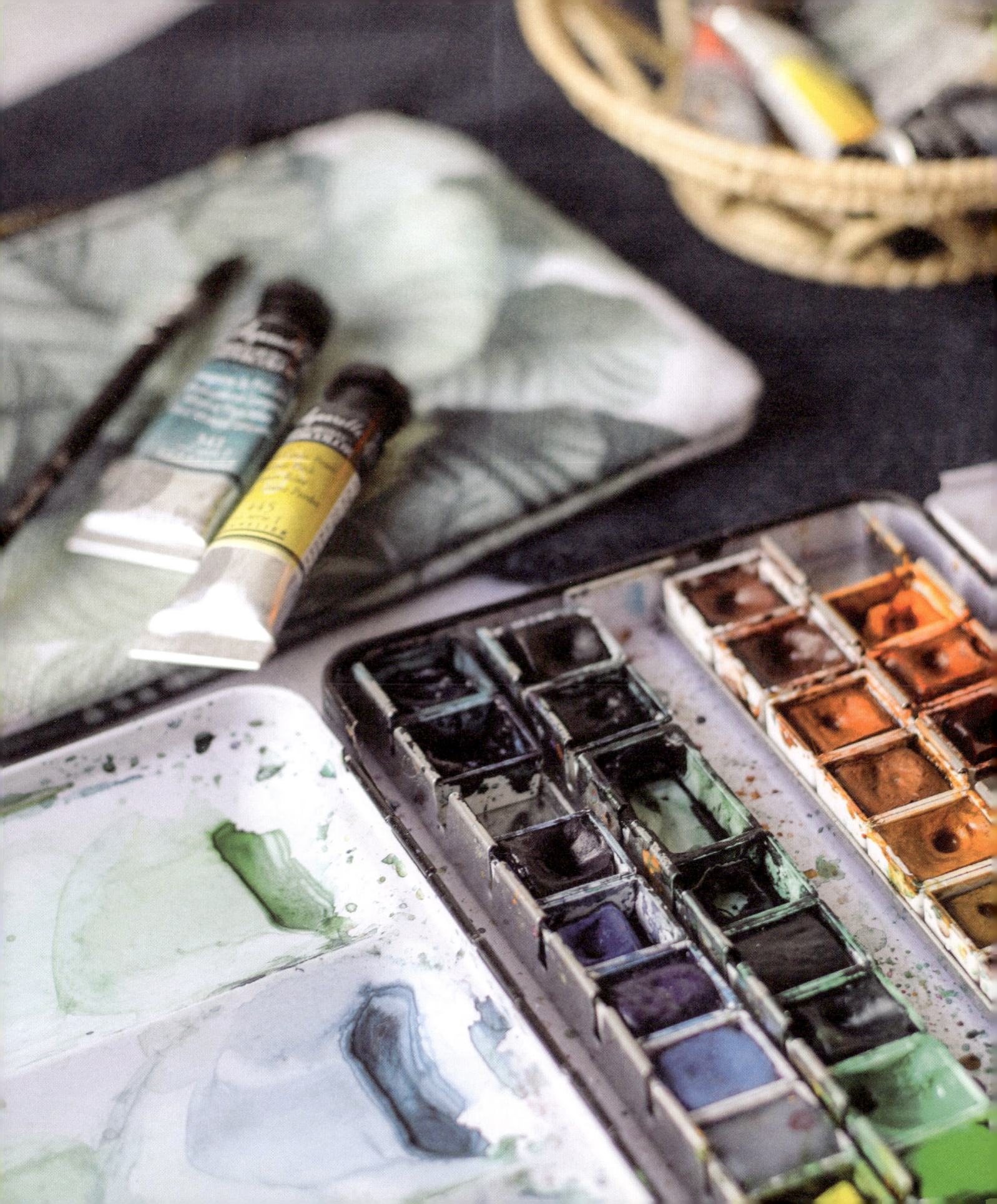

CREATING A
color chart

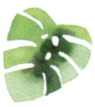

TO START DISCOVERING MORE ABOUT YOUR PALETTE, I SUGGEST YOU CREATE YOUR OWN COLOR CHART. THIS WILL HELP YOU GET TO GRIPS WITH USING THE RIGHT AMOUNT OF WATER AND FAMILIARIZE YOURSELF WITH THE COLORS. FOR EACH PAN, MAKE THREE COLUMNS WITH DIFFERENT CONCENTRATIONS OF PIGMENT: STRONG, MEDIUM AND WEAK.

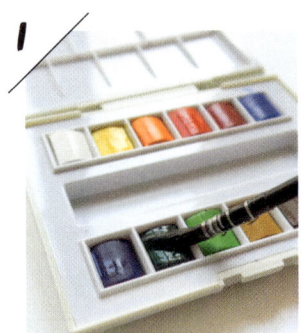
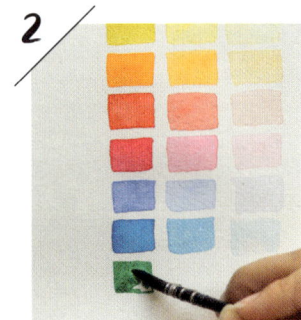
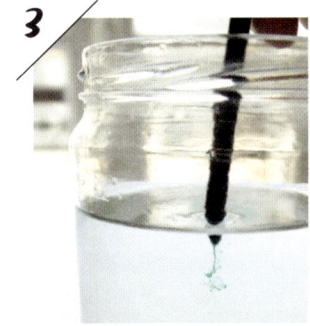
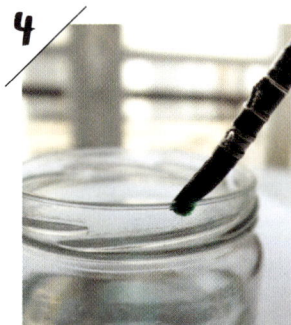

1. Sweep a wet brush over a pan (in this case Deep Green) several times, briskly, without hesitation, to load it with as much pigment as possible but without scraping the pan.

2. Then paint this color in the first column. Here I've chosen to do rectangles.

3. Dip the tip of your brush in the water as shown. The aim is to reduce the amount of pigment without rinsing it off completely. Do not stir the brush.

4. Remove excess water against the rim of the jar then paint a rectangle in the second column. Repeat stages 3 and 4 for the last rectangle. Continue your color chart with each of the colors in your palette.

THE TWELVE COLORS IN THE SENNELIER "LA PETITE AQUARELLE" SET

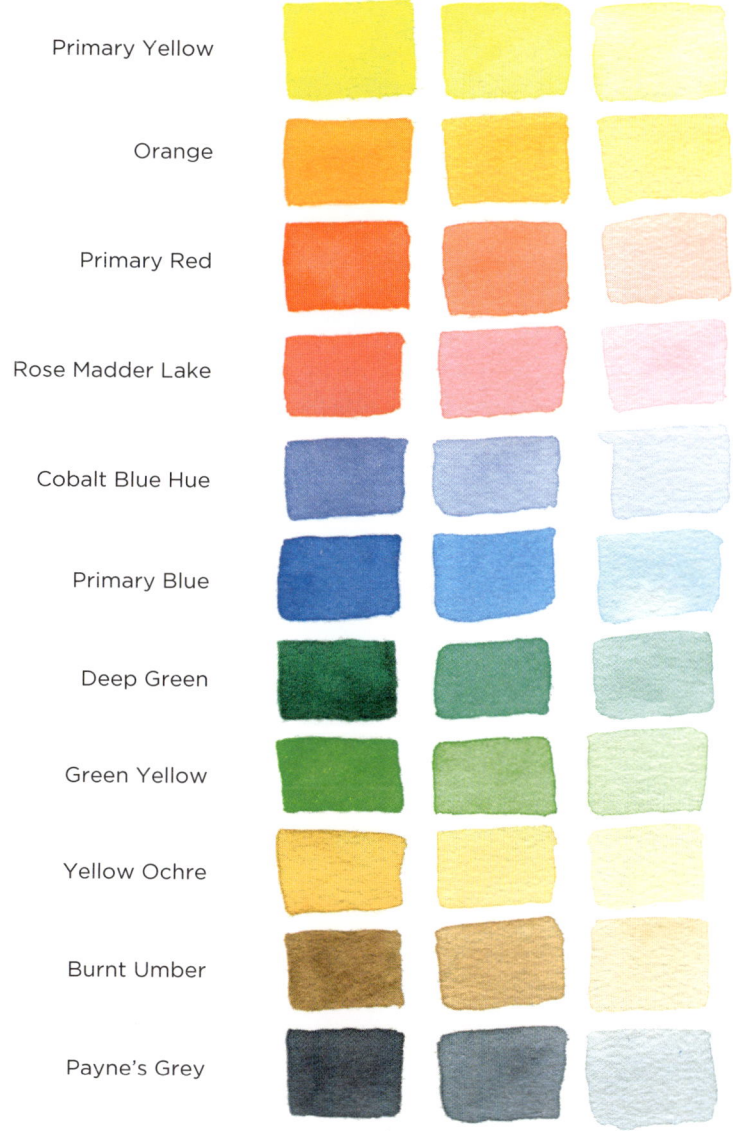

Primary Yellow

Orange

Primary Red

Rose Madder Lake

Cobalt Blue Hue

Primary Blue

Deep Green

Green Yellow

Yellow Ochre

Burnt Umber

Payne's Grey

Titanium White (not shown)

This exercise is not as easy as it appears. Take your time getting the precise proportions. If you have rinsed your brush too much and two rectangles look alike, try to add pigment by tapping gently with your brush. Apart from light colors like yellow, it is possible to obtain three different concentrations. I have not shown white as it is a color I do not use. With watercolors, the paper and water act as white.

WATER
usage

THE PREVIOUS EXERCISE DEMONSTRATED HOW THE AMOUNT
OF WATER AFFECTS THE COLOR. BUT HOW MUCH SOLUTION
SHOULD YOU APPLY TO THE PAPER? WITH PRACTICE, YOU
WILL OF COURSE LEARN TO JUDGE WHETHER YOUR MIX IS TOO
LIQUID OR TOO DRY. I'VE EXPLAINED IT HERE TO HELP YOU.

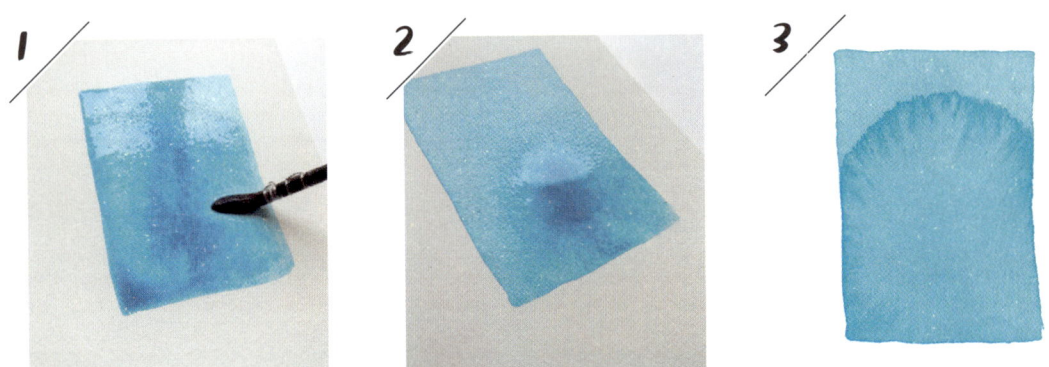

As you can see in picture 1, I've just applied a lot of liquid to the sheet of paper. As a result, it is not drying evenly. Generally, it starts at the edges (picture 2). There is still a damp area, whereas the rest is already almost dry. The area where there appears to be surplus water pushes the pigment outwards, creating a darker fringe of concentrated pigment. Once it is all dry (picture 3), the result is what we call a halo effect. Most of the time, we avoid obtaining this effect by controlling the amount of water applied to the paper.

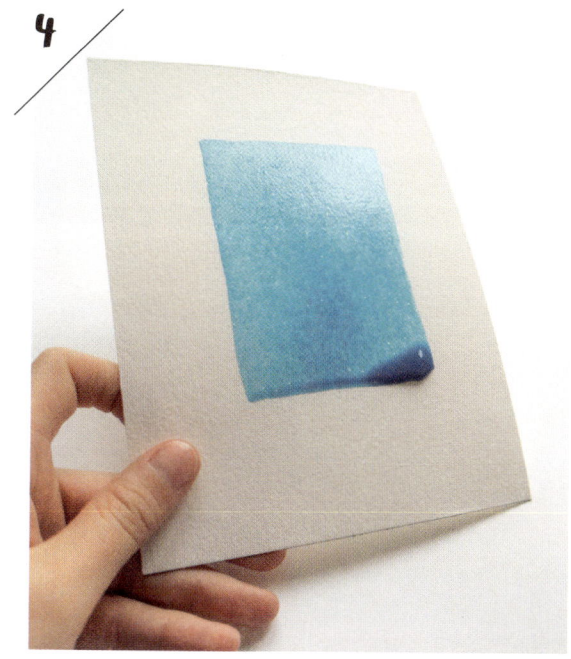

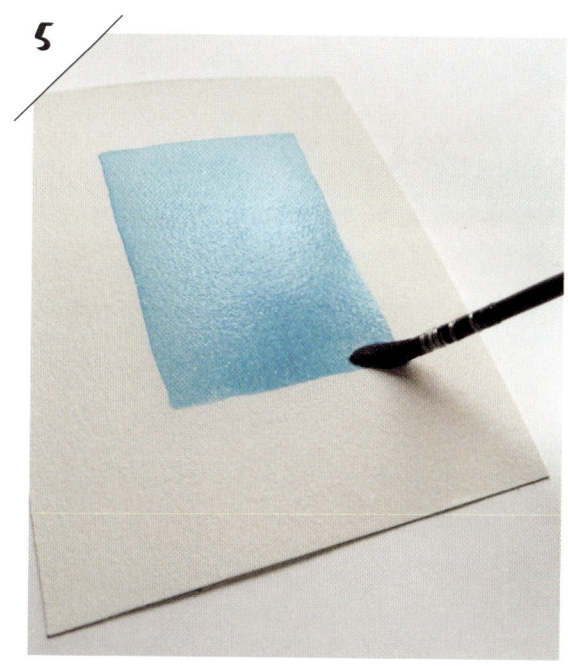

How do you know how much water to apply for an even result? There's a simple technique that consists of just tilting the sheet to one side. If a bead of water forms at the bottom, it means there is too much liquid (picture 4). This surplus just needs to be removed using a dry brush. Rinse your brush well, squeeze it on a cloth then gently mop up this bead of water (picture 5). The result will be even, as in picture 6. Also look closely at the appearance of the blue area when there is too much water (picture 1) and the right amount of water (picture 5). You are seeking a wet but not too sparkling look, which can be seen by tilting the paper.

Over time, you will gain a more intuitive understanding of how much solution (mixture of paint and water) to apply to your paper. And practice is the only solution!

MIXING
colors

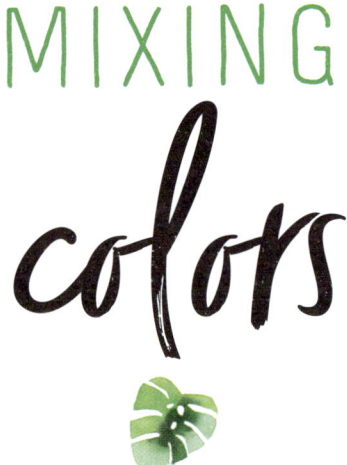

YOU CAN OBTAIN THOUSANDS OF SHADES FROM TWELVE COLORS. HERE I SHOW YOU HOW TO CREATE A MIX EASILY AND PROVIDE THE KEY TO OBTAINING INTERESTING COLORS.

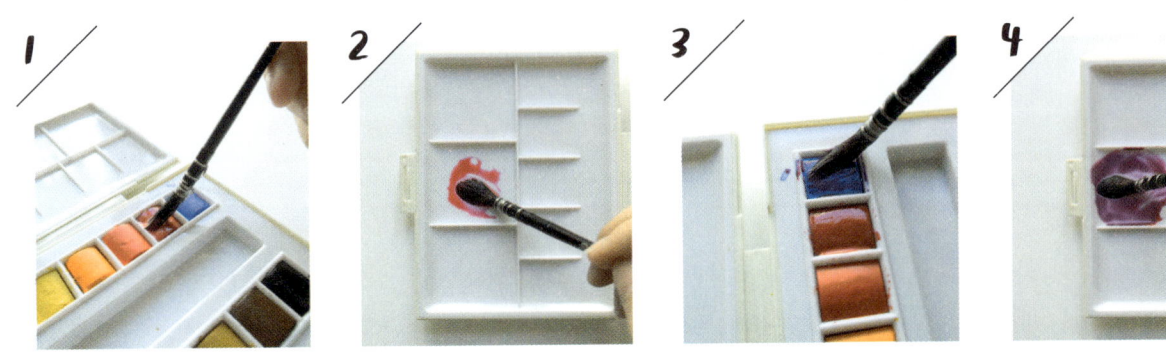

1. Sweep a wet paintbrush over the color of your choice (here I used the Rose Madder Lake). There is no point in loading up the brush with as much pigment as possible, as it is better to proceed with small touches.

2. Transfer the color to the mixing palette. Some colors are highly pigmented, as you will have noticed when making your color chart. Your mixes will not necessarily be made of two colors in strictly equal proportions.

3. Then immediately get some of another color, here it is the Cobalt Blue Hue. It does not bother me if the colors mix together on the surface of the pans. If I need a pure color for a mix, I rinse my brush, sweep it over the dirty pan and then rinse the brush again.

4. Transfer the second color to your mixing palette, on top of the first, and mix them together. Add water or other colors to get the desired shade. Then apply the color to the paper.

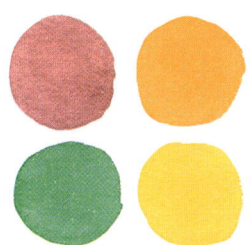

CREATING NEW COLORS

Mix two of three colors together and observe the result. Even if a mix has dried out, you can still reuse it by adding water. If you need to clean your mixing palette, hold it under running water and gently rub it with the brush. Speaking personally, I rarely clean my palette as I have marked out a separate area for warm colors and another for cool colors.

LIGHTEN

To create lighter colors, you just need to add water to your mix. Do this gradually, starting with a little water and adding more if needed. When you're just beginning, you tend to not use enough water. And yet by using light and dark tones, you can create the most beautiful contrasts.

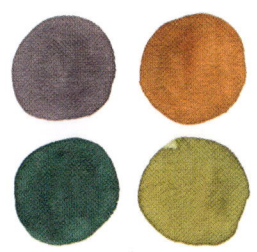

DARKEN

To darken a color, you can add black or grey, depending on what you have on your palette. You can also increase the concentration of pigment in your mix (less water).

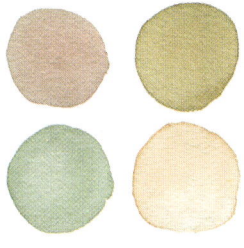

DESATURATE

The colors in your palette are generally very vivid. But if you only use vivid colors, the result risks being garish and not particularly elegant. Feel free to desaturate your colors, that is to say make them a little duller. To do this, take the color that you want to desaturate and then add a little of its complementary color. As a reminder, complementary colors are the ones that are opposite each other on the color wheel, for example, purple and yellow. If you want to desaturate an orangy red, add a little blue-green.

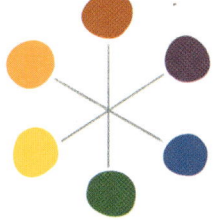

EXPERIMENT

I encourage you to experiment with the mixes for yourself. Test them out and paint colored rounds side by side. Try to obtain darker or lighter colors and with varying degrees of brightness and vividness. Vary the concentrations between two different pigments: 50/50, 70/30, 10/90, etc. You can try to replicate the colors below, all obtained using the twelve-color "La Petite Aquarelle" set from Sennelier.

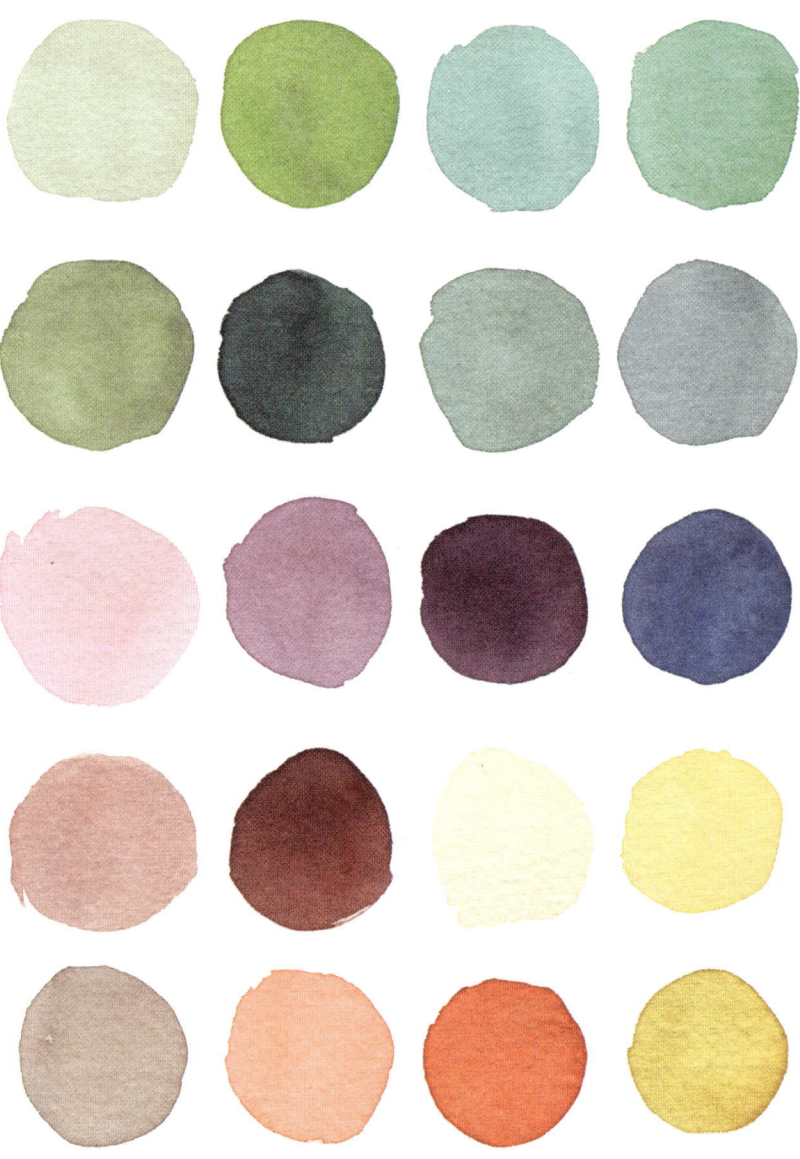

USEFUL MIXES

In the demonstrations shown in this book, I use pure extra-fine colors. There is no need to buy exactly the same colors as me. Use your own to get similar shades. I have given you a suggested guide below for approximating my colors, but you may possibly find different combinations that produce the same result. Make sure you are not restricted by the materials available to you and make the most of them to explore further!

FINE COLOR MIXES TO OBTAIN THE EQUIVALENT OF EXTRA-FINE COLORS

 Greenish Umber = Deep Green + Yellow Ochre + Payne's Grey

 Olive Green = Green Yellow + Yellow Ochre + Burnt Umber

 Emerald Green = Primary Blue + Green Yellow + Titanium White

 Brown Green = Green Yellow + Yellow Ochre

 Hooker's Green = Deep Green + Yellow Ochre

 Alizarin Crimson = Primary Red + Burnt Umber + a little Payne's Grey + Orange

OTHER USEFUL MIXES

 Dark or diluted blue-green (fine quality) = Deep Green + Burnt Umber
or
 Phthalocyanine Turquoise + Greenish Umber (extra-fine) Add water to dilute.

 Cool pink (fine quality) = Rose Madder Lake + Primary Red + Cobalt Blue Hue
or
Carmine + Indigo (extra-fine)

 Peach (fine quality) = Rose Madder Lake + Burnt Umber + Orange
or
Carmine + Burnt Sienna (extra-fine)

 Light green (fine quality) = Green Yellow + Cobalt Blue Hue
or
Olive Green + Emerald Green (extra-fine)

JUNGLE
palettes

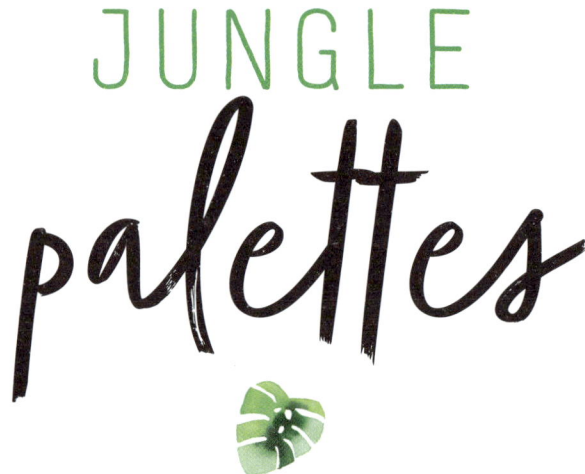

CREATING A JUNGLE-THEMED PALETTE IS NOT SO EASY. THE AIM IS TO AVOID GARISH GREENS COMBINED WITH VIVID COLORS, SO THE RESULT IS ELEGANT. FOR EACH PALETTE, AUTOMATICALLY TRY TO COMBINE DARK, LIGHT AND MIDTONE SHADES.

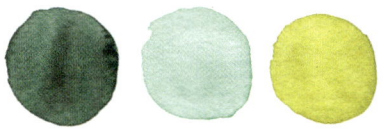

This is my favorite combination of colors, which you will see on numerous occasions throughout this book. I select various shades of green: a yellowish green and blue-green but avoiding "pure" green. Here I used: Greenish Umber, Emerald Green and Brown Green (extra-fine colors from Sennelier).

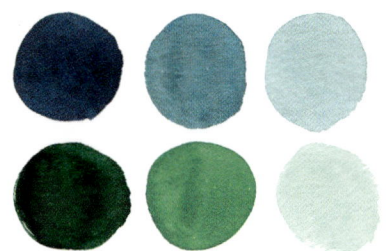

MONOCHROMATIC COLOR SCHEME

Cool monochromatic tones (blue and blue-green) form an elegant combination for a jungle theme. Exotic plants can be visually complex, so using just one color makes it easier to interpret your creation.

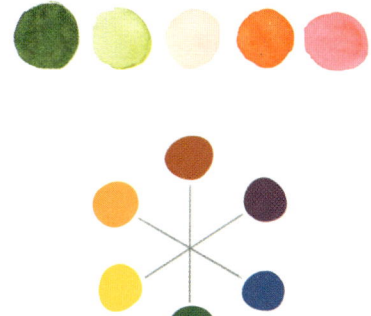

COMPLEMENTARY COLORS

In general, a simple solution for putting together a palette is to use complementary colors, i.e. those positioned on opposite sides of the color wheel from one another.

"Jungle" palettes almost automatically contain a green shade. Red is its complementary color. You have two options:
• Green verging on yellow + pinkish red verging on purple
• Green verging on blue + red verging on orange (French Vermilion)

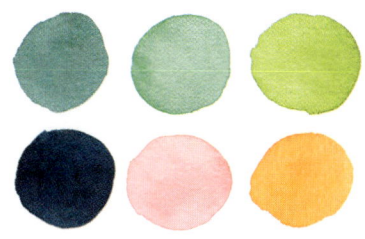

COMPLEMENTARY DUOS

For a more complex palette, you can combine two pairs of complementary colors. Here we've got green + pink (a tinge of red) and blue + orange. I particularly like this palette which I have used throughout this first chapter. When you use palettes with a lot of colors, as here, make sure they do not all have the same level of saturation (see page 21). Here the two blues are desaturated in comparison with the other colors.

ANALOGOUS COLORS

Another solution for getting inspiration is to select a set of colors that are near one another on the color wheel: analogous colors like, in this case, green, yellow and orange. In any event, take artistic liberty in adapting palettes as you wish. There are no hard and fast rules, these are just suggestions that work well.

MASTERING
transparency

ONE CHARACTERISTIC OF WATERCOLOR IS THAT IT IS
INFINITELY MORE TRANSPARENT THAN ANY OTHER MEDIUM.
LEARN TO USE LAYERING TO GIVE THE EFFECT OF DEPTH.

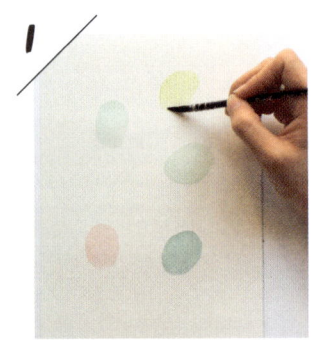

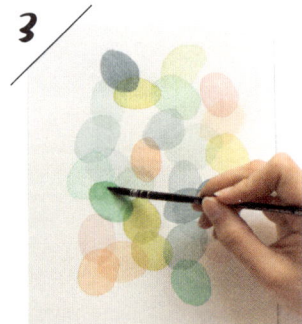
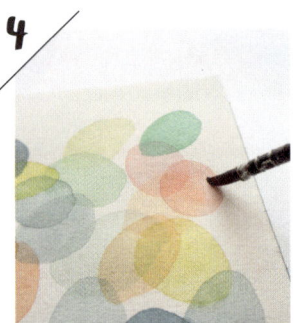

1. Start this exercise by painting several circles in a light color. To get a neat result and avoid smudges, you need to work as in the picture seqence above, increasing the concentration of pigment as you increase the number of layers.

2. Wait until the first layer is properly dry before moving on to the next. Use a blow-dryer to speed up the process. Don't use a large amount of pigment straight away, but do a second layer that is not very concentrated.

3. Even if the paint seems dry, wait a few seconds longer. The paper may, in fact, be dry on the surface but still damp within.

4. Continue adding one layer after another, gradually increasing the pigment concentration. I've opted for the "Complementary Duos" palette shown on page 25.

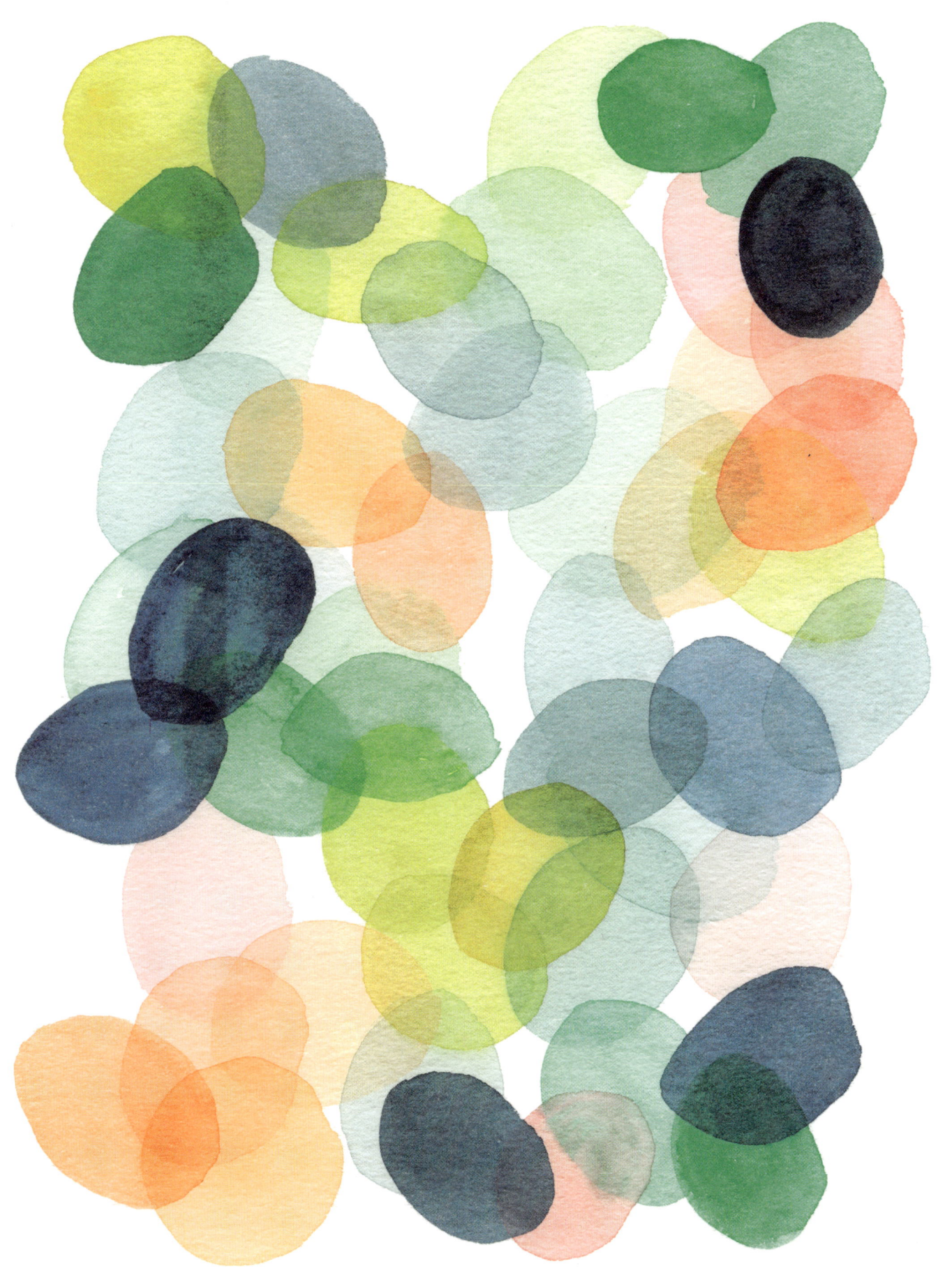

WORKING
in the wet

WORKING "IN THE WET" IS AN ESSENTIAL WATERCOLOR TECHNIQUE. WHILE THE PAPER IS STILL WET, YOU WILL CREATE BEAUTIFUL EFFECTS. THESE TECHNIQUES WILL BE THE ONES USED MOST IN THIS BOOK.

Result when dry

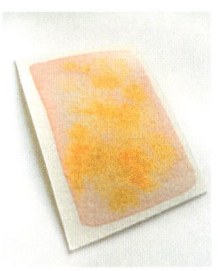

EXERCISE 1 - WET-IN-WET

Take an area of color that is still wet (here it's pink) and add pigments of a second color (here it's orange) by tapping the brush gently. You are applying wet pigment to a wet area. The pigment will disperse and create beautiful random effects. It is important to just tap and not do large strokes. Leave it to work by itself. It's very tempting to move the pigment yourself but if you do that, you will end up with a uniform appearance and the effect will be less interesting.

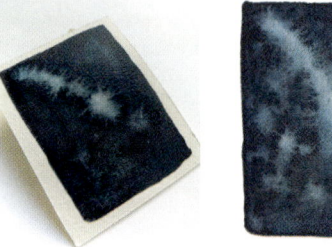
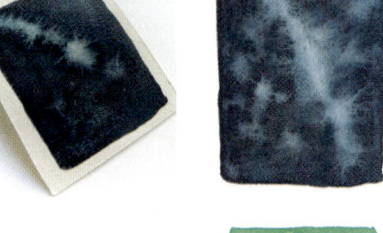

Rinse your brush and apply clear water over an almost-dry dark colored area (drier than in the previous example). The water will repel the pigment. Remove any surplus water with a dry brush if necessary.

EXERCISE 2 - SALT

Sprinkle salt over an area that is still really wet. The technique works best with coarse salt crystals or fleur de sel. Wait until everything is dry before removing the salt crystals and observing the formation of star patterns.

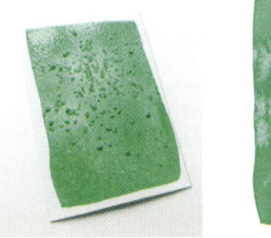
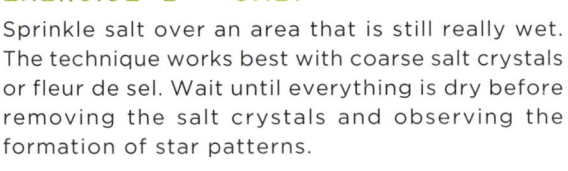

EXERCISE 3 – GRADATION EFFECT

Working "in the wet" also lets you create lovely gradation effects. I use this technique very often in my work, for example to paint large leaves.

1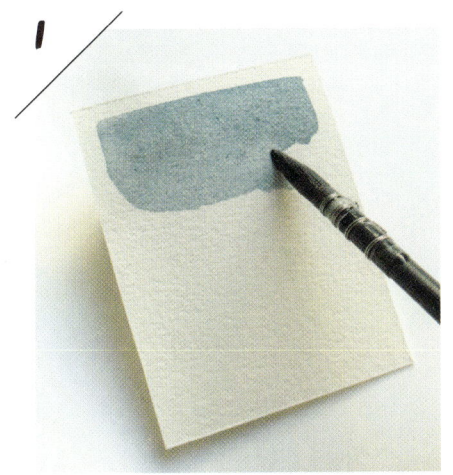

Start by painting an area using an initial color. Work fast as everything has to stay wet to get an even result.

2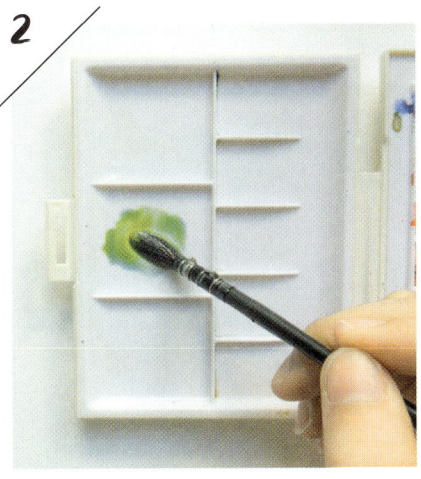

In your palette, mix a second color with the first one. It is important not to forget this stage so the color gradient is gentle.

3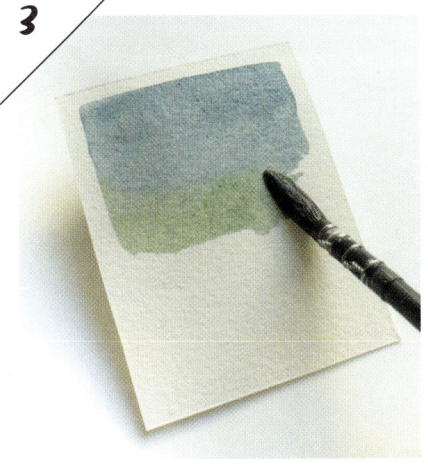

Continue painting with the mix obtained. Tilt your sheet slightly to ensure any surplus solution runs to the bottom of the painted area so you can absorb the water as you paint and ensure the work dries without any halo effect.

4

Finish by using just the second color. When you reach the bottom, make sure to remove any surplus solution if necessary, using a brush that has been rinsed and wiped dry.

Note

You can use this technique to create a gradation effect with one color and water, sometimes called a graduated wash. This procedure will be used on page 149 for painting shadows.

EXERCISE 4

The aim of this exercise is to get you to work fast using the wet-in-wet technique. You're going to paint little rounded lozenge shapes all over the page. Start with an initial color (here it's pink), which you will prepare on your mixing palette. Then add a second color to create a mix. Always put your colors in the same spot on the palette to facilitate the color gradient effects as in exercise 3. Add to this mix as the work progresses: a bit of color no. 2, a little water, move on to a third color, and so on. Do not prepare too much solution in advance. It doesn't matter if it's not perfect as the aim is for everything to stay wet as long as possible so lovely gradation effects and blends can form. This exercise forces you to just let go.

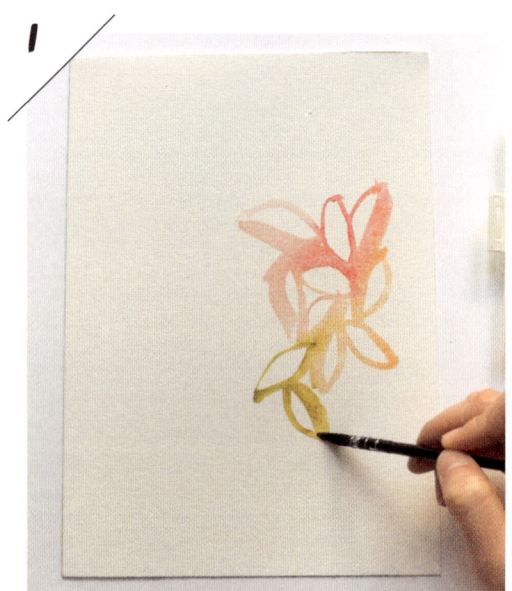 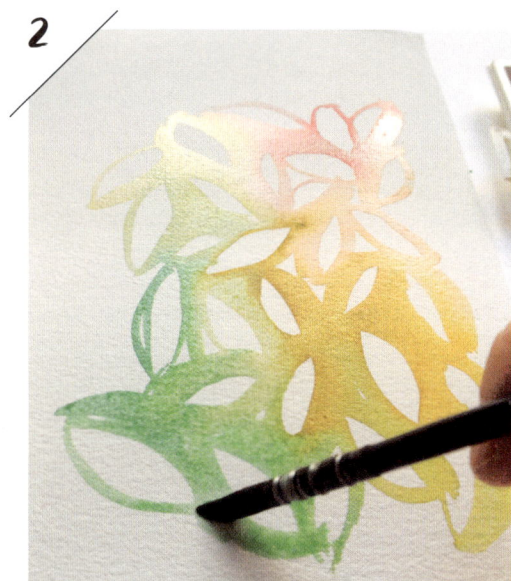

CORRECTING MISTAKES

Watercolor is regarded as difficult as it leaves little room for mistake. It is impossible to touch up an error on a watercolor artwork by adding a layer of white, as the paper and water are the white. If it's dry, you need to start again. However, slipups can be rectified if you react while everything is still wet. If you make a mistake, such as an unintentional patch of color, rinse your brush thoroughly and apply a generous amount of this clear water to the patch. Pay particular attention to the stained area to separate the colored pigment from the paper. Then use a clean cloth to mop it up. Wait until everything is dry before going over it again. It will not be as good as initially but you will be able to get rid of the stain almost entirely!

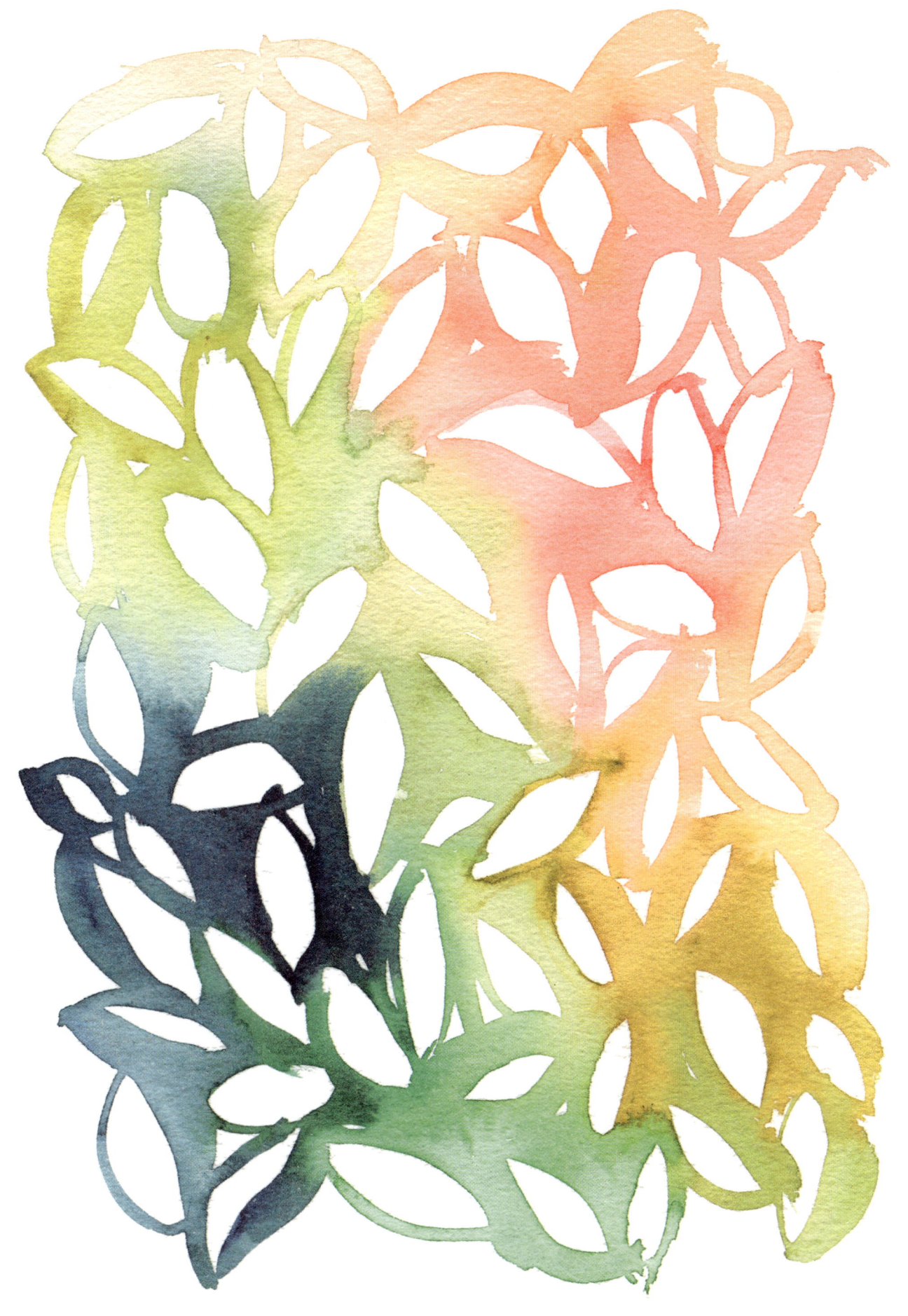

EXPERIMENTING WITH *overlays*

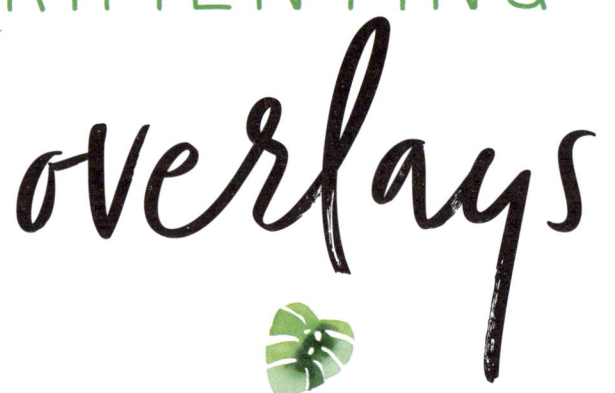

THIS LAYERING TECHNIQUE IS SIMILAR TO THE ONE FOR TRANSPARENCY. YOU'RE GOING TO PAINT SEVERAL LAYERS ON TOP OF EACH OTHER TO GET DIFFERENT EFFECTS THAT WILL ENHANCE YOUR CREATION.

EXERCISE 1

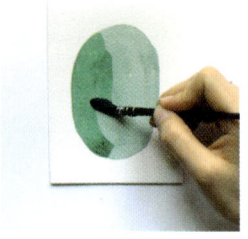

Select a color and paint a shape; I opted for an oval. Leave it to dry, using a blow-dryer to speed things up. Add a layer of the same color with virtually the same pigment concentration. Repeat this process four or five times. You will then realize the color density you can obtain through layering.

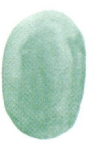 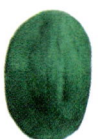 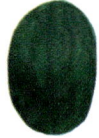

1 layer   3 layers   5 layers

EXERCISE 2

Once again, select a color and paint four similar circles. Once everything is completely dry, paint a different colored layer over each circle (here I used Rose Madder Lake, Orange and Green Yellow). Observe the interesting shades you can create using layering.

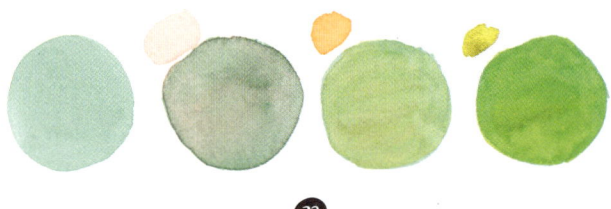

EXERCISE 3

Start in the same way as for exercise 2, with three similarly colored circles. Once everything has dried, instead of applying a uniform color, add a layer as a graduated wash over the second circle, using dark green and water (see page 29). For the third circle, add several colors using the wet-in-wet technique.

EXERCISE 4

A second layer can allow you to add details. This is a technique I use very frequently. The pictures below show a simple banana leaf (one layer) and a more detailed leaf (two layers). The second layer also intensifies the color.

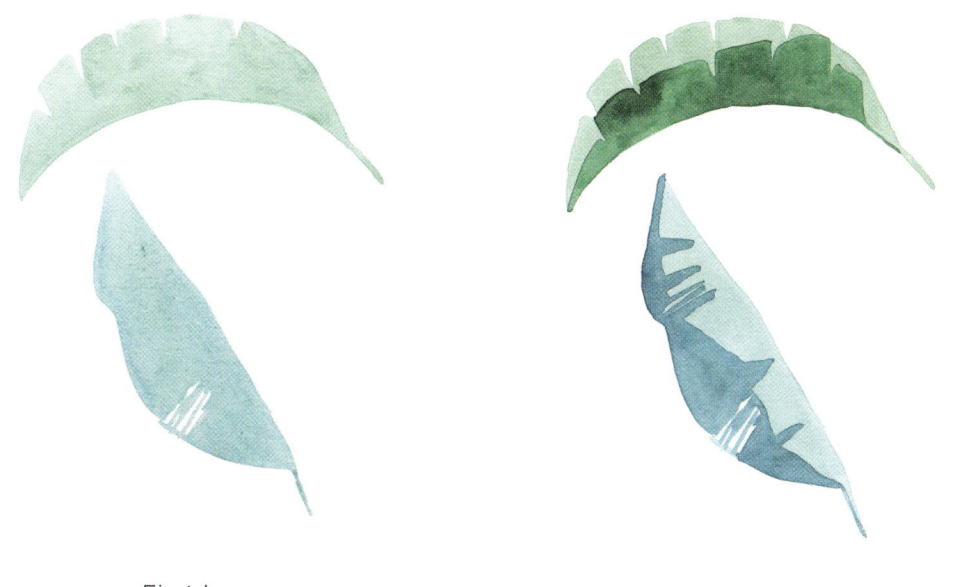

First layer   Second layer

33

NEGATIVE
painting

NEGATIVE PAINTING IS A VERY INTERESTING WATERCOLOR METHOD THAT USES LAYERING. THIS TECHNIQUE ADDS GREAT DEPTH TO A PAINTING. IT IS A SIMPLE PRINCIPLE: INSTEAD OF PAINTING AN OBJECT, DELINEATE ITS OUTLINE. LEARN MORE ABOUT THIS TECHNIQUE WITH THE FOLLOWING EXAMPLE.

1

Start with the lightest colored layer. Remember that this layer will form the foreground. Paint a big circle.

2

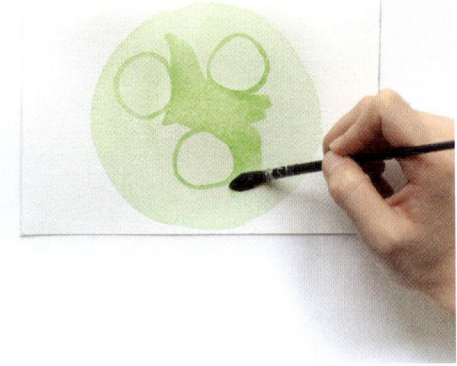

Then paint objects in the foreground, in this case, three circles. Fill in the rest of the space with the same green color with a low level of pigmentation.

3 /

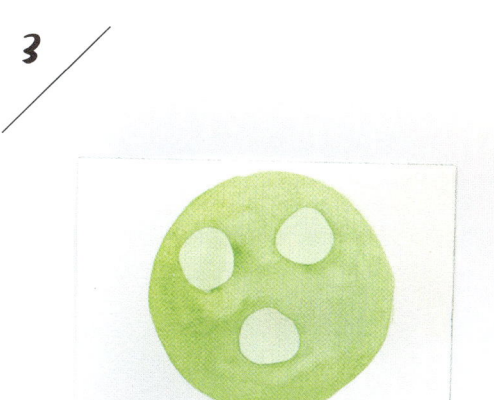

Use the techniques shown earlier to ensure even drying. Remember that a color is always noticeably lighter when dry than it is when wet.

4 /

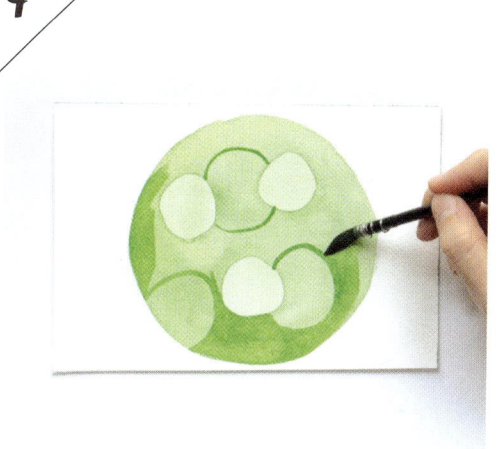

When it has dried (compare the color difference with the previous stage), continue by marking out three more circles. They will appear to be below the first three.

5 /

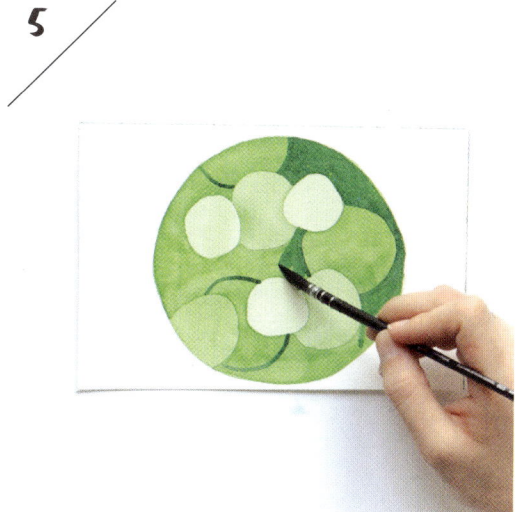
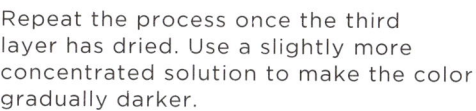

Repeat the process once the third layer has dried. Use a slightly more concentrated solution to make the color gradually darker.

6 /

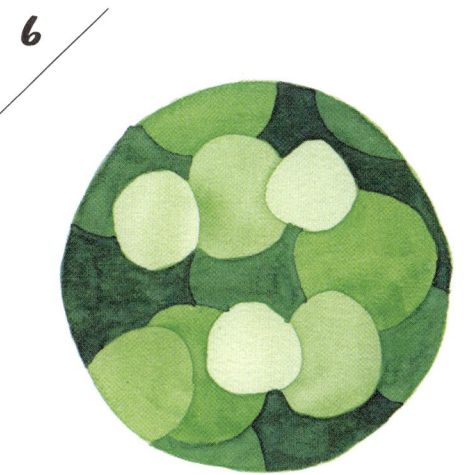

To finish, add five more circles, four of them near the rim of the main circle, with just part of them visible, and one in the center, using a dark green solution. Color the rest with the same solution.

KEEPING BRUSHWORK
fluid

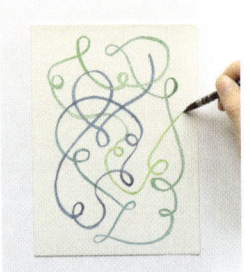

TO INCREASE SPEED AND PRECISION, YOU NEED TO GET MORE COMFORTABLE HANDLING THE BRUSH. USE THESE EXERCISES TO INCREASE THE FLUIDITY OF YOUR BRUSHWORK AND EXPLORE THE POSSIBILITIES IT OFFERS. THIS IS A REALLY KEY STAGE IN GAINING CONFIDENCE.

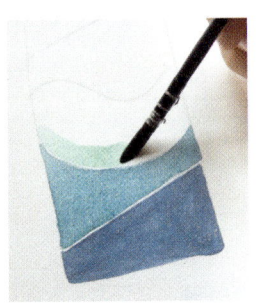

EXERCISE 1

The purpose of this exercise is to get you working on the precision of your brushwork. Start by using a drawing pencil or watercolor pencil to outline a large rectangle, with several dividing lines to create differently shaped inner sections, as in picture 1. Starting at the bottom of the rectangle, fill in the first section. Continue working your way up to the top of the rectangle, leaving a slight gap between each area. The aim is for the areas to be as close to each other as possible but without actually touching (result shown in picture 2).

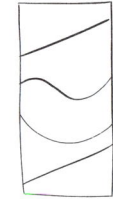 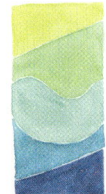

1   2

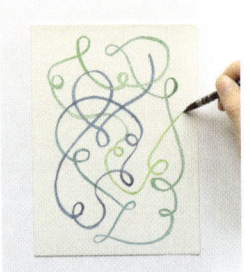

EXERCISE 2

Imagine you are drawing a long piece of string on the paper. It forms lots of loops, kinks and twists. Work on your mixes to vary the color of the string subtly, without any clear visible transition. Sometimes I just paint the outlines of elements (see page 66) to lighten a composition. This exercise will help you gain confidence to achieve this.

EXERCISE 3

Experiment with the different marks made by the brush. My approach to watercolor painting relies very heavily on these brushstrokes. Vary the pressure and angle of the brush on the paper and observe the result.

1 /

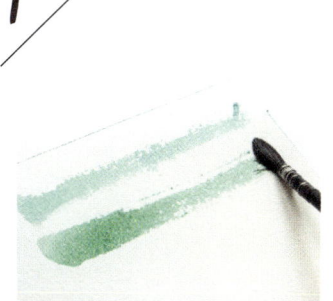

Applying strong pressure to the brush while holding it flat against the paper produces textured effects.

2 /

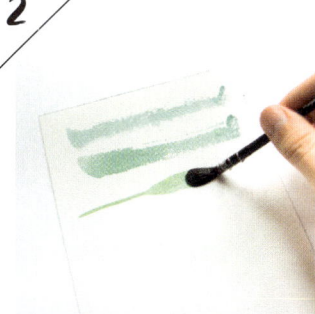

Paint a thin line without pressing down, then increase the pressure to get a broad stroke.

3 /

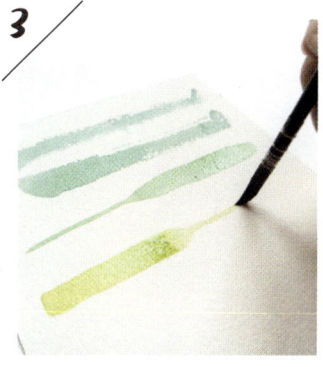

Do the opposite: start with a lot of pressure to get a broad stroke, then gradually reduce the pressure to make it thinner.

4 /

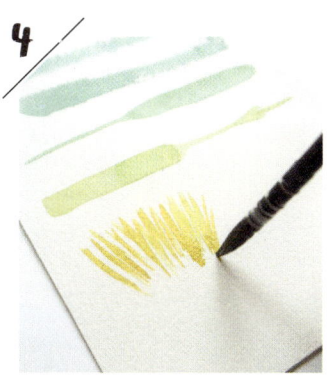

Use the tip of the brush, without applying pressure, to paint short, quick strokes close together.

5 /

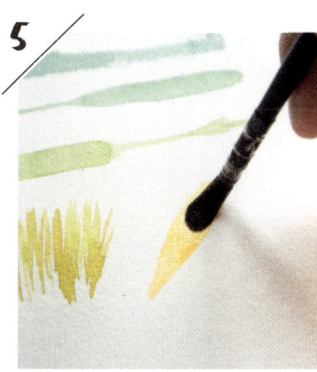

Create a leaf by applying pressure as you draw the brush away from you.

6 /

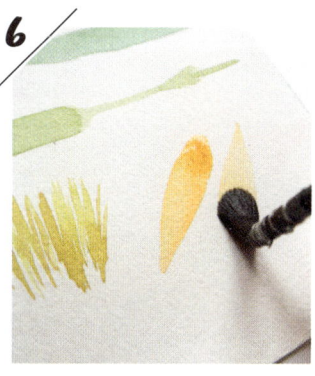

Conversely, create a leaf by applying pressure as you draw the brush towards you.

IDEAS FOR
compositions

LEARNING TO PAINT "JUNGLE" PLANTS IS A GOOD STARTING POINT FOR BUILDING CONFIDENCE. THE NEXT STAGE INVOLVES WORKING ON YOUR COMPOSITIONS. USING THE FOLLOWING TIPS, YOU WILL BE ABLE TO ASSEMBLE AND ARRANGE VARIOUS ELEMENTS TOGETHER TO PRODUCE REAL PAINTINGS.

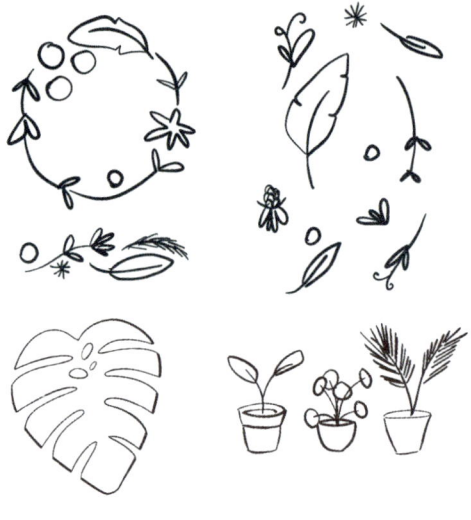

ARRANGEMENT

Start by choosing how you want to arrange the plants on the paper. You can assemble them in a ring, as a frieze, or a pattern, frame, bouquet, etc. You can see many examples in this book. You can also depict a single plant element in far greater detail in the center of the paper, such as a leaf from a Swiss cheese plant or a torch ginger flower. Lastly, you can paint potted tropical plants, as in chapter 4.

SIZE

Vary the size of the different elements chosen for your composition. Try to combine large, medium and really small elements, such as berries or splatters.

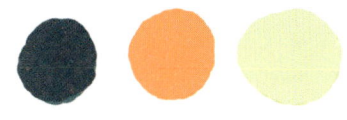

DIRECTION

To add consistency to your composition (bouquet, frieze or pattern), give it direction: the templates shown in this book will give you examples.

The jungle theme lends itself well to a dense, lush pattern. So as not to lose your way, choose the following directions: either from top to bottom (picture 1), or two converging directions (picture 2).

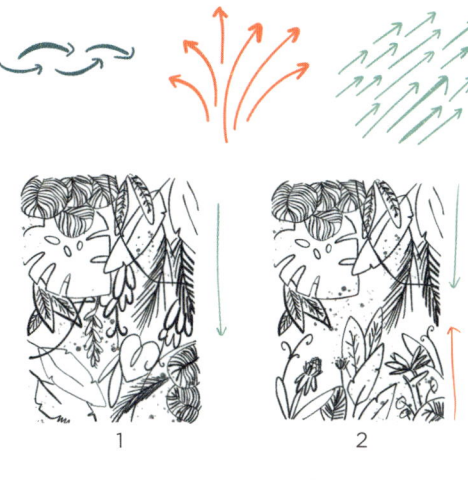

1   2

COLORS

Make sure you have a color palette that combines light, midtone and dark colors to avoid a drab result.

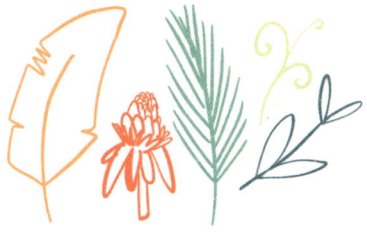

CONTRAST

To create contrast, try to paint very light and very dark areas close together but not actually touching. Thanks to the brushstroke exercises, you're now more accurate!

SHAPES

If you choose to paint several plants, combine a wide variety of striking shapes - simple, composite, angular, rounded, etc. - to make the result more interesting and avoid monotony.

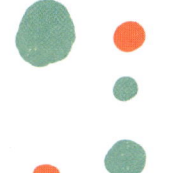

BALANCE

Avoid pairs. Opt instead for one or three elements. Also avoid alternating sizes and shapes in too regular a manner.

IDEAS FOR
framing

THE CHOICE OF FRAMING HAS JUST AS GREAT AN INFLUENCE ON THE RESULT AS DOES THE COMPOSITION. TIGHT FRAMING, WIDE FRAMING, NEGATIVE SPACE, LAYOUT WITH TEXT, ETC., YOUR PAINTING WILL HAVE MORE IMPACT IF YOU THINK ABOUT THESE OPTIONS UPFRONT.

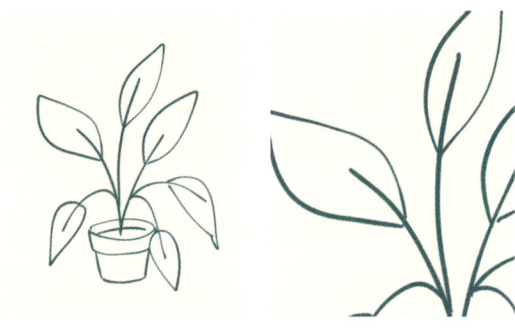

CLOSE-UPS

Regardless of your choice of composition, you can vary the degree to which you focus in on the subject. To show the entire subject, choose a wide framed view (see Calathea orbifolia, page 147) or to explore details, opt for a close-up (see Caladium, page 137). In the case of a close-up, be sure to cut off part of the subject, to give the impression it is spilling out of the frame.

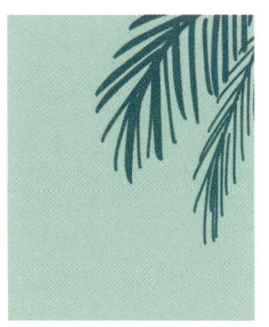
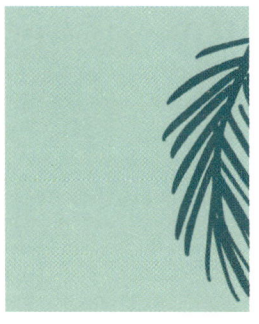

OFF-CENTERING

Play with negative space (empty space, blank paper) and do not always position the subject in the center of the sheet. For example, try to position your subject in a corner or just on one side. This produces very elegant creations that make perfect posters.

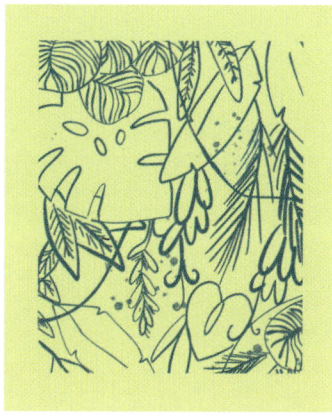

BORDERS

If your composition will have a particularly heavy concentration of graphic elements, before you start painting think about creating a frame for them with a border, using negative space to let your creation breathe. I recommend you use masking tape for this, after first pressing it against your clothing a few times to reduce its adhesiveness. By doing this, I never tear the paper when removing the tape once I've finished my painting.

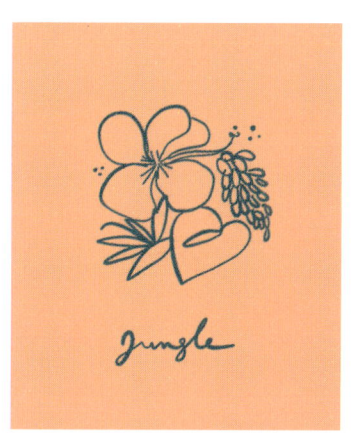

ADDING TEXT

I love turning my watercolors into greetings cards, invitations, announcement cards and posters. This can be done by adding a bit of text to a painting as an attractive finishing touch. Here are two easy ways of adding text:

- Below a central painting, for example in a rounded shape;
- In the middle of a frame (made using masking tape, before you start to paint), or in a ring (see page 108) or a border.

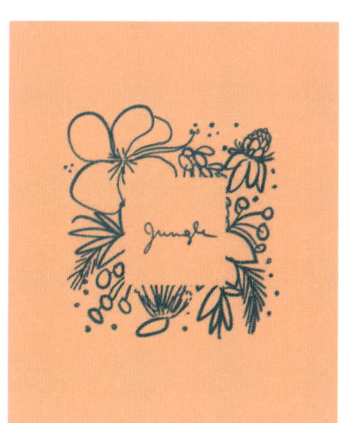

MY

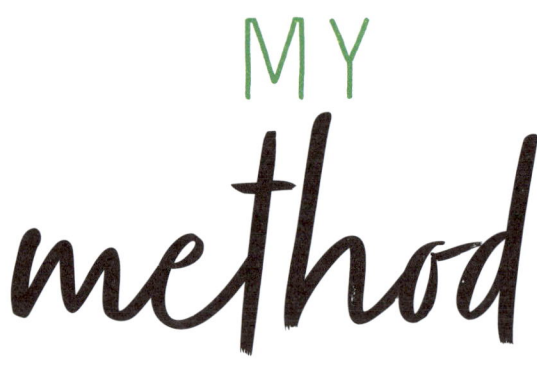

method

I AVOID LETTING MYSELF BE INTIMIDATED BY WATERCOLORS (AFRAID OF MAKING A SLIP OR WASTING MATERIAL), BY TAKING TIME TO PREPARE FOR MY MOST POLISHED CREATIONS THROUGH DOING RESEARCH, DRAFTS AND EXPERIMENTS. I HOPE THAT SHARING MY METHOD WITH YOU WILL GIVE YOU CONFIDENCE.

Most of the time, I paint in a more spontaneous way, straight onto the paper. However, there are times when I need to give more thought to putting together a creation and then I follow the method described on the opposite page (but remember, it is just a suggestion).

FINDING INSPIRATION

The contents of this book already provide a good basis for inspiration. Once you feel more comfortable with the techniques shown, feel free to further your knowledge by researching additional sources of inspiration. I'm sure you will be able to depict other plants and even animals or fruits. Work from photos and practice simplifying the shapes you observe.

THINK AHEAD

If you don't know where to start for creating your own jungle painting, use these four pillars as your base: Vegetation (picked from chapters 2, 3 or 4); Techniques (wet-in-wet, transparency, negative, brushwork, etc.); Composition (see page 38); Framing (see page 40).

For example: paint bird of paradise and Heliconia flowers together with banana leaves using the wet-in-wet technique, with a palette of analogous colors to form a pattern with a white border.

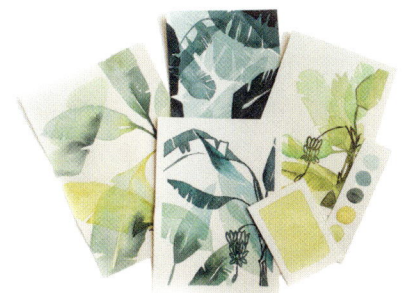

RESEARCH AND EXPERIMENT

I have a vague idea of what I want to do (here the painting on page 75: banana leaves, using the transparency technique, covering the whole page), and I start my research. I experiment with several leaves in draft format (on the back of pages I've already used, for example) or on a large board (see page 49). I do not impose any restrictions on myself in my experimentation as regards palettes, compositions, shapes, etc. I carry on until I've found a concept I like.

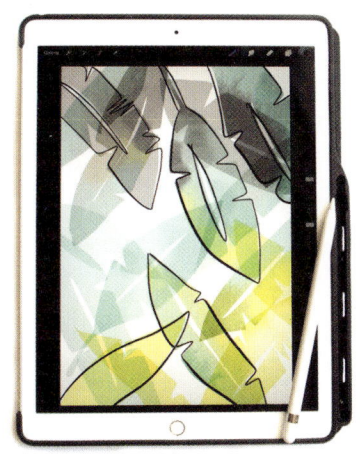

DRAFT

I test out my idea with a draft. The colors and composition are defined. This stage increases my knowledge of the plan and lets me refine the details. Personally, I often use my iPad for this stage.

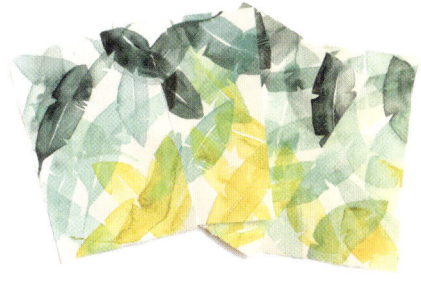

PAINT WITHOUT WORRYING ABOUT MISTAKES

I then start painting with confidence, holding all the keys. If my painting is not to my liking, I just start afresh. Don't worry about mistakes. The sooner you make mistakes, the sooner you will progress as you'll have learnt something.

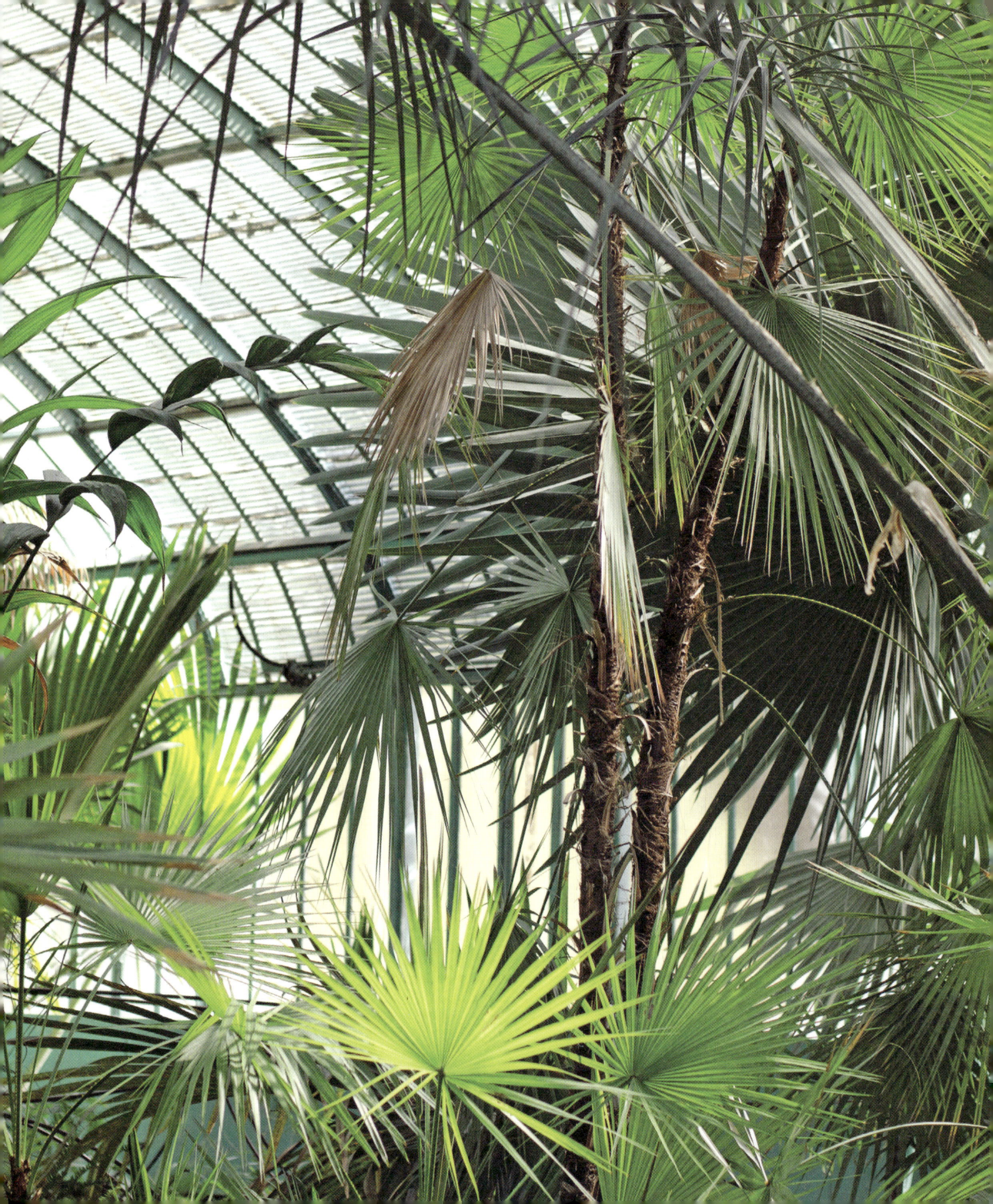

CHAPTER 02

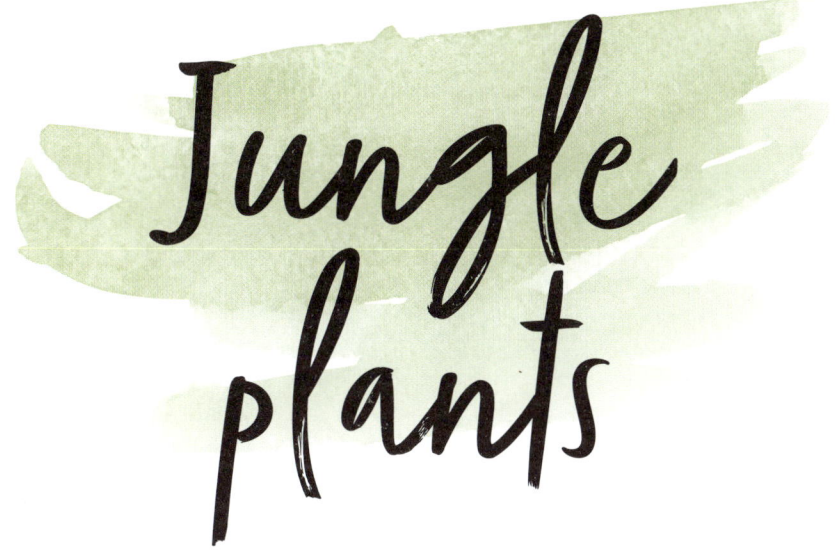

Jungle plants

NOW YOU'RE MASTERING THE BASIC PRINCIPLES OF WATERCOLOR, YOU'RE GOING TO DISCOVER HOW TO PAINT THREE PLANT FEATURES THAT WILL INSTANTLY GIVE YOUR PAINTINGS A JUNGLE LOOK. THEY ARE THE LEAVES FROM A BANANA TREE, A SWISS CHEESE PLANT AND A PALM TREE, ALL THREE OF WHICH COMPLEMENT ONE ANOTHER WELL FROM A GRAPHIC POINT OF VIEW.

BANANA *tree*

BANANA LEAVES HAVE A VERY INTERESTING APPEARANCE.
WE WILL DEPICT THEM FACE-ON BUT ALSO FROM VARIOUS
ANGLES, AS YOU WILL DISCOVER IN THIS CHAPTER.

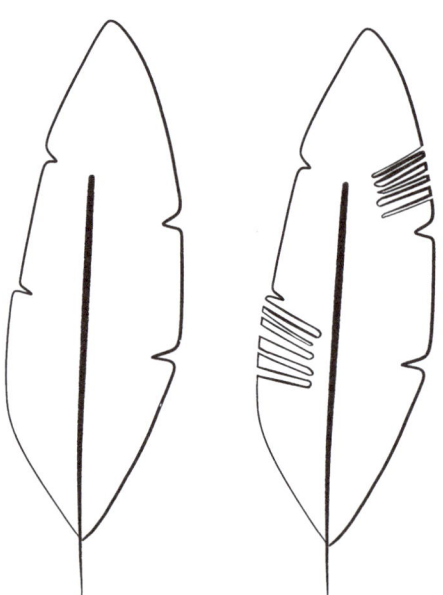

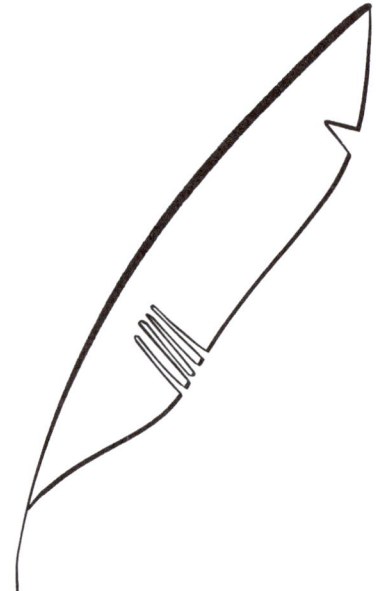

UNDERSTAND

This is the shape of a banana leaf. It is elongated, resembling a feather and is slightly pointed at the tip. The leaf usually looks like it has notches cut into the sides. Try not to depict it too symmetrically either side of the central vein.

To paint a side-on view of a leaf, I mark out the slightly curved central vein and then just one of the sides.

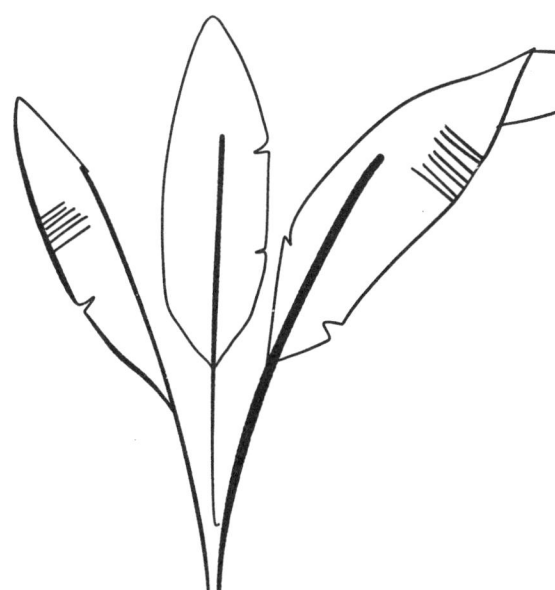

Leaves in a group can be shown from different angles, for greater realism. It is even possible to depict them bent over widthways (see leaf on the right of this picture).

Here is a slightly more complex way of depicting leaves bent lengthways. Start by painting the central vein and then both parts of the leaf seen from the same side. I use the layering technique to depict these leaves (see page 33).

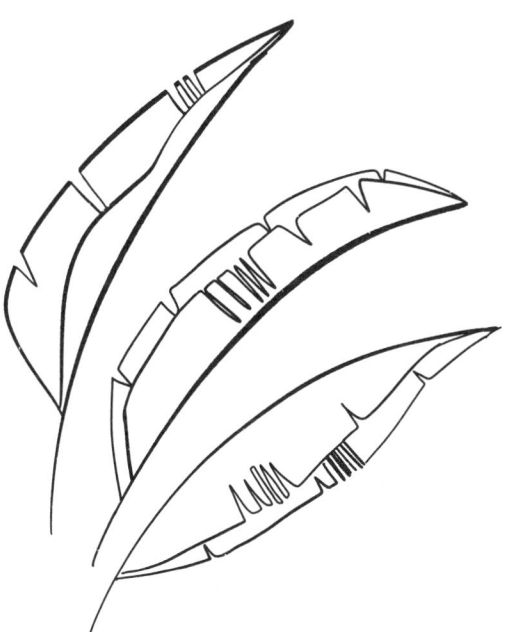

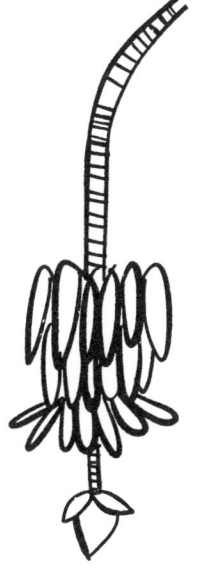

Here is my way of depicting bunches of bananas growing in clusters. Under the weight of the fruit, the whole thing often hangs down on one side of the banana tree.

1 /

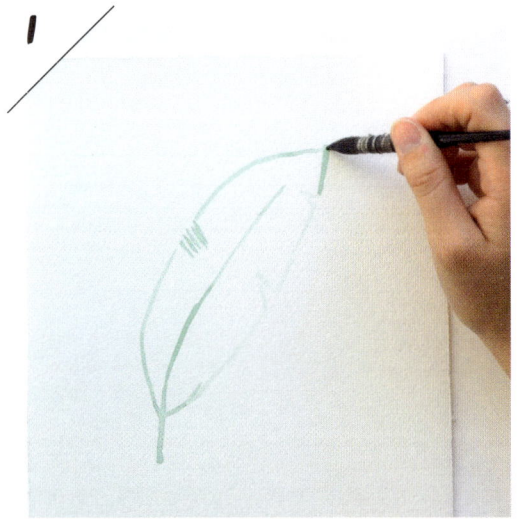

My method of painting a banana leaf is very simple. Start by painting the outline of the leaf using a diluted blue-green solution (see page 23). Refer to the previous sketches to help you get the right shape.

2 /

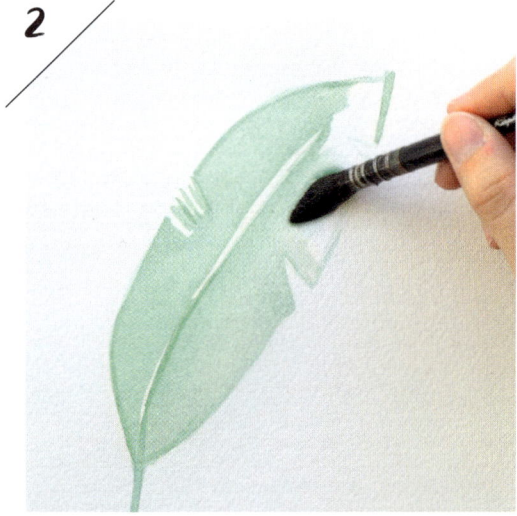

Fill in this shape with the same light blue-green solution, working fast so the outlines do not have time to dry. Be sure to leave a white line along the center of the leaf to represent the vein.

3 /

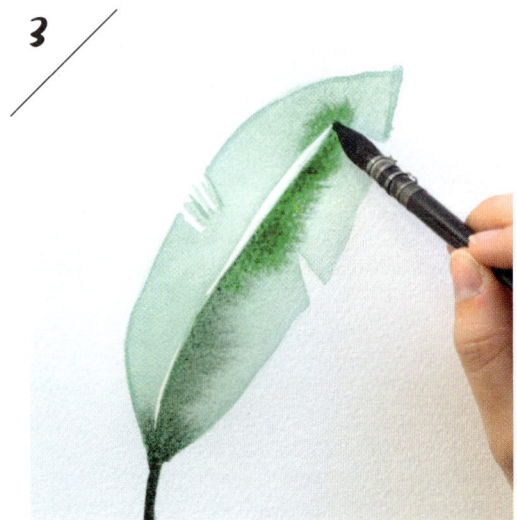

While everything is still wet, add dark green pigment along the length of the vein to create a lovely contrast with the white space that you left.

4 /

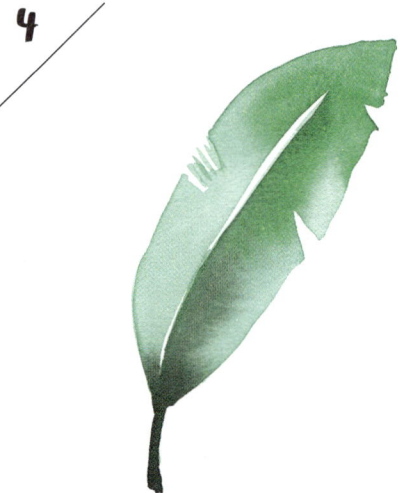

Here is the result when dry. The picture opposite shows a research board with various experiments (see My Method, page 43).

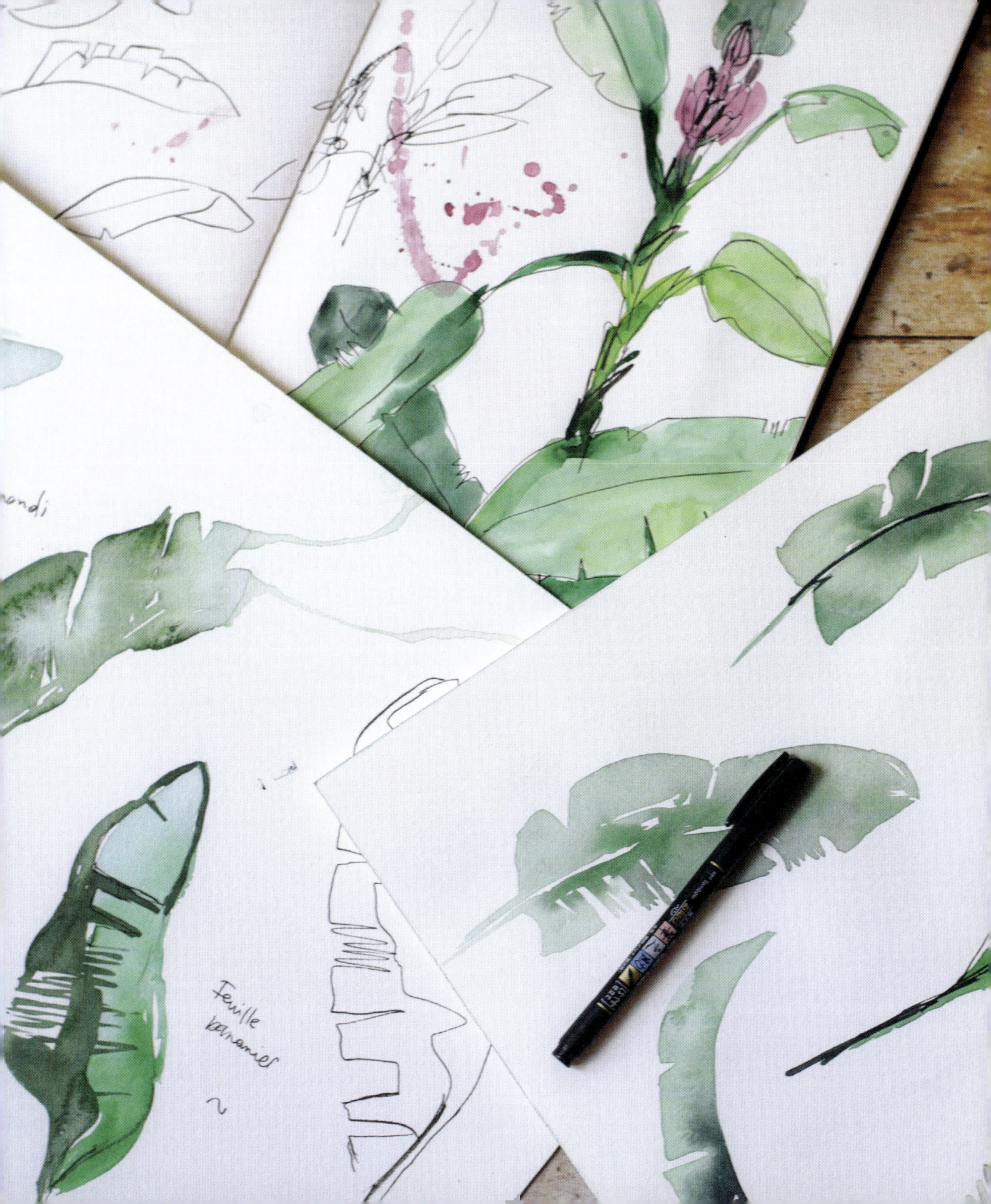

SWISS
cheese plant

THE LARGE LEAVES OF A SWISS CHEESE PLANT, OR MONSTERA, ARE VERY STRIKING AND ADD GREAT INTEREST TO A PAINTING. HERE IS MY EASY METHOD FOR PAINTING THEM WITHOUT MARKING EVERYTHING OUT IN ADVANCE. PAY ATTENTION TO THE DIFFERENT VISUAL CLUES HIGHLIGHTED TO ENABLE YOU TO REPEAT THE RIGHT BRUSHSTROKES FROM MEMORY.

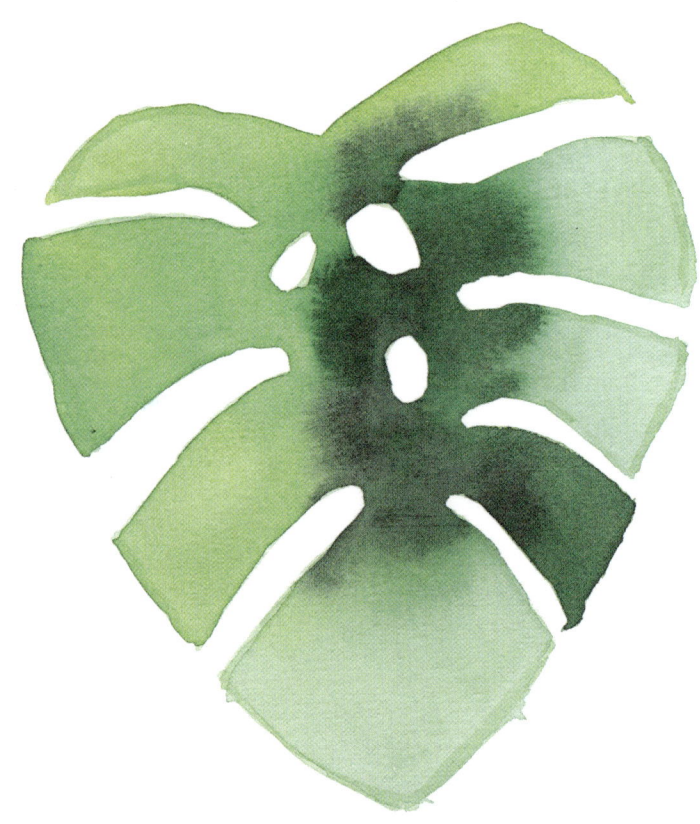

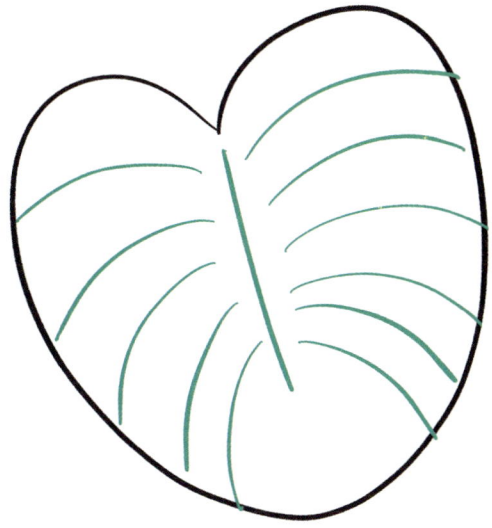

Start by observing the leaf. Its overall shape resembles a heart. There are obvious slits, arranged almost symmetrically. Remember their layout, which reminds me of a ribcage.

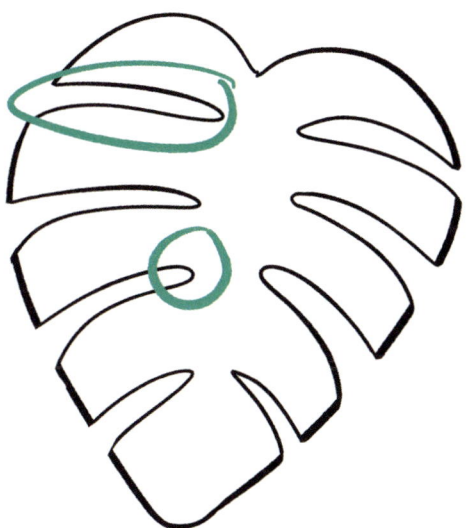

Now focus on the spaces between the slits. At the edge of the leaf, the cut out is angular whereas it is rounded near the center of the leaf.

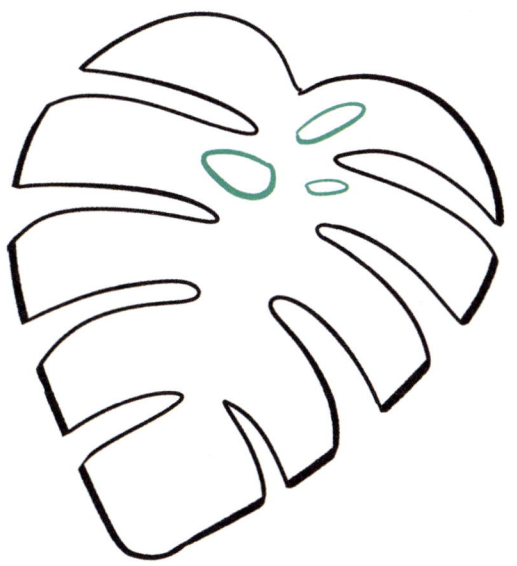

Lastly, at the top, near the stem, the leaf has perforations of varying sizes. Be aware that the more the leaf grows, the more holes it develops.

PAINT

1 /

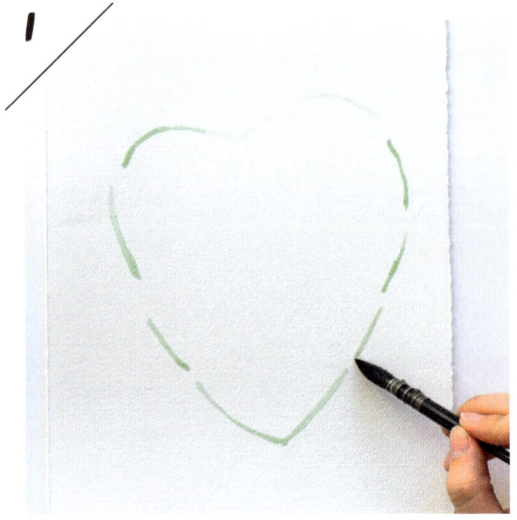

Using a very light green solution (see page 23), start by marking out a heart shape with large dashes. Paint the bottom of the heart with a solid line, denoting the bottom of the leaf.

2 /

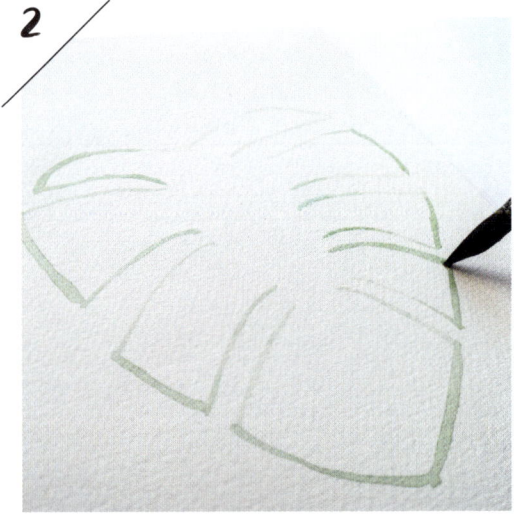

For each slit in the leaf, paint two lines in the direction studied previously, as if you were painting ribs. Don't extend the lines all the way to the center of the leaf.

3 /

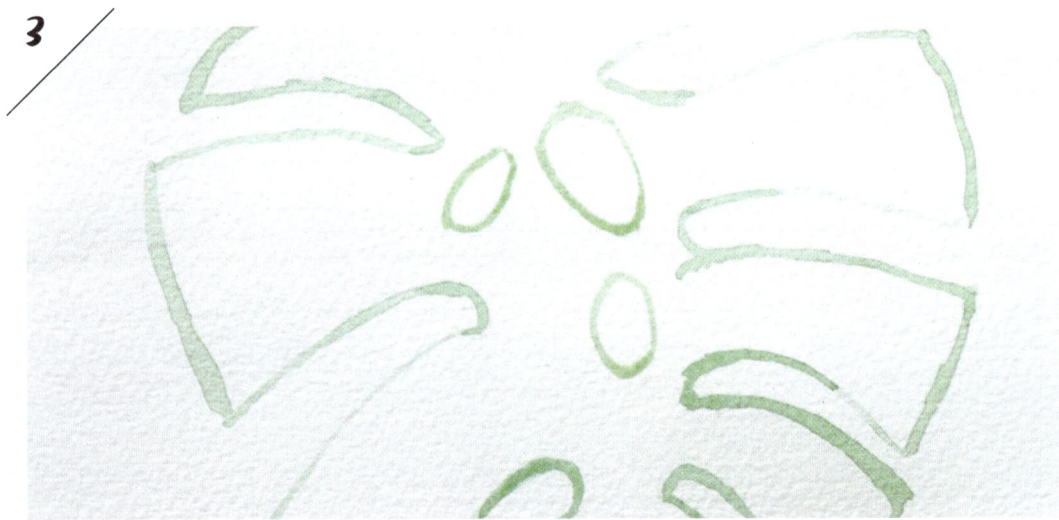

Connect your lines with a curve and add several perforations to the center.

4

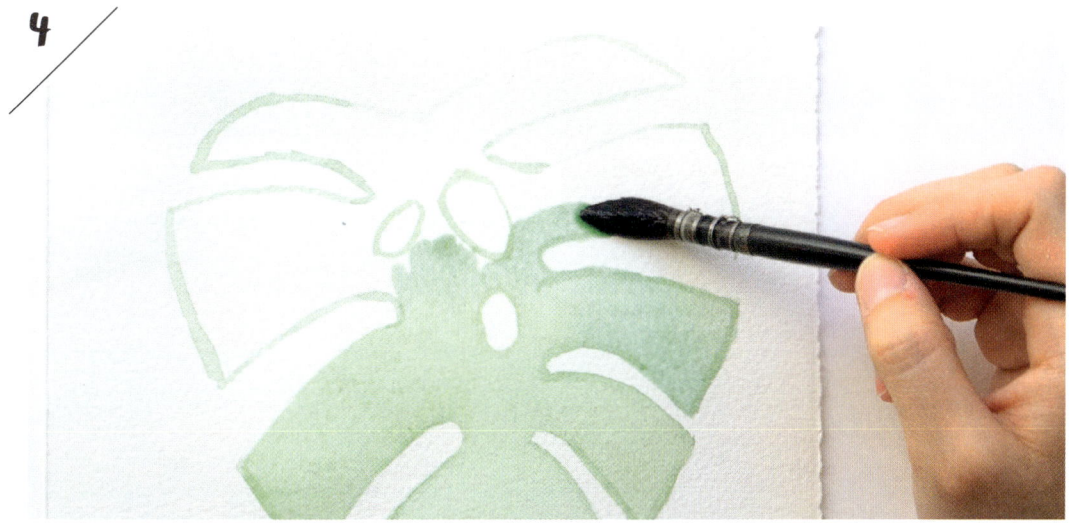

Now completely fill in your leaf with the same light green solution. Use the explanation on page 19 to fill it in evenly.

5

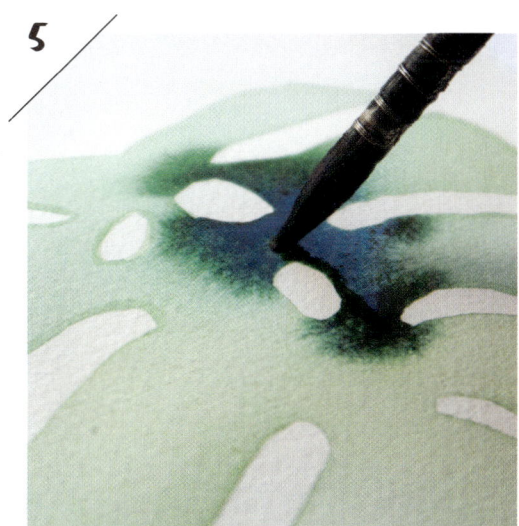

In the same way as for the banana leaf, add dark green pigment in several places, especially near the perforations.

6

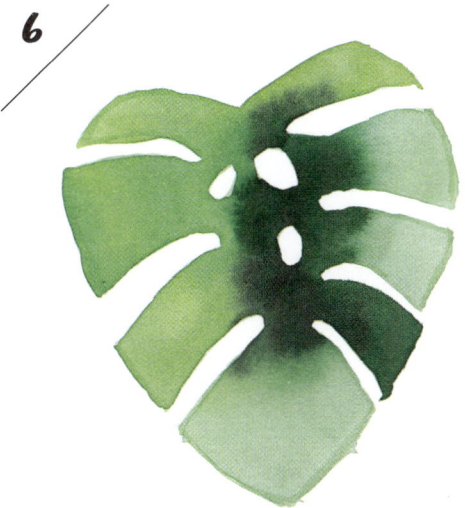

You can also add other shades of green to give your watercolor greater depth and a more three-dimensional appearance (here I used Hooker's Green, Greenish Umber and Olive Green).

PALM
tree

LEAVES CAN COME FROM MANY SPECIES OF PALM TREE.
HERE WE WILL FOCUS ON LONG, THIN PINNATE LEAVES
(IN THE SHAPE OF A FEATHER OR COMB), BUT THERE ARE
ALSO FAN-SHAPED PALMATE LEAVES (SEE PAGE 122).

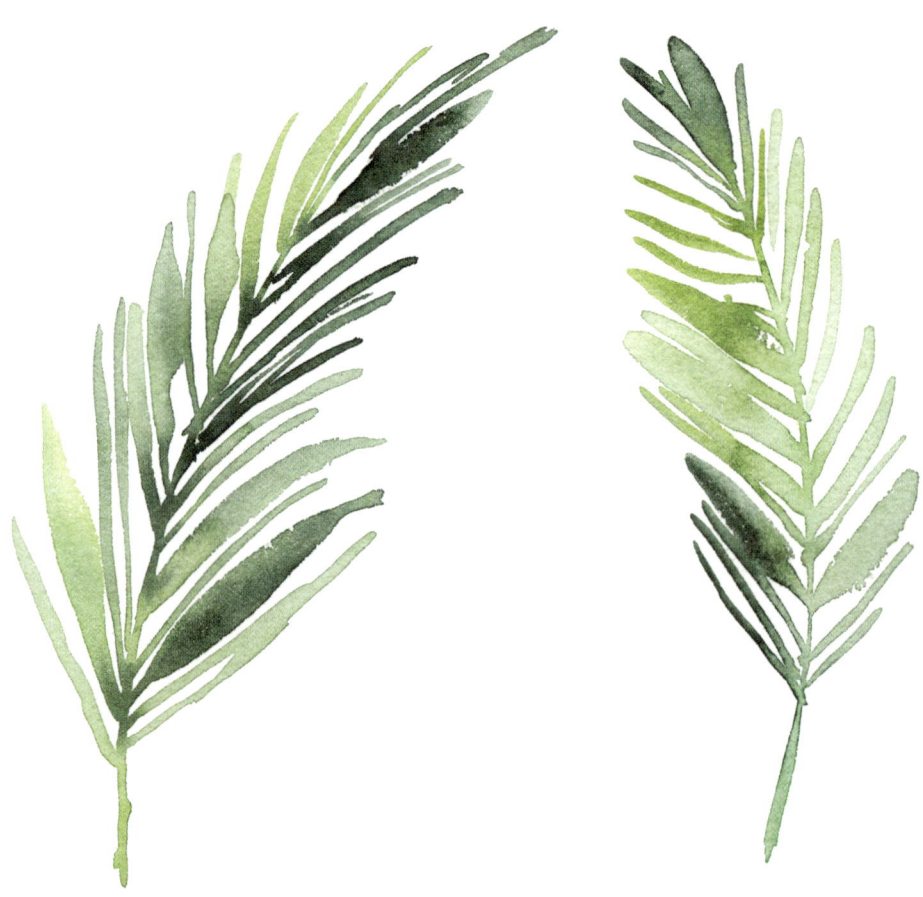

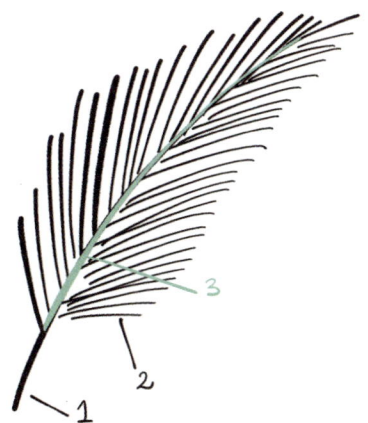

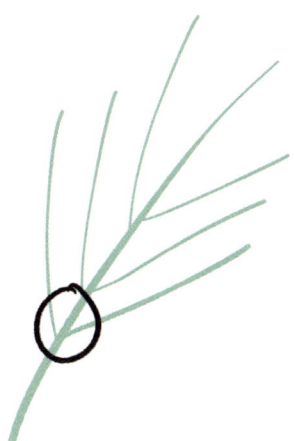

1. Petiole
2. Leaflet
3. Rachis

The first tip for drawing a palm leaf concerns the angle between the leaflets and the rachis (central vein). It is about 45°. Avoid drawing right angles as this would not look natural for pinnate leaves.

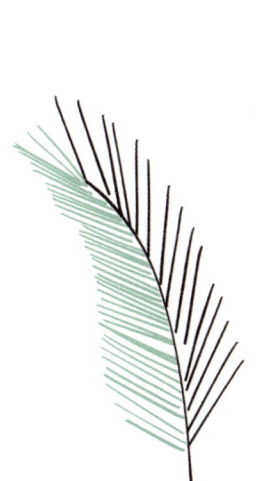

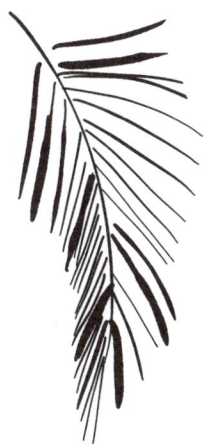

The second tip to remember is to make sure the petiole (the bare part) and its continuation, the rachis, are both curved. On the concave side (on the inside of the curve, shown in green), the leaflets are more tightly packed together, so paint more of them to give that impression.

The final tip is to vary the thickness of the leaflets. Even though, in real life, they are regular, when seen from a distance, some will be pointing at different angles. Experiment with the brushstrokes to use for thick versus thin leaflets described overleaf, then try to use a combination of strokes.

THICK LEAFLETS

1

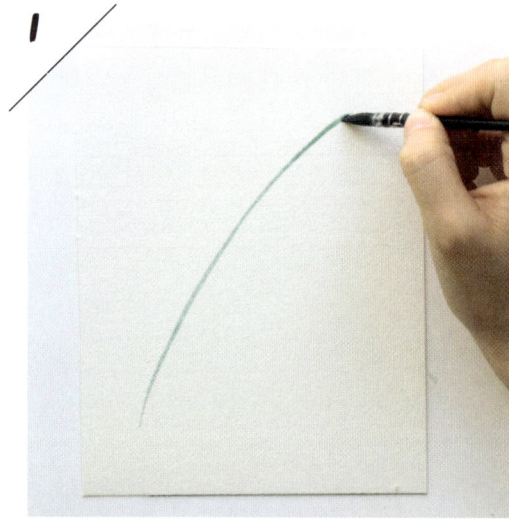

Start by painting the petiole and rachis of your leaf in a light solution. As with the banana leaf, try to avoid making the line too straight.

2

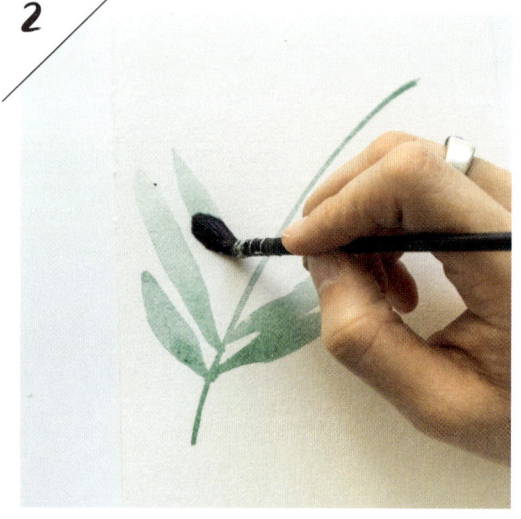

To paint thick leaves, start your brushstroke at the outer end of the leaflet, moving in towards the rachis. Start by applying only slight pressure and then press harder for the central part of the leaflet, before finally releasing pressure as you get to the rachis.

3

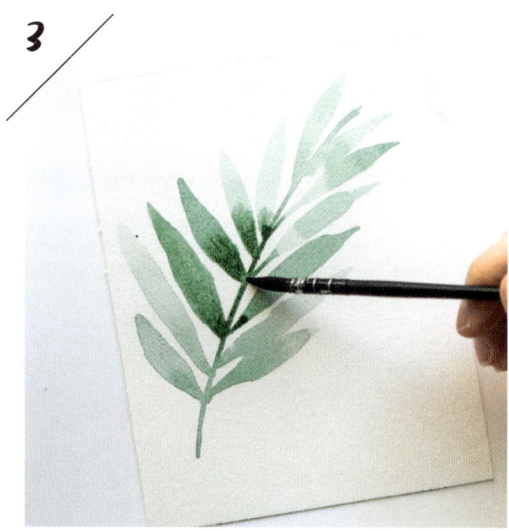

Paint different leaflets using the same method. Those at the end of the rachis are shorter. While everything is still wet, apply darker pigment on and near the rachis to create a gradation effect.

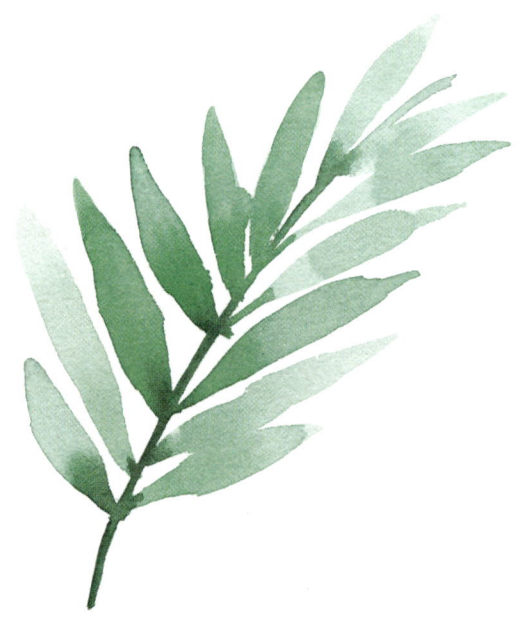

THIN LEAFLETS

1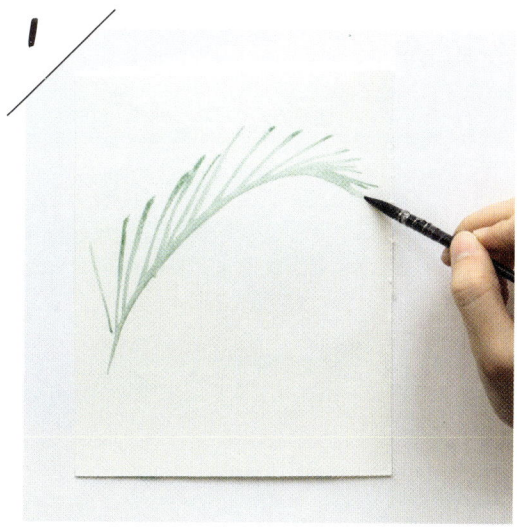

Once again, paint the petiole and rachis of your leaf in a light solution. This time, paint the leaflets with brushstrokes starting at the rachis and working outwards to the tip, applying light pressure to continue creating a thin line.

2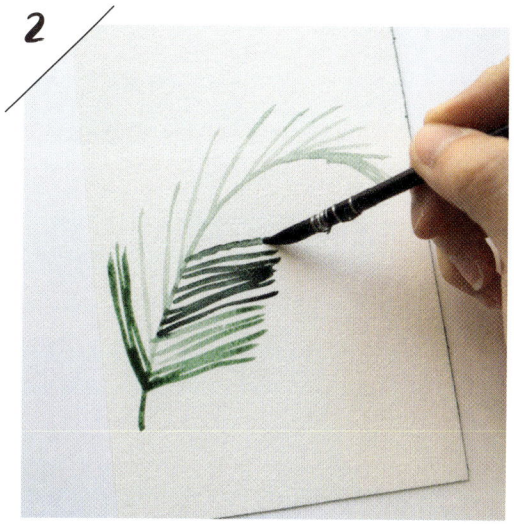

The leaflets are denser on the side of the stem that is more curved. The faster you paint them, the surer you will be of producing a random, but also more expressive palm leaf. It's up to you to determine the desired effect.

3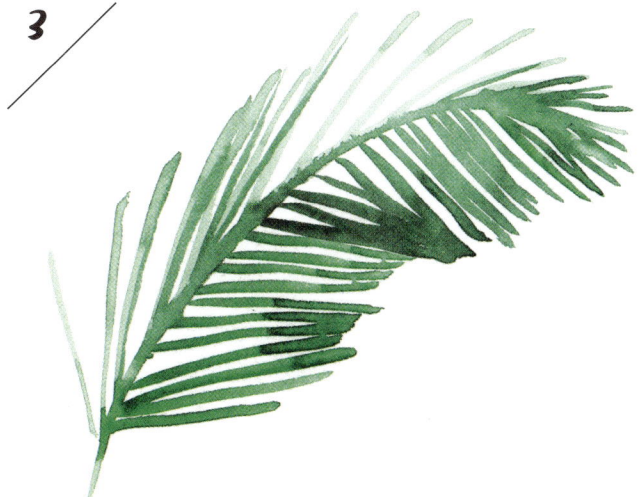

Vary the pigment concentration and size of leaflets as you get closer to the end of the rachis. Feel free to do a mixture of thin and thick leaflets on the same palm leaf (see page 117).

OTHER JUNGLE *plants*

THE JUNGLE IS TEEMING WITH UNUSUALLY SHAPED LITTLE PLANTS, FLOWERS AND FRUITS. TO RECREATE THIS CROWDED EFFECT, FEEL FREE TO USE THE FOLLOWING LITTLE PLANT ELEMENTS, WHICH WILL ADD EVEN MORE CHARACTER TO YOUR PAINTINGS.

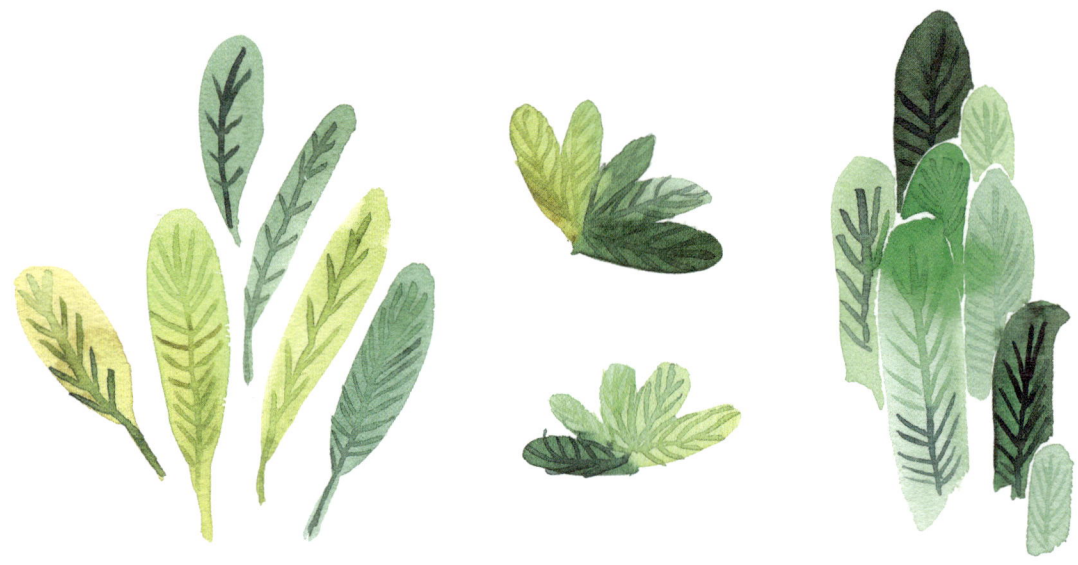

ROUND LEAVES AND VEINS

Paint fairly long, rounded leaves by pressing firmly on the brush as you work from the stem end to the outer tip (see page 37). Once everything is dry, add veins using a more concentrated solution, applying only slight pressure to your brush. See my suggestions above for different ways of arranging the leaves.

BRANCHING AND SPIRALS

Increase the complexity of stems by showing them branching. Move from one individual stem (top row, left) to a combination of several stems. Don't think too much about where this branching occurs, so that the overall effect will be more natural. I also recommend you add little spirals in various places, as shown on some of the examples below. I find this gives the plant a lush look.

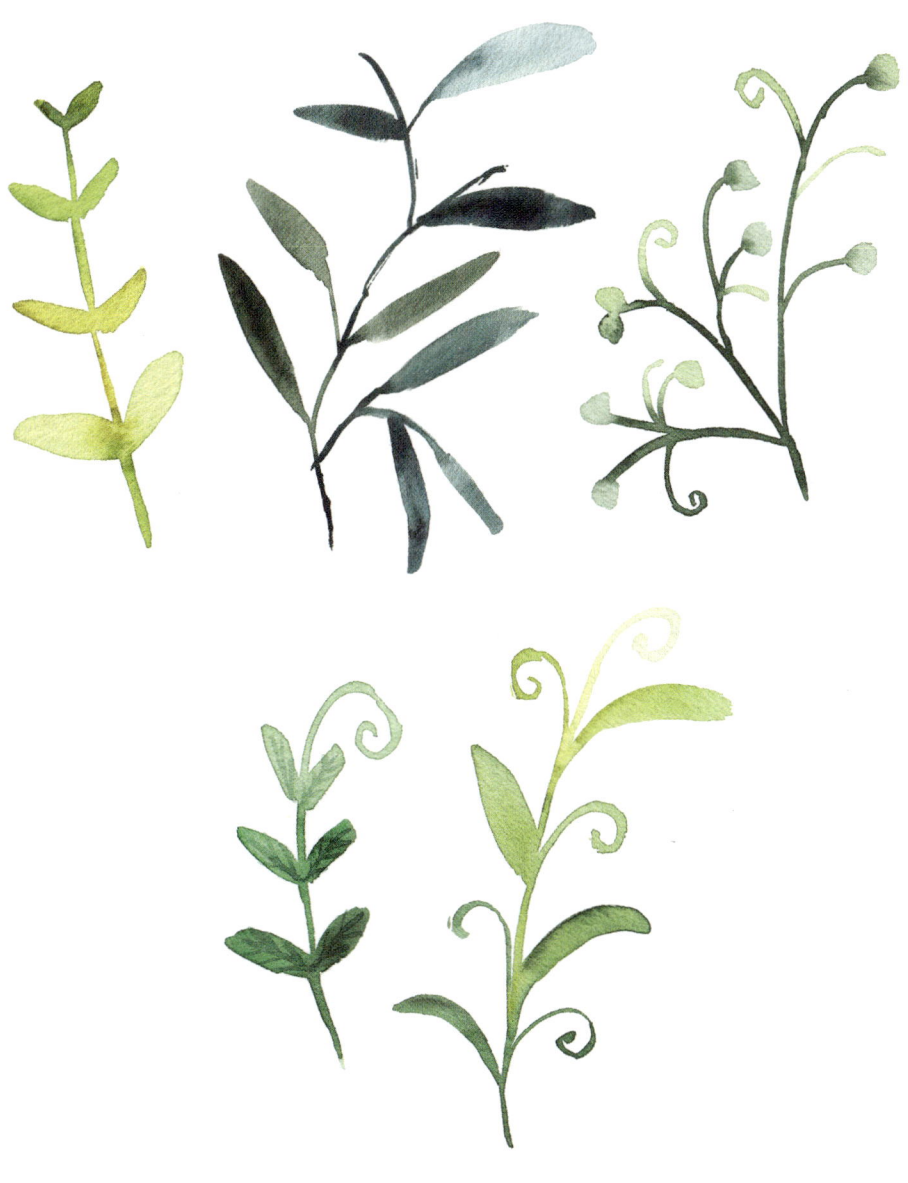

FLOWERS AND LINES

Feel free to add little flowers to your compositions. I very often create "pompoms" by painting lots of expressive strokes grouped together. See the examples below for inspiration to add to your creations.

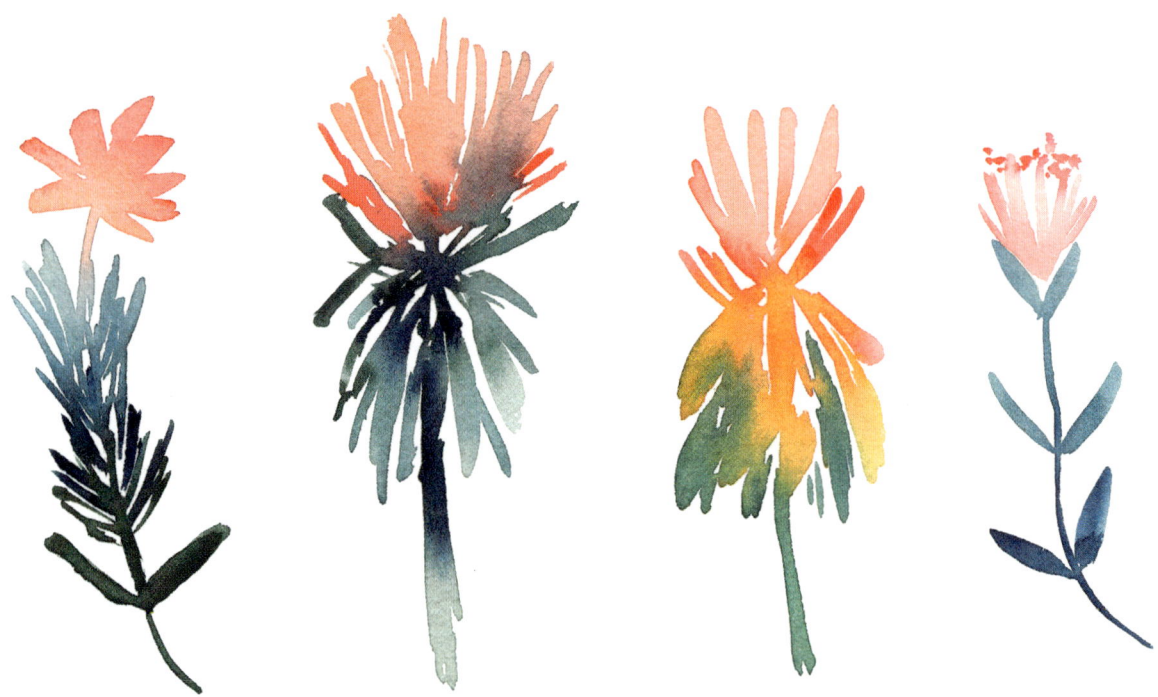

FRUITS AND SEEDS

Fruits and seeds make a perfect addition to a jungle creation. You can group them together on a stem or paint them individually, dotted about your creation. See below for inspiration on stems. Keep things simple when depicting fruit (I do simple circles) as most flowers and leaves are already pictorially complex. This will provide balance. Feel free also to paint little dots that are reminiscent of seeds. You can do this by applying gentle pressure to your brush or by creating colored spots (see page 69, stage 12).

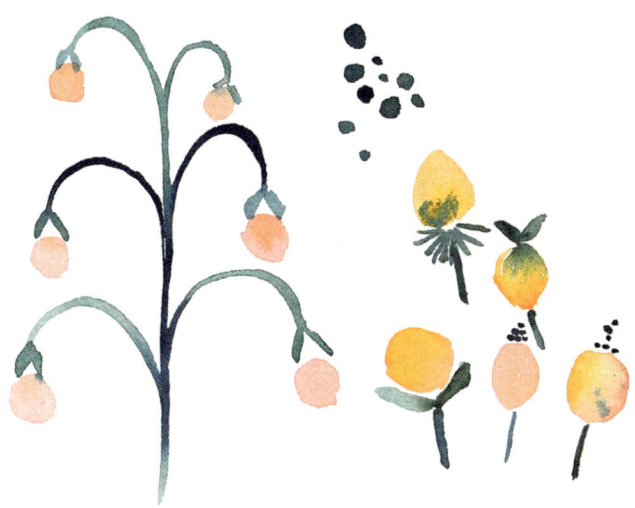

VINES

I really love adding vines and creepers to my jungle pictures. You can paint simple strokes of varying thickness. You can also draw inspiration from the suggestions shown below: a vine with fruits, flowers or leaves, or with a striped effect to add visual interest.

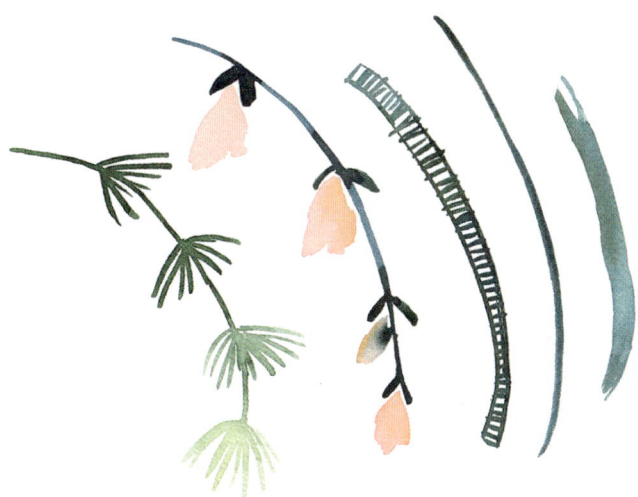

A VARYING
pattern

FOR YOUR FIRST WATERCOLOR, YOU'RE GOING TO CREATE A
PATTERN MIXING BANANA, SWISS CHEESE PLANT AND PALM LEAVES,
ALONG WITH SMALL PLANT ELEMENTS TO FILL OUT THE PATTERN.

THE MAIN COLORS

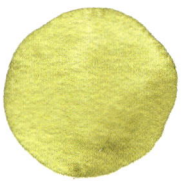 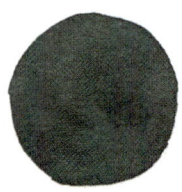 

Brown Green   Greenish Umber   Diluted blue-green
(see page 23)

Remember

- To simplify the creation of a pattern, give it a direction: running diagonally from bottom right corner to top left.
- Give the impression of some elements extending beyond the page to reinforce the pattern.
- Use a variety of pictorial techniques (lines, filling in, splatters) to add even more interest.

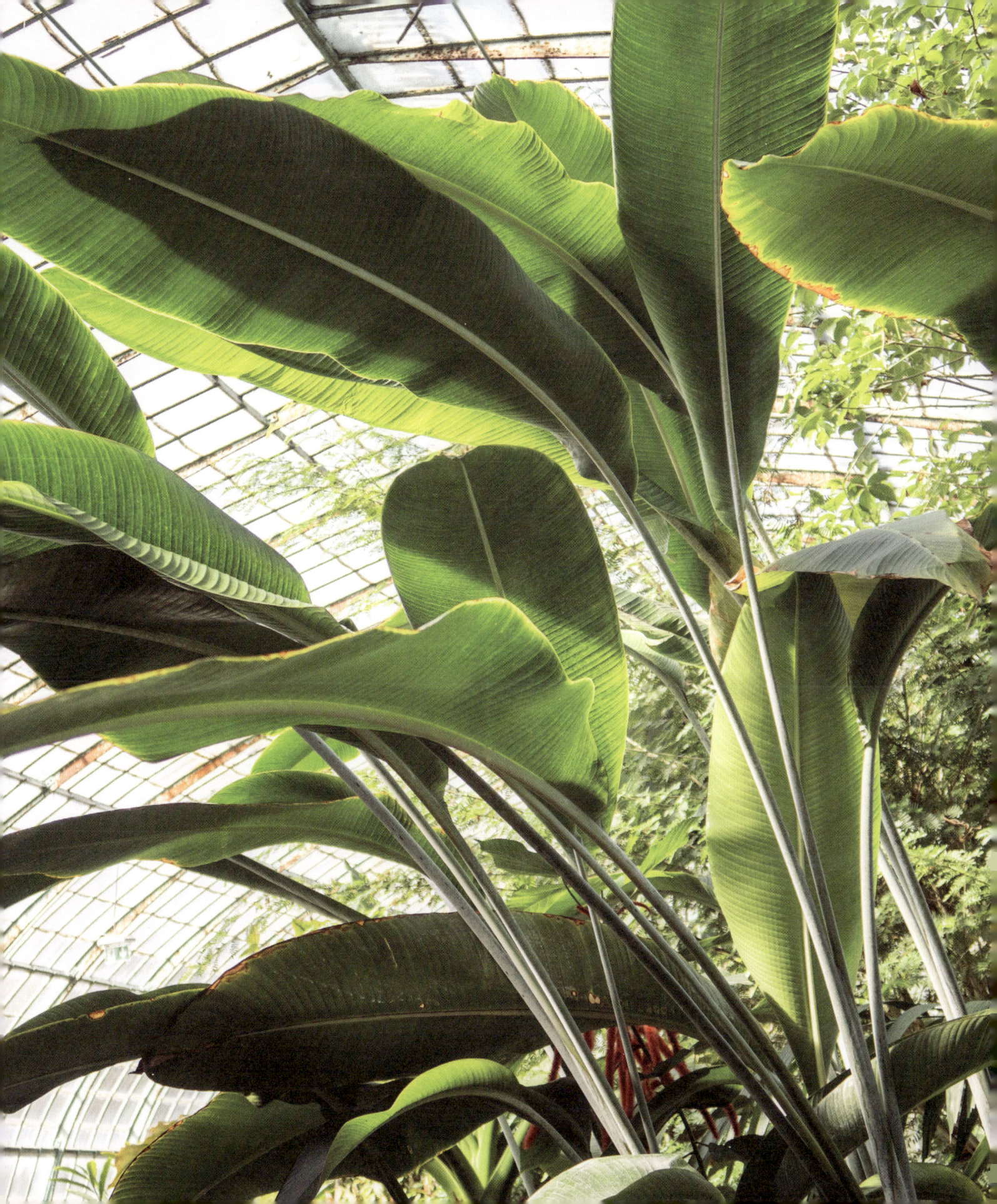

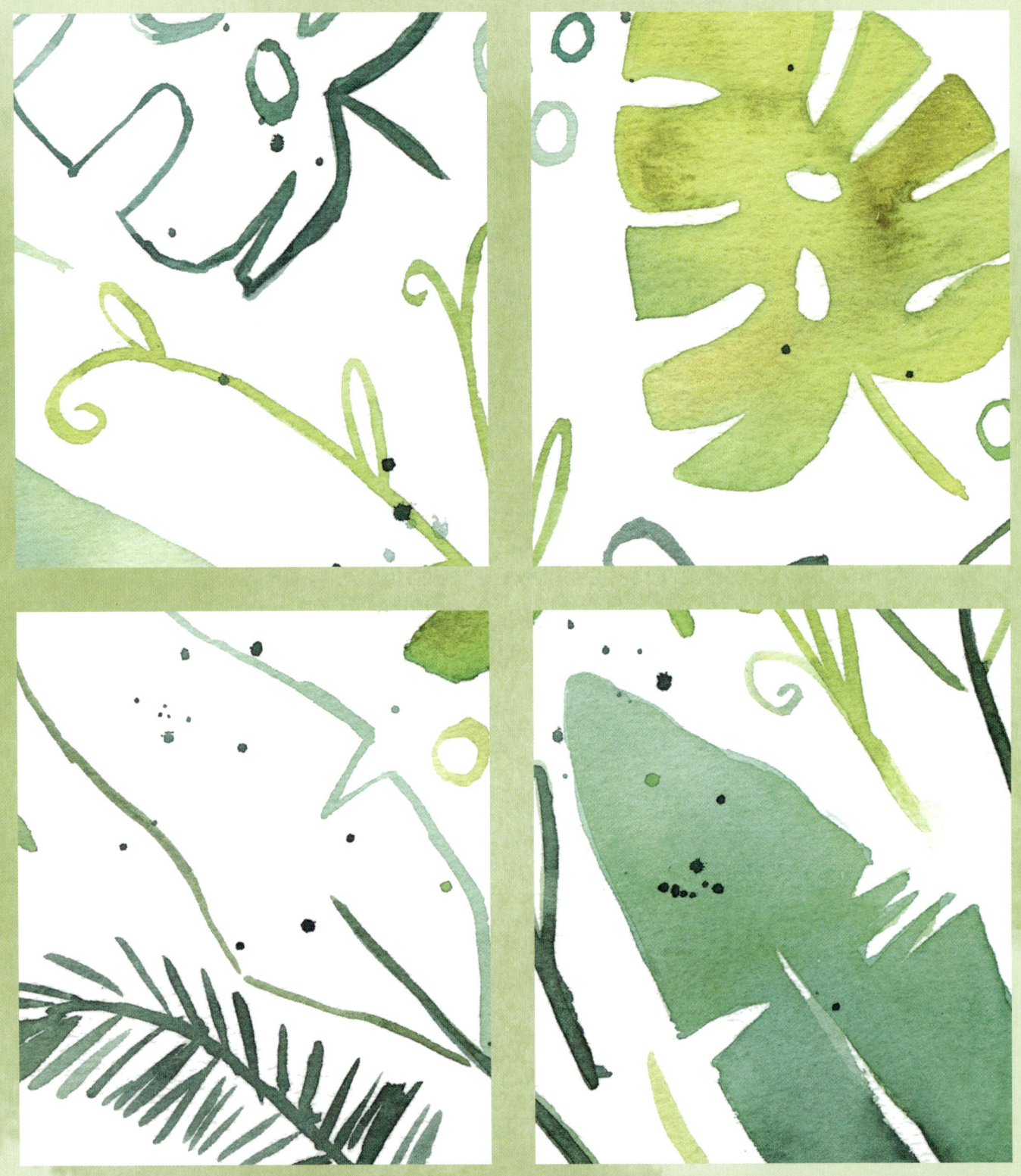

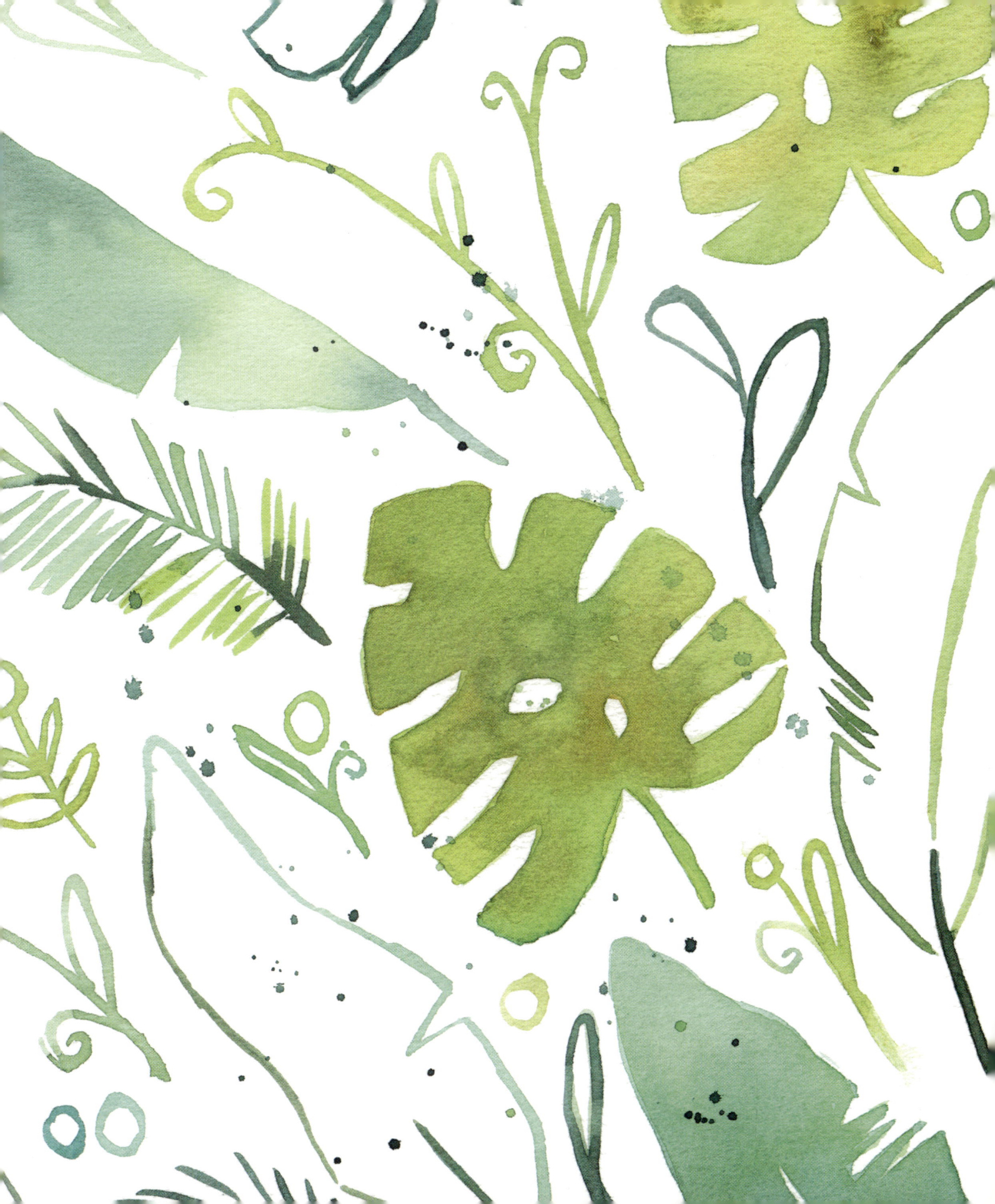

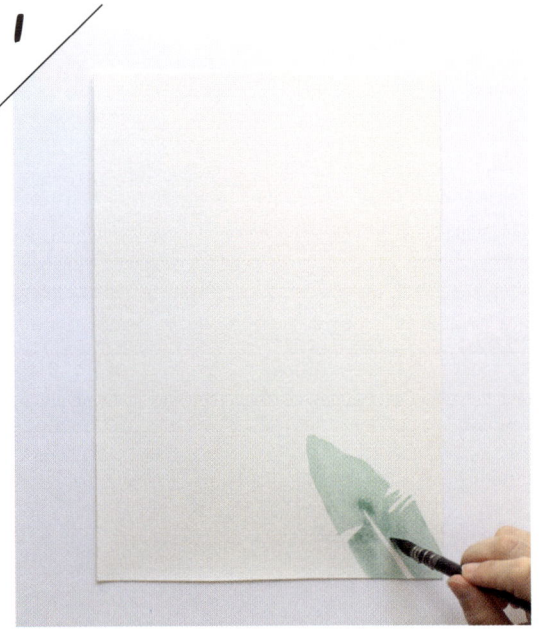

1

Start the pattern with a banana leaf, bottom right of the page, as though it extends beyond the frame. Use a blue-green solution and vary the tones while the area is still wet (I added Emerald Green here).

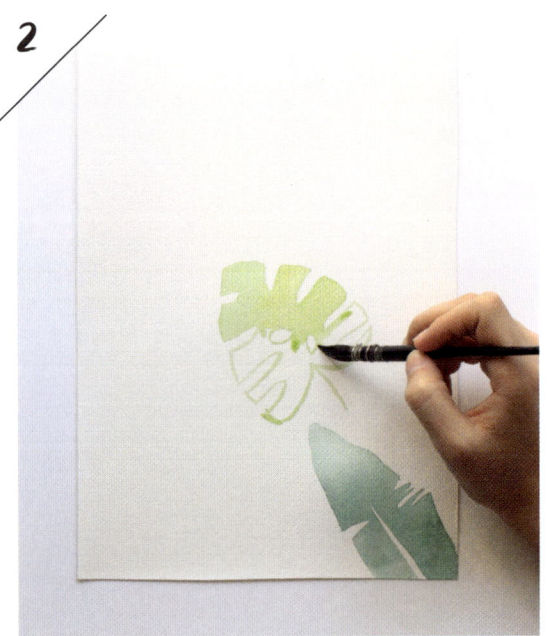

2

Paint a Swiss cheese leaf diagonally in yellowish green tones. The leaf is pointing in the same direction as the previous one, towards the top left corner of the page.

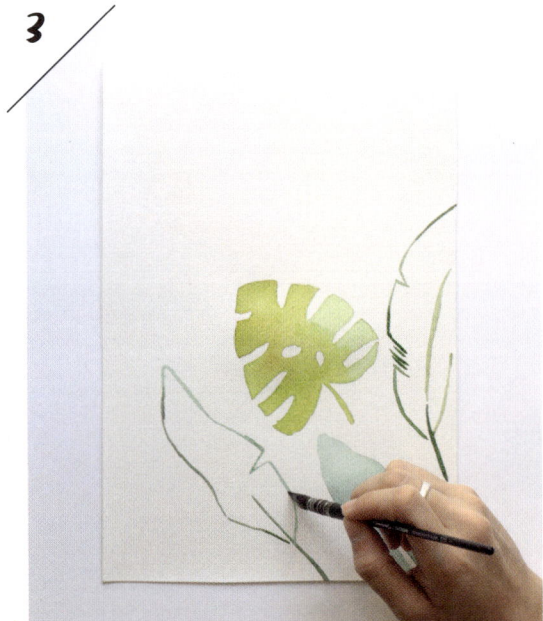

3

Paint more banana leaves in outline form only, to keep the pattern light (see exercise 2 on page 36). Vary the colors: blue-green, Greenish Umber, Emerald Green, etc.

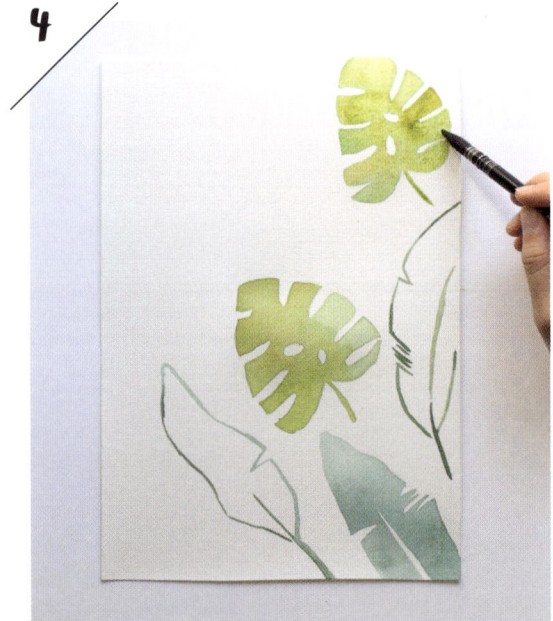

4

Mark out a second Swiss cheese leaf, similar to the first, in the top right corner. Paint close to the edge of the page and cut off part of the leaf if necessary.

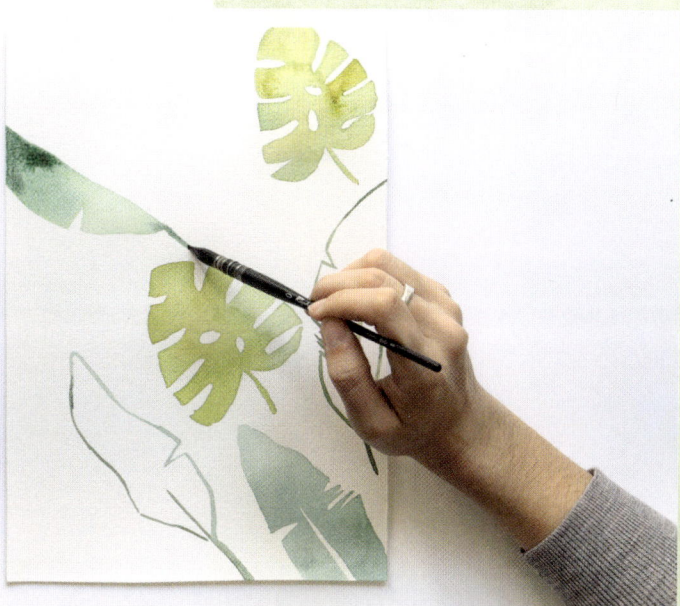

Paint another banana leaf, similar to the first, in blue-green tones. Before everything has dried, add pigment of varying degrees of concentration to create lovely color gradations using the wet-in-wet technique.

6 /

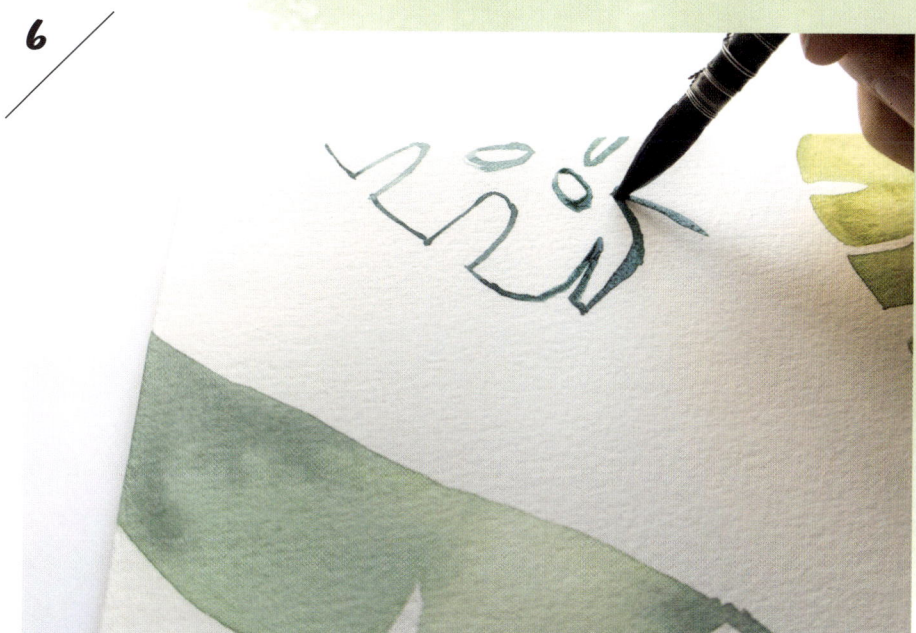

Create another Swiss cheese leaf close to the top left corner of the page. Use a dark blue-green solution (I used Greenish Umber and Phthalocyanine Turquoise here) and just paint the contours. The shape of the partly cut off leaf can be made out to give the illusion of the pattern continuing.

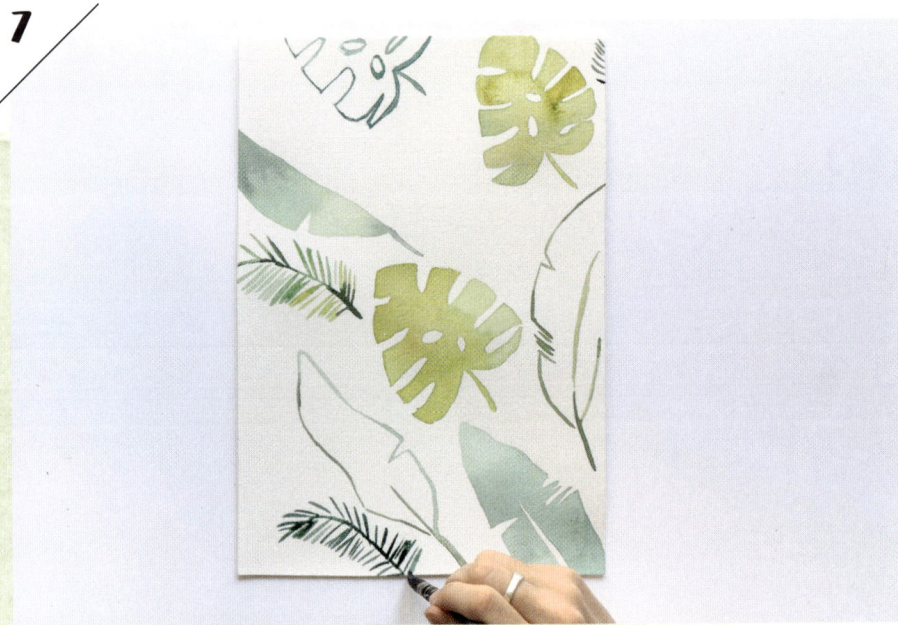

Balance up the pattern with three palm leaves in the same dark blue-green solution. Continue to position each leaf in the chosen diagonal direction to increase the effect of movement.

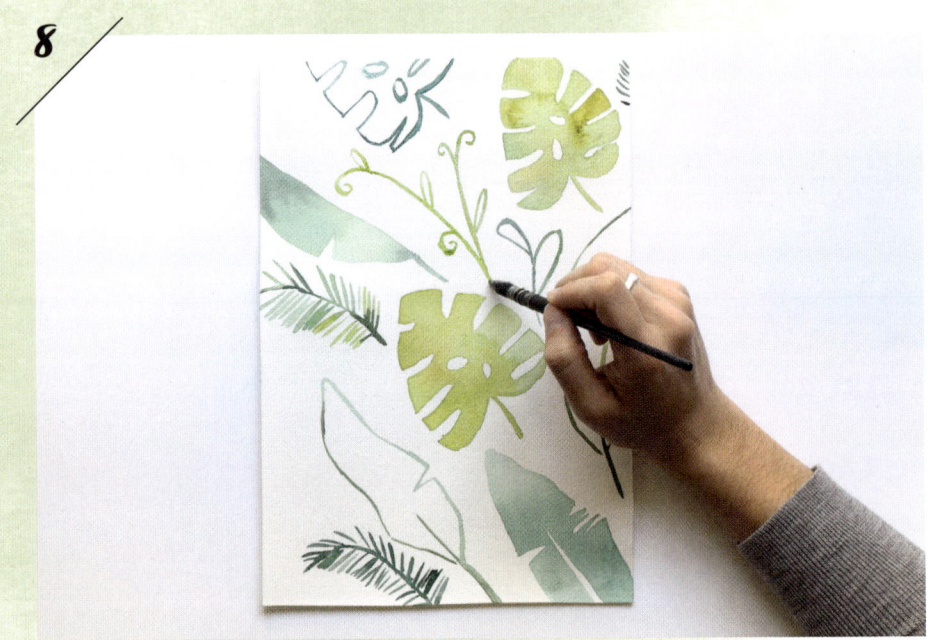

Add small elements such as fruits, leaves and stems in a jungle spirit, as shown on page 59. Make sure to use several colors for each line to make it more interesting.

9

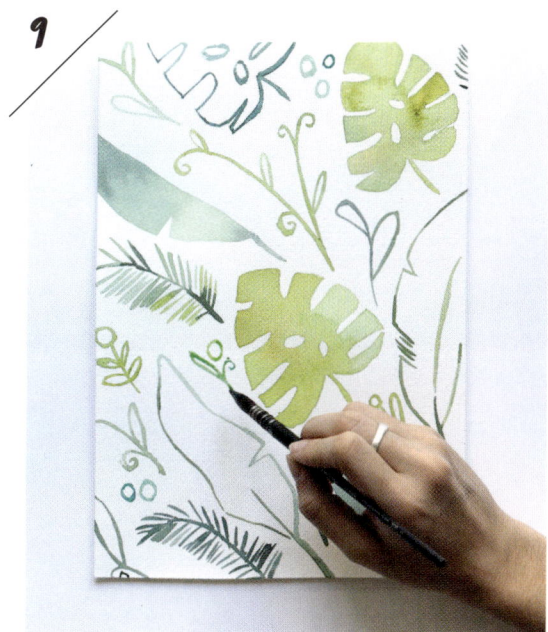

Add little circles to fill in empty areas of the pattern, continuing to use a variety of tones.

10

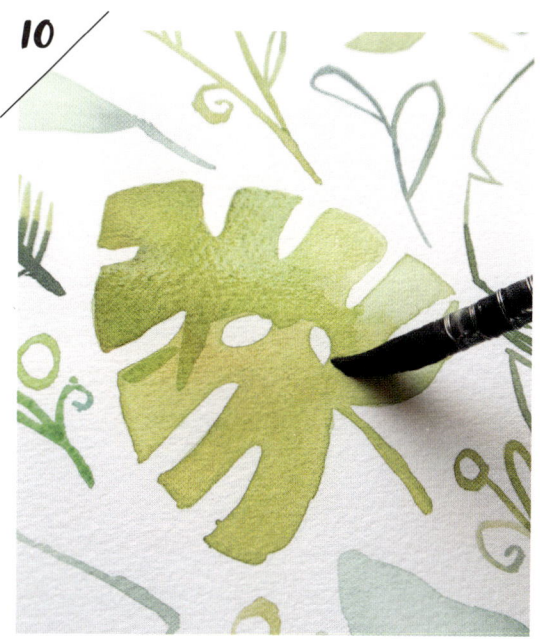

Once the largest leaves are dry, add another layer, using several shades of green. This will give the leaves greater depth and add contrast.

11

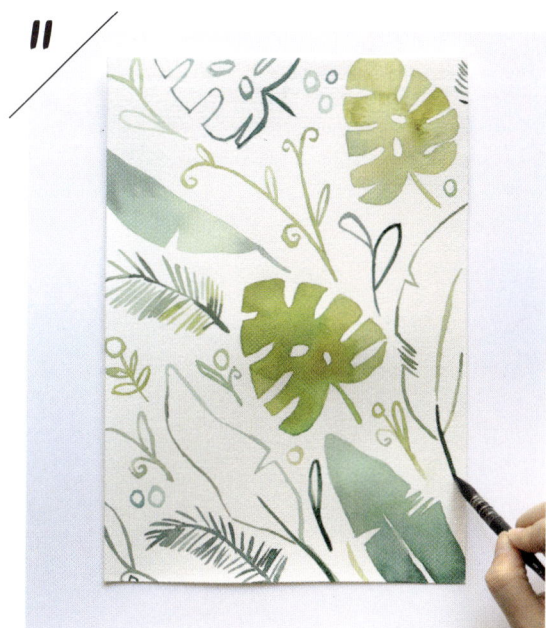

Go back over certain lines on the pattern with a dark green solution for greater color density.

12

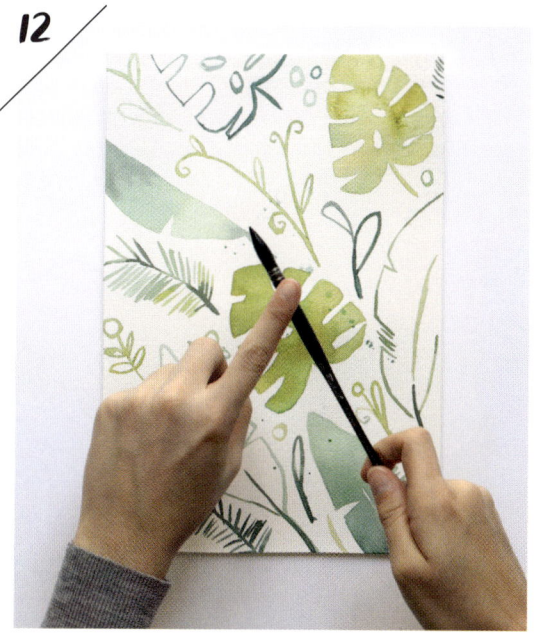

Finish off your painting by spattering random spots of paint. Load up your brush well with color and while holding it in one hand, almost at the end of the handle, tap the brush with one finger of your other hand, as illustrated above.

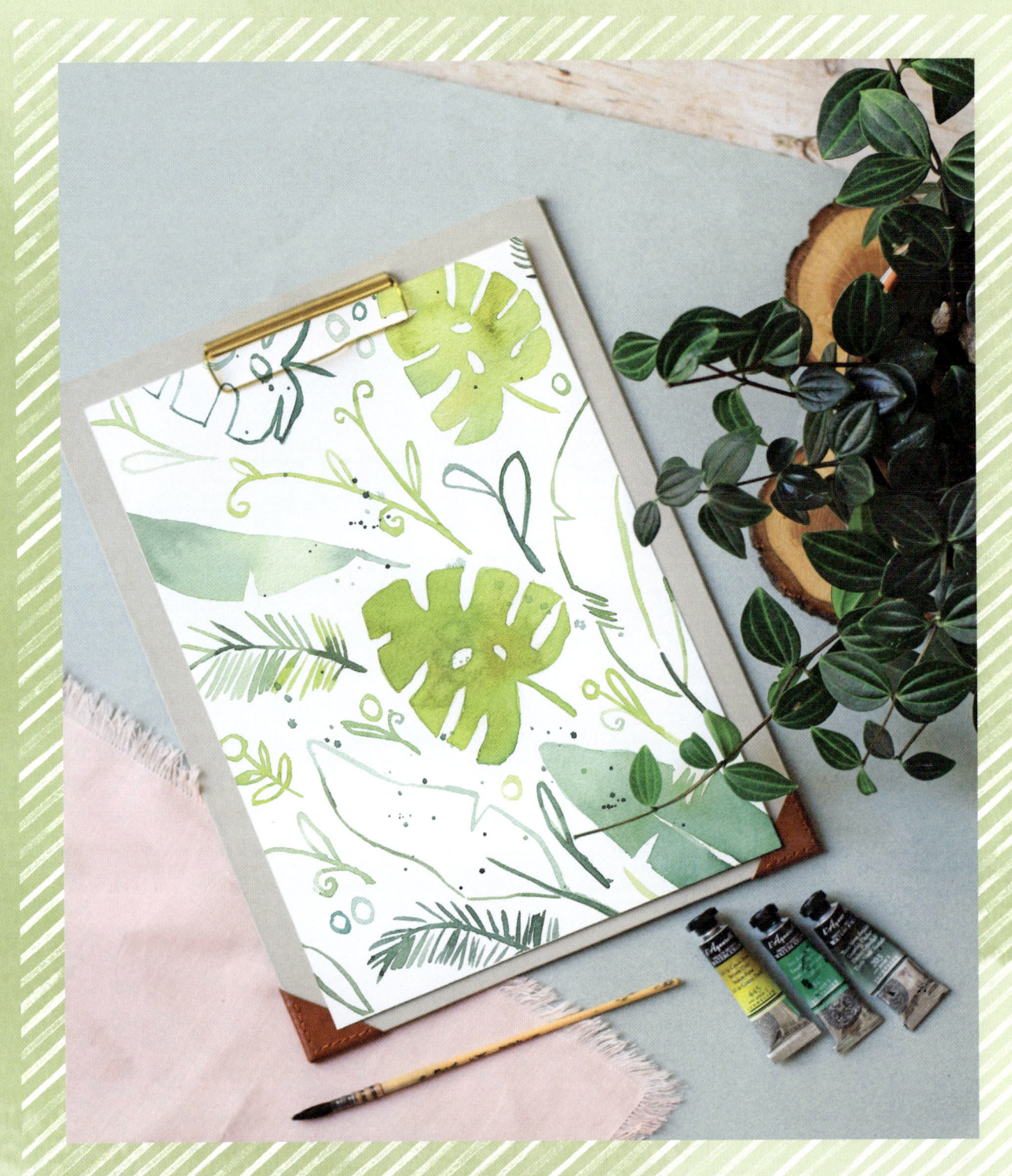

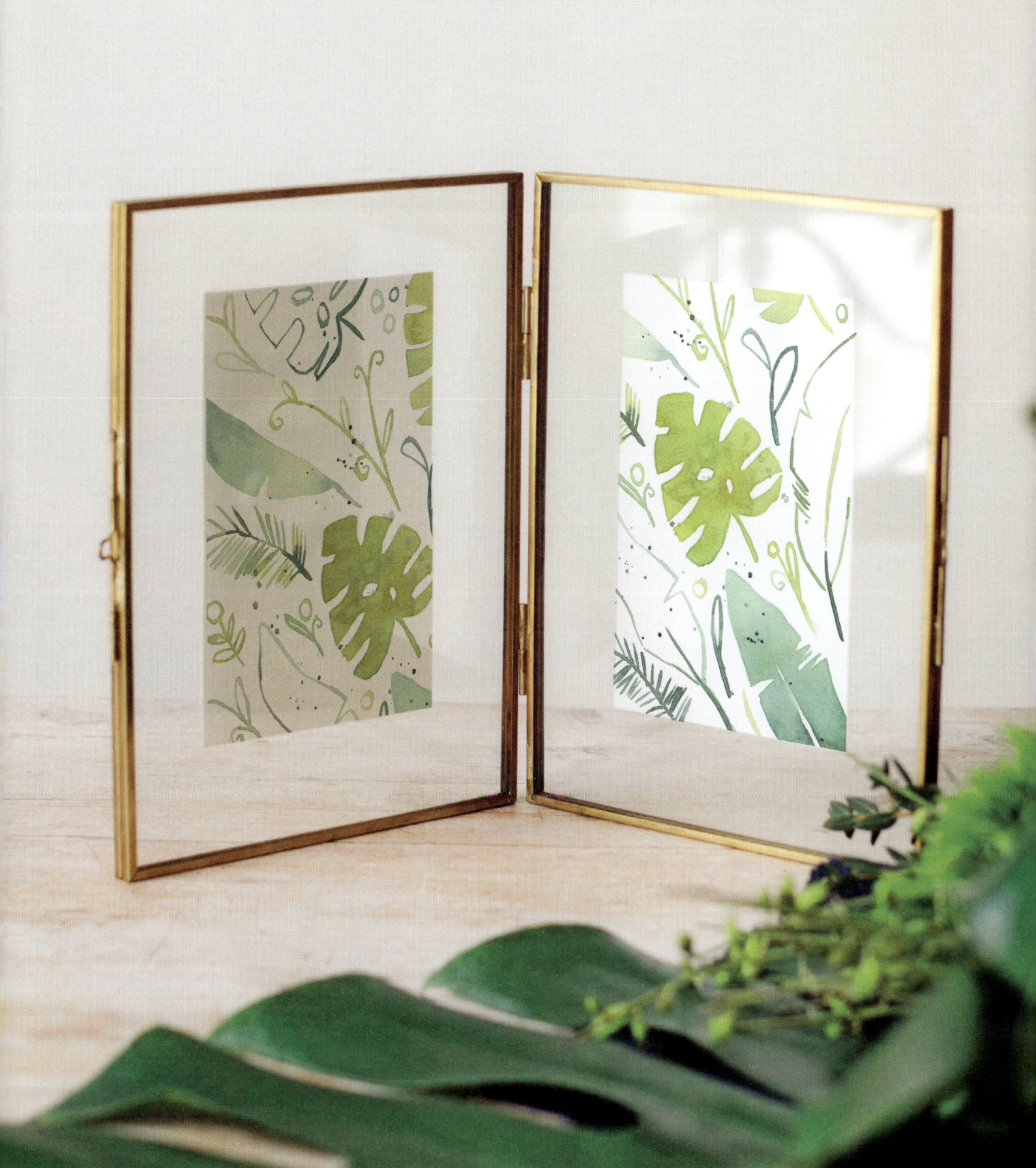

TRANSPARENT
jungle

I GOT THE INSPIRATION FOR THE FOLLOWING PAINTING FROM THE PLAY OF LIGHT OBSERVED THROUGH OVERLAPPING LEAVES IN THE MAJORELLE BOTANICAL GARDEN IN MOROCCO. IT'S NOT ALL THAT EASY TO EXPERIMENT WITH WATERCOLOR TRANSPARENCY. TO SIMPLIFY THINGS, I HAVE CHOSEN TO USE JUST ONE TYPE OF LEAF, THE BANANA LEAF, WITH THREE COLORS AND A DIAGONAL DIRECTION ONCE AGAIN, WHICH HELPS TO GIVE CONSISTENCY TO MY CREATION.

THE MAIN COLORS

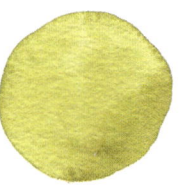

| Brown Green | Greenish Umber | Emerald Green |

Remember

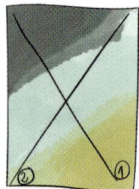

- The colors are split into three separate areas (see sketch).
- The selected directions are diagonal, referred to as 1 and 2 for ease of explanation.

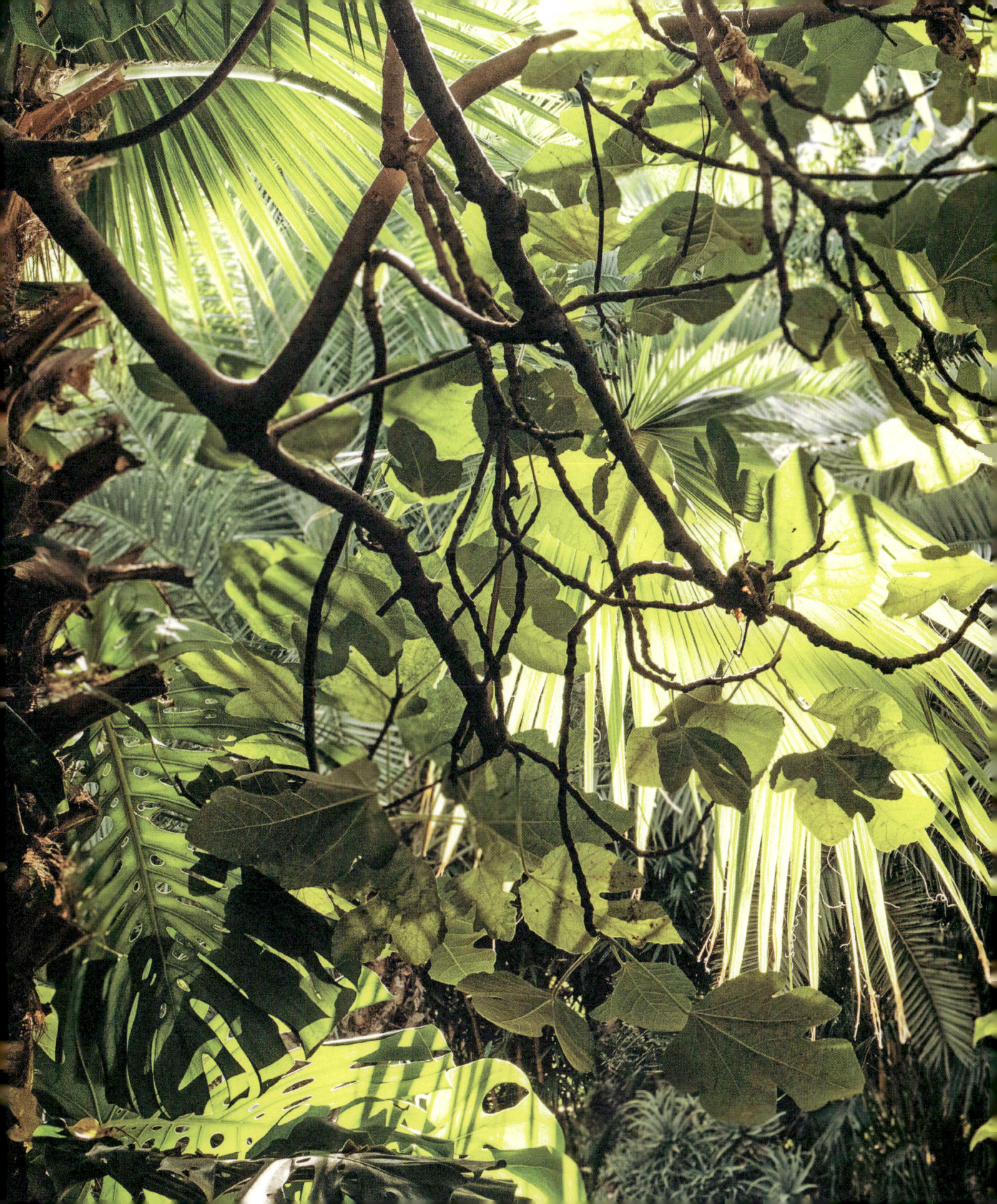

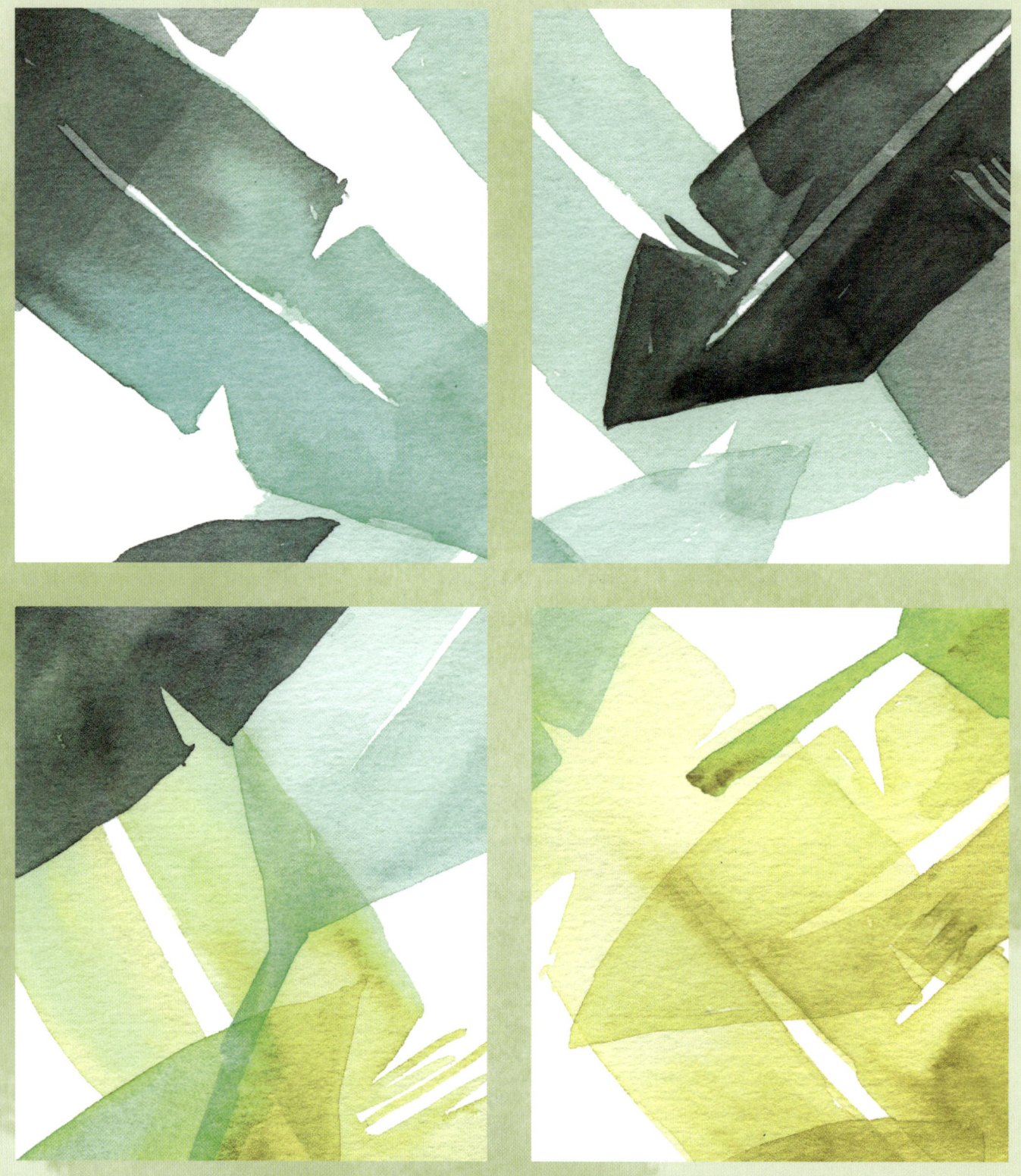

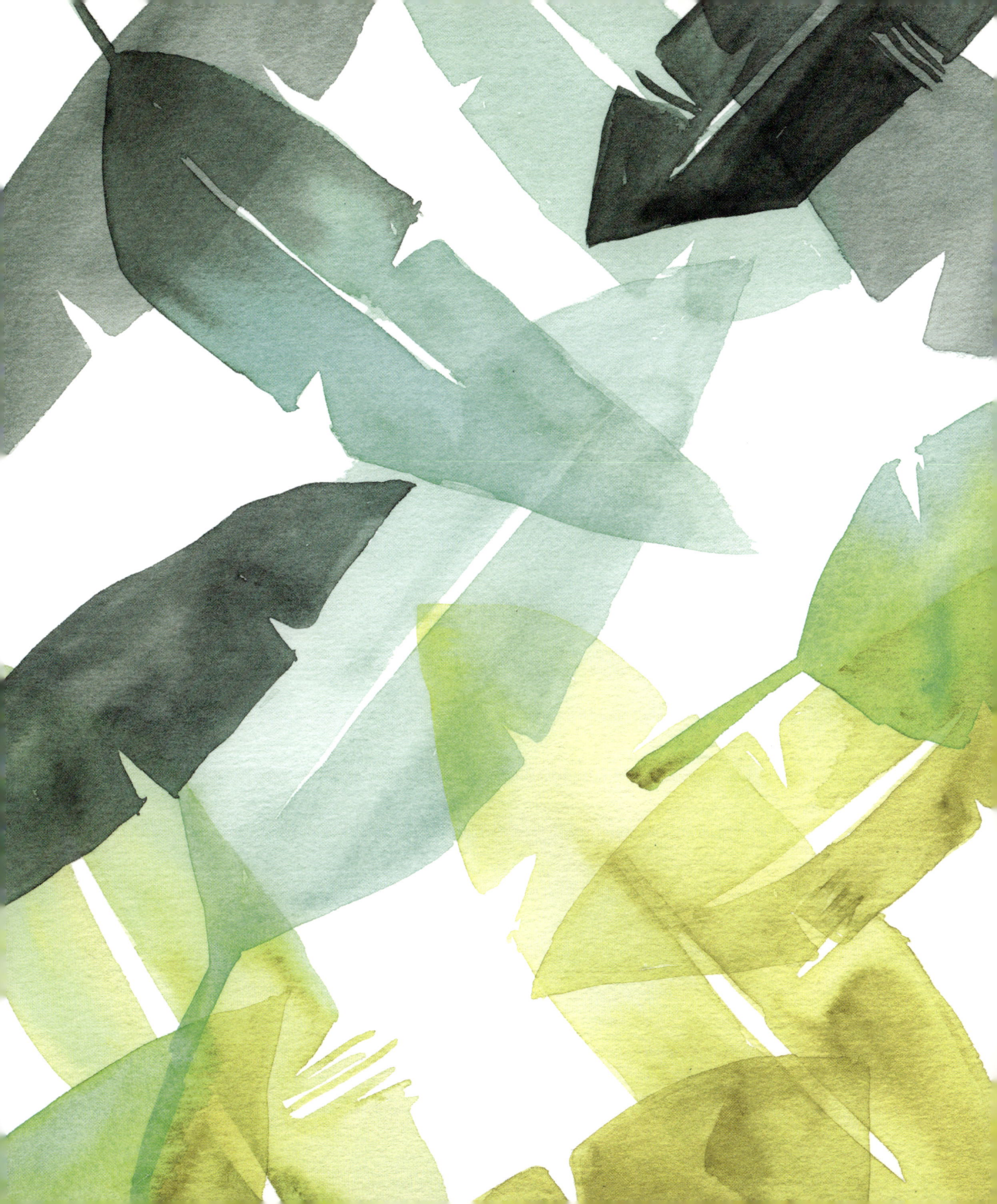

1

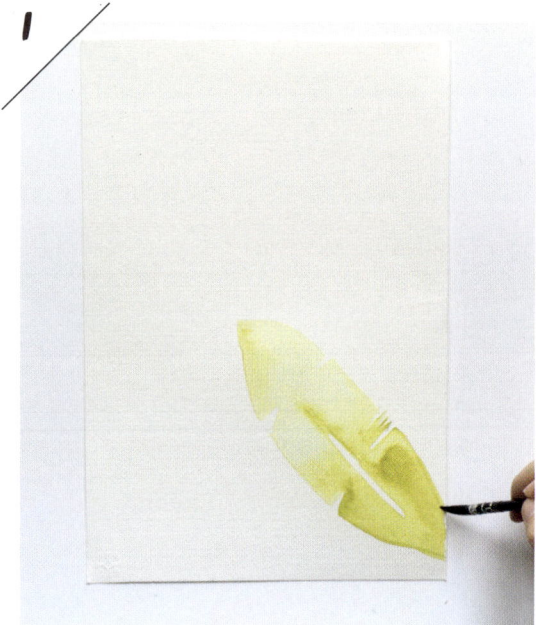

Start with a banana leaf in the bottom right corner, using a greenish yellow solution (shown here in Brown Green). The direction is diagonal 1.

2

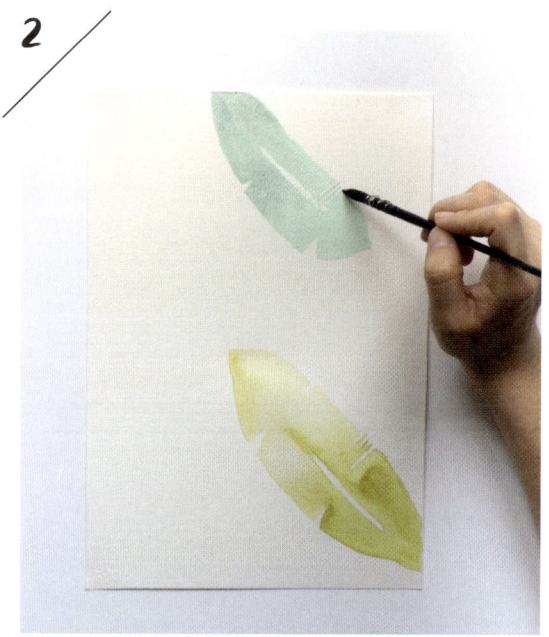

Paint a banana leaf in the same direction at the top of the page, with blue as a dominant color (Emerald Green) but also with a touch of grey-green (Greenish Umber).

3

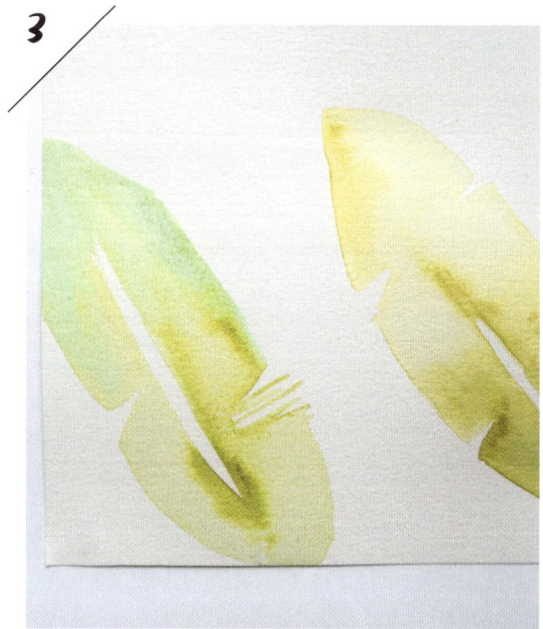

Paint a leaf close to the first, adding a few touches of blue. These first leaves are quite light. Remember that pigment concentration will increase as we add more layers (see page 26).

4

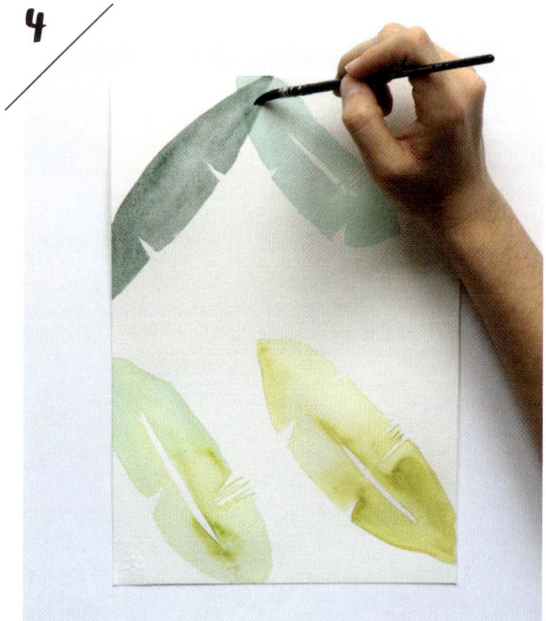

Paint a grey-green leaf seen from the side, and pointing in the opposite direction from the others, called diagonal 2. Varying the direction and shape of the leaves adds interest to the end result.

5 /

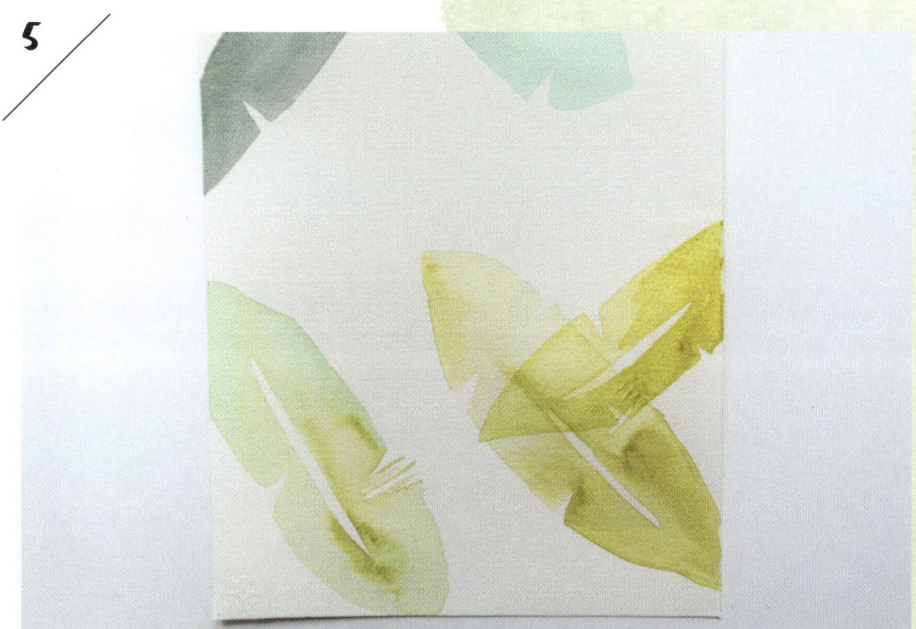

When everything is dry, return to your first leaf and paint another in greenish yellow tones, following the line of diagonal 2.

6 /

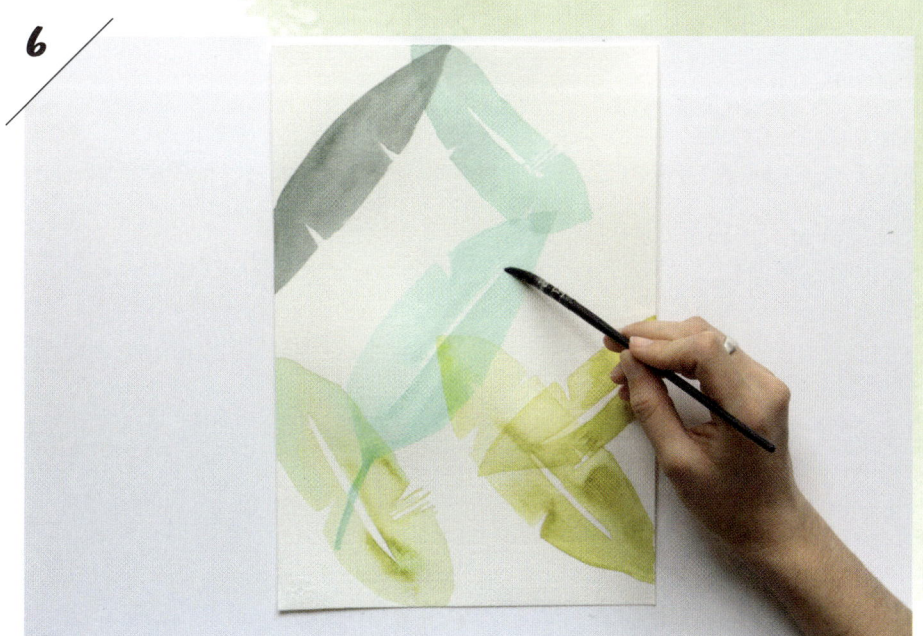

Continue by adding a new blue-green leaf in the middle of the page. Be careful not to linger on areas that have already been painted as, although they are dry, going over them with a wet brush may cause smudges.

7 /

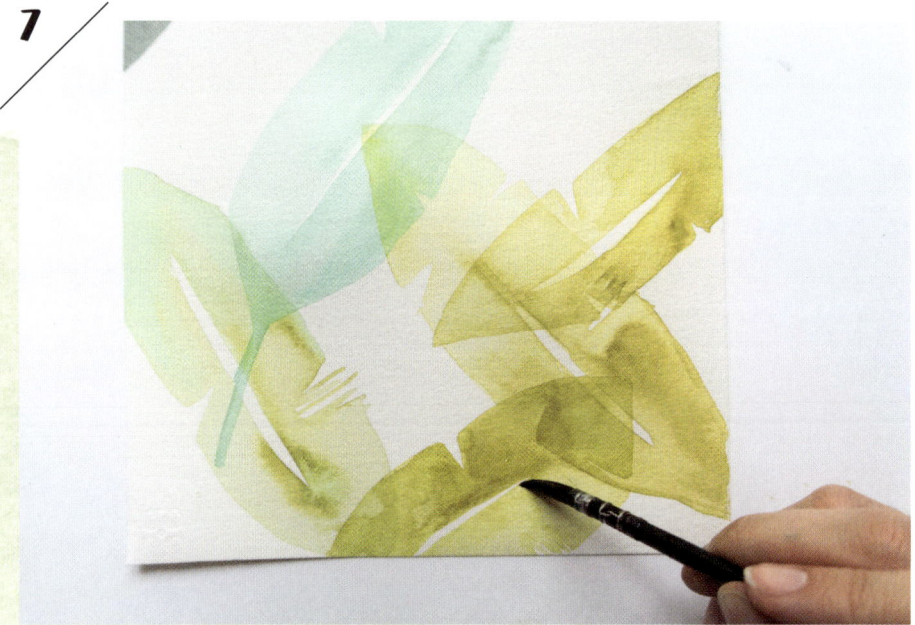

Add another greenish yellow leaf at the bottom of the page, with part of the leaf cut off. Start increasing the amount of pigment used. I always use the same three colors (Brown Green in this case).

8 /

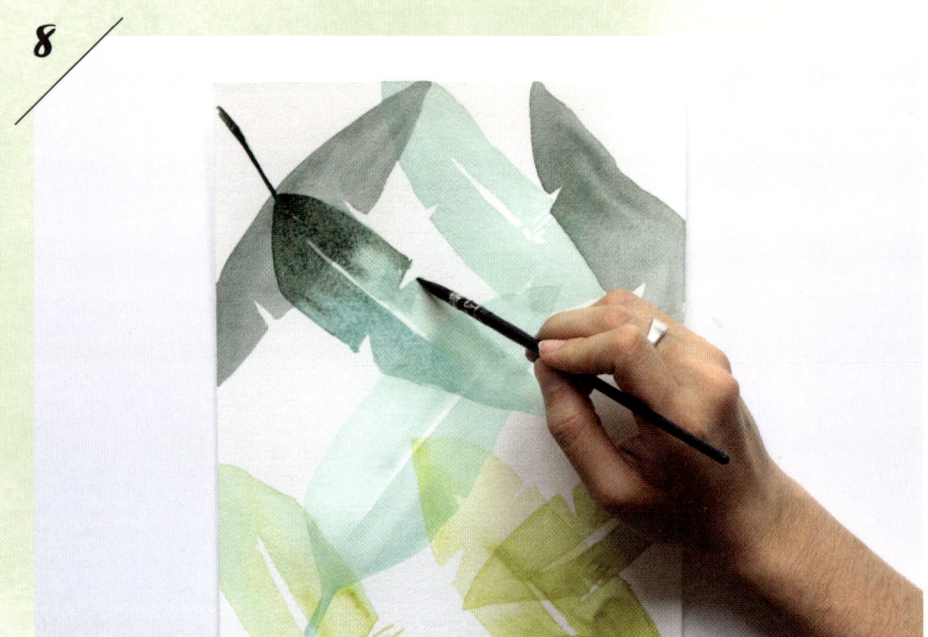

Paint an overlapping leaf following the line of diagonal 1, using blue and grey tones. Don't forget to leave some white space to represent the central vein, if it is a face-on view.

9

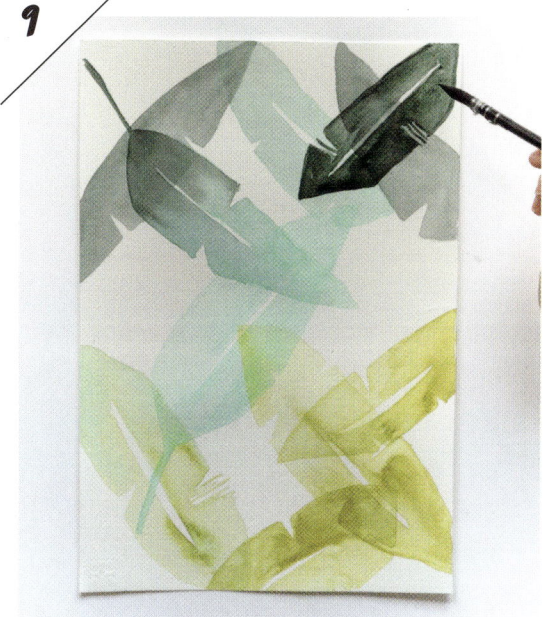

In the top right corner, add another grey-green leaf using a concentrated solution.

10

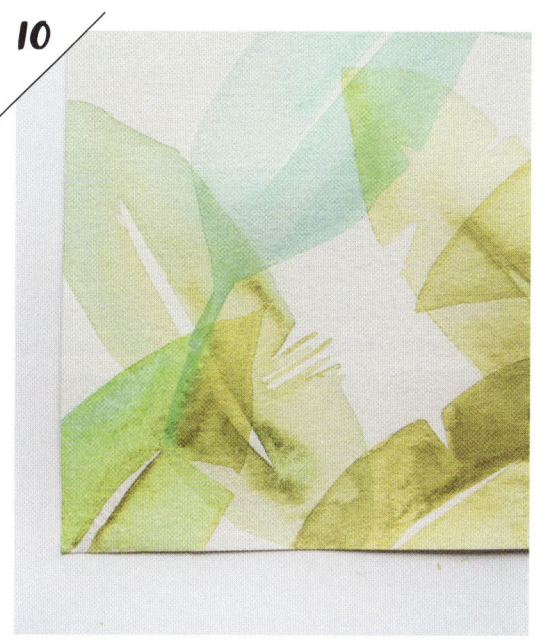

In the bottom left corner, add part of a predominantly greenish yellow leaf. Using the wet-in-wet technique, feel free to add in blue-green dots.

11

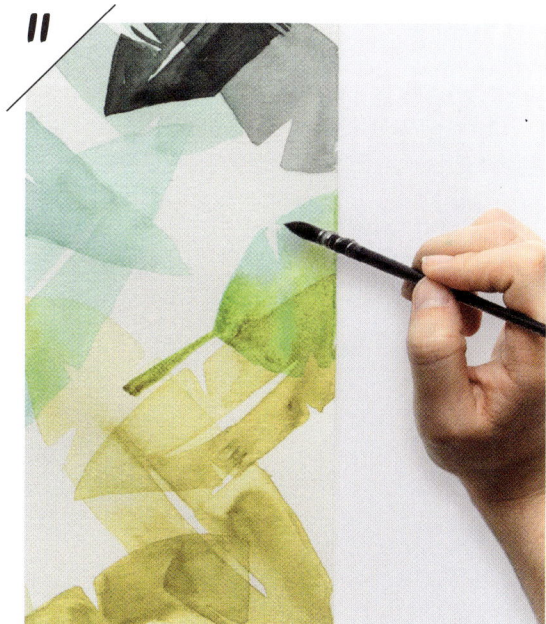

Do the same with a leaf on the right-hand side of the page, positioning it so it is only partly visible.

12

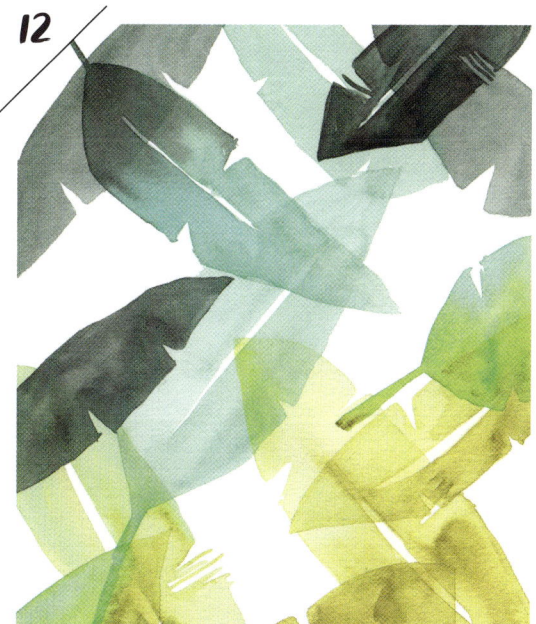

On the left, finish off with a grey-green leaf seen from the side, using a highly concentrated solution.

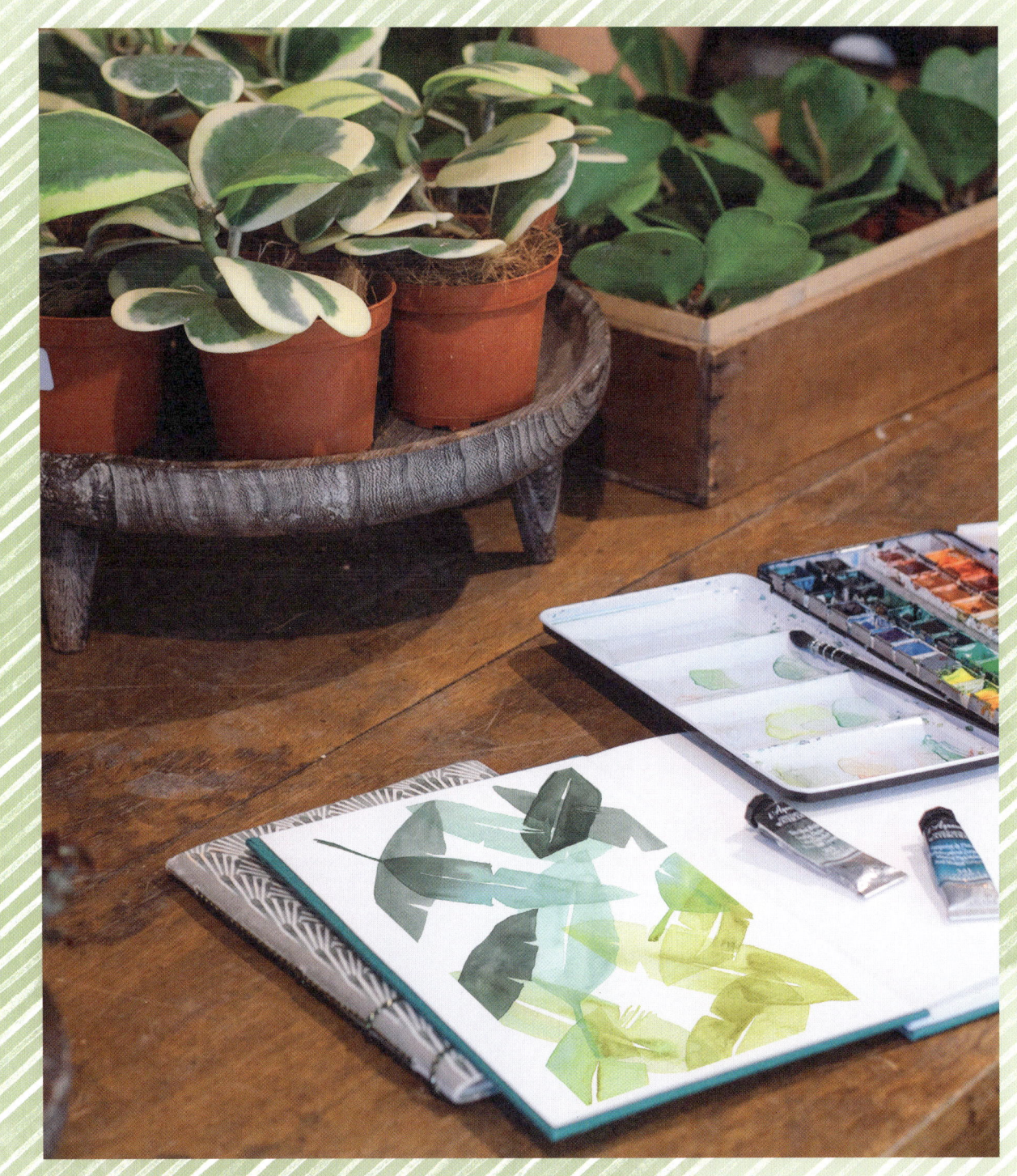

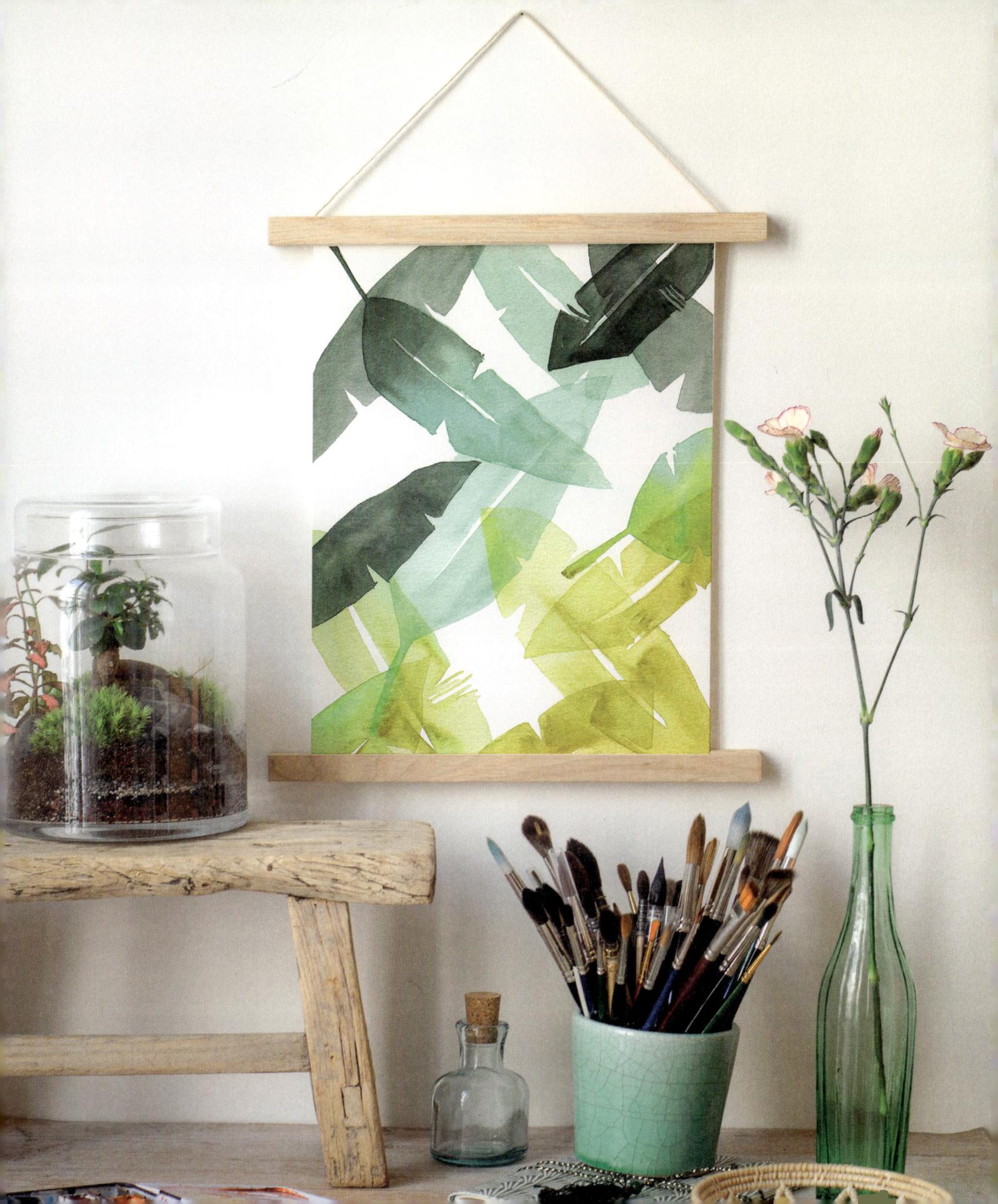

OTHER
ideas

DISCOVER NEW CREATIVE IDEAS WITH THE EXAMPLES BELOW.

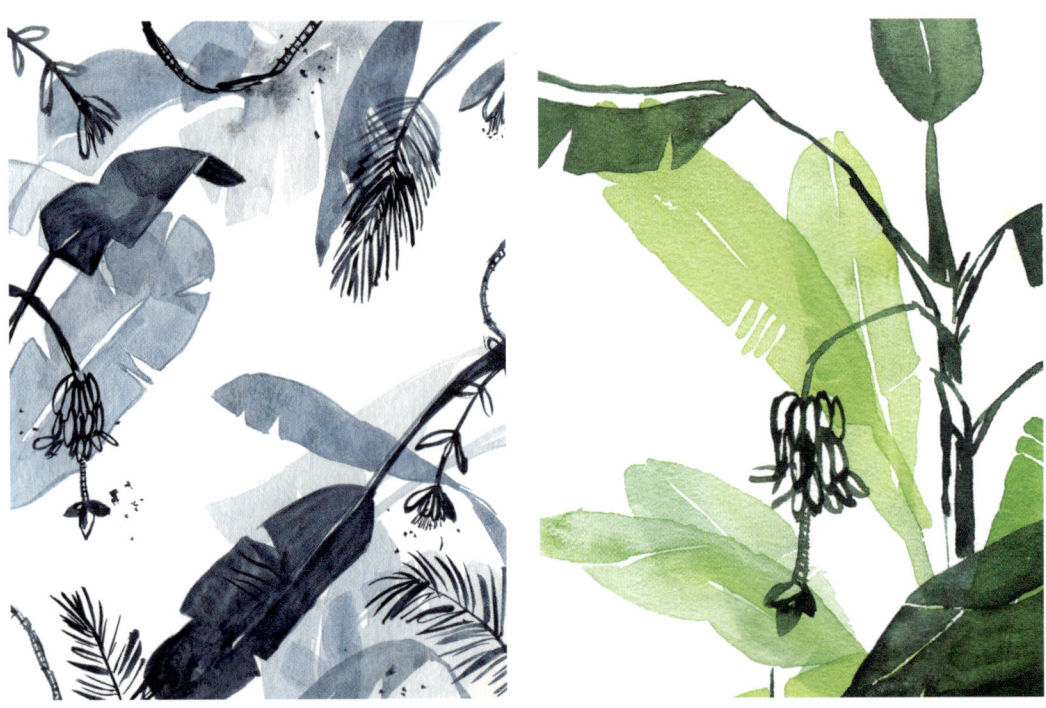

Combine the three leaves you've learnt about in this chapter in a monochromatic painting that also experiments with the transparency of watercolors. Start with light layers and finish with the darkest layers. Details like small plants, vines and a cluster of bananas are also painted in the darkest color to accentuate depth.

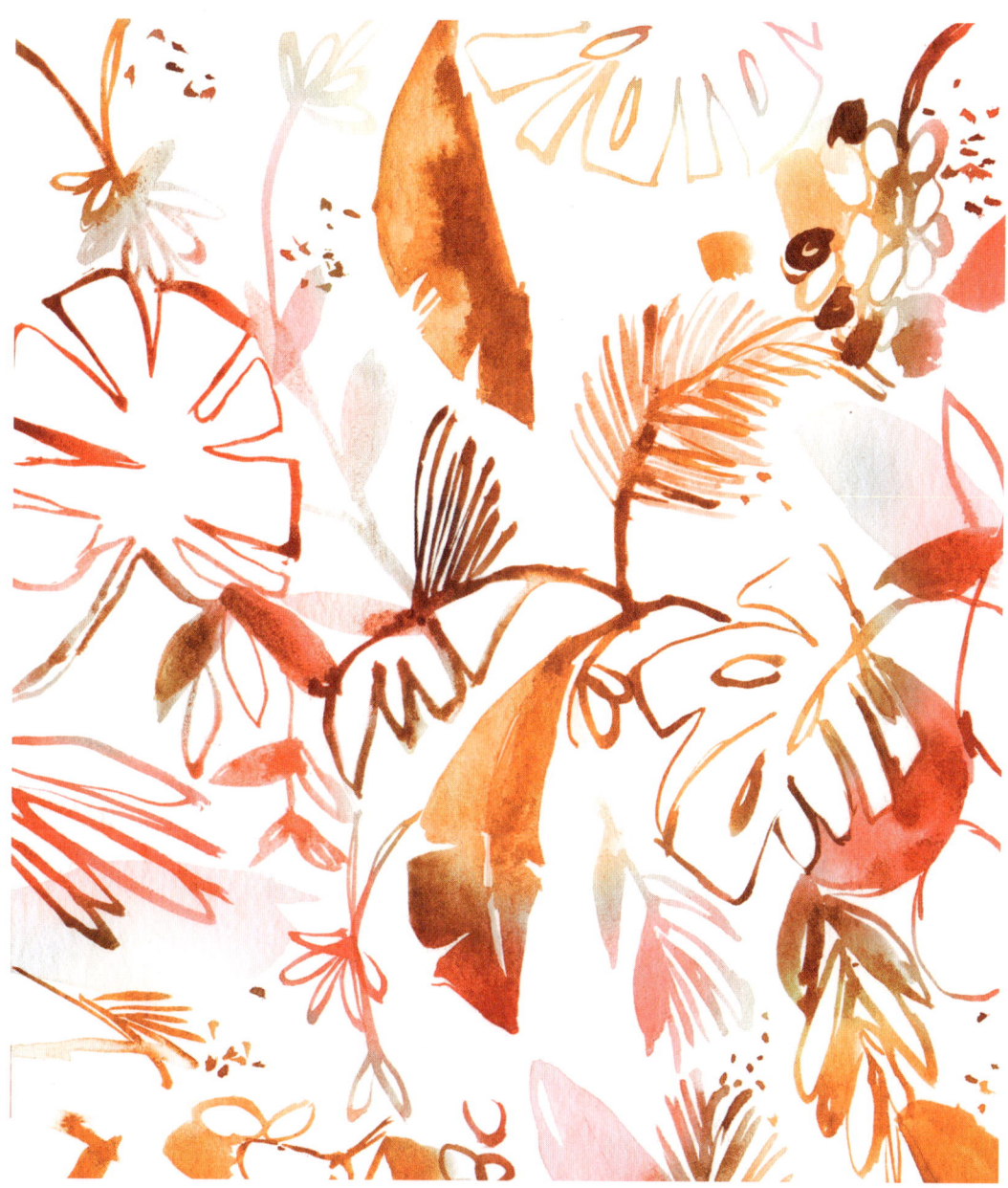

This painting was done very quickly. I experimented with the hallmarks of watercolor painting and replicated the exercise from page 30 but with plants instead of the lozenge shape. Some of the plants are not perfect, but that's the spontaneous result that interests me. Everything merges together and gives a lush jungle effect.

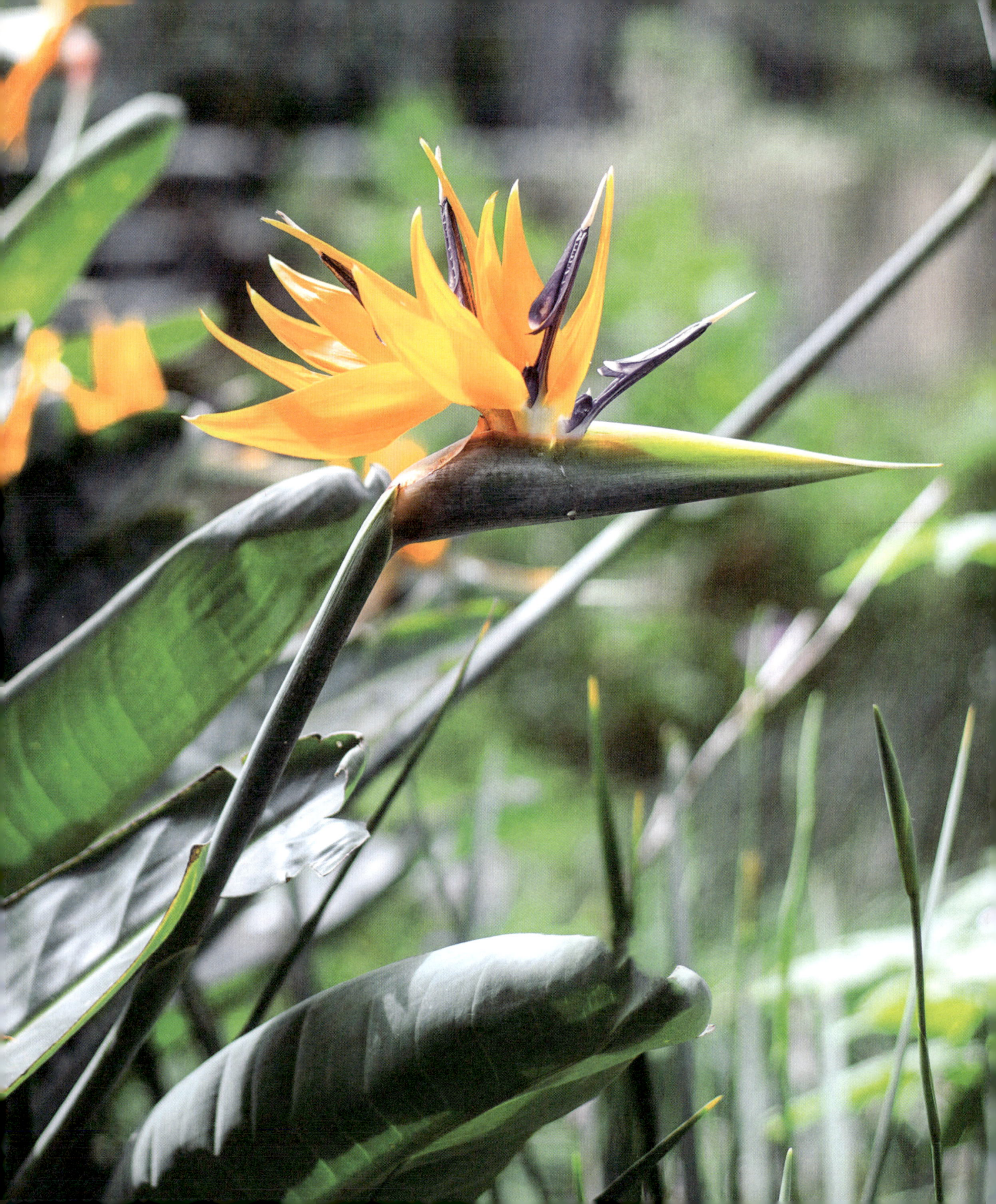

CHAPTER 03

Tropical flowers

TROPICAL FLOWERS COME IN UNUSUAL SHAPES AND VIVID COLORS THAT ARE FASCINATING TO PAINT, BUT OFTEN THESE FLOWERS ARE A DIFFERENT PART OF THE PLANT. SINCE IT IS EASIER TO PAINT A PLANT FEATURE THAT YOU PROPERLY UNDERSTAND, I'VE DONE SEVERAL LITTLE SKETCHES FOR YOU TO FAMILIARIZE YOURSELF WITH THE PLANT AND ITS SOMETIMES COMPLEX BOTANICAL VOCABULARY.

Hibiscus

THE HIBISCUS IS A BEAUTIFUL FLOWER THAT IS OFTEN MONOCHROMATIC OR TWO-TONE. IT HAS FIVE PETALS, OUT OF WHICH RISES THE PISTIL, SET WITH STAMENS.

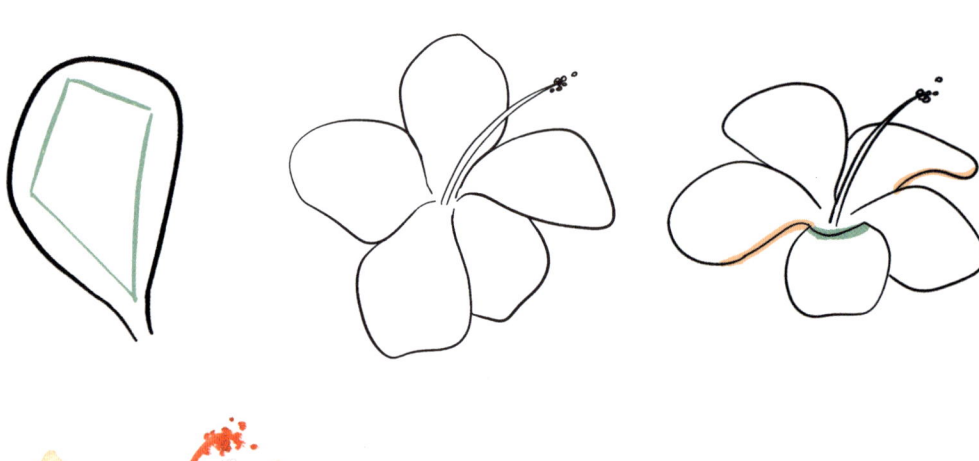

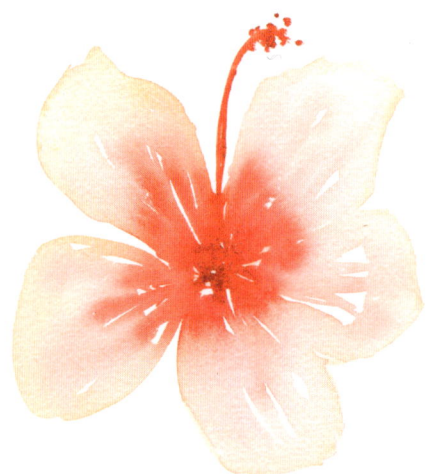

In this demonstration, I explain how you paint a front-on view of a hibiscus. Think of its petals as kites with flattened corners. To depict a sideways view of it, use the help of the orange and green markers above for the best representation of this flower.

1 /

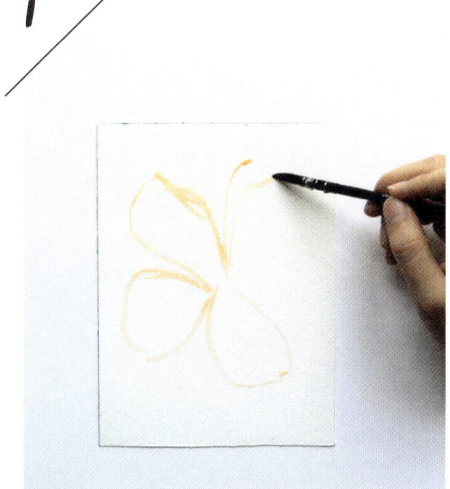

Start by painting the overall outline of the flower using a very light solution. The petals have an elongated yet rounded shape that reminds me of a kite.

2 /

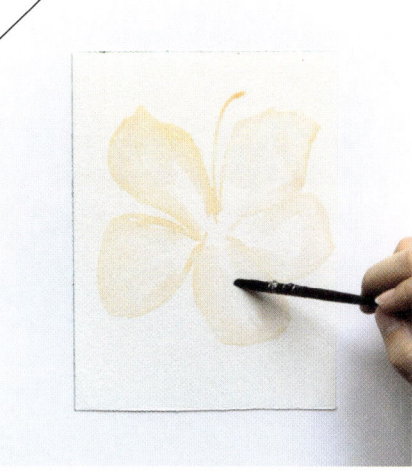

Thicken the contours of the flower with the same solution. Everything needs to stay wet throughout the procedure to get the best possible result.

3 /

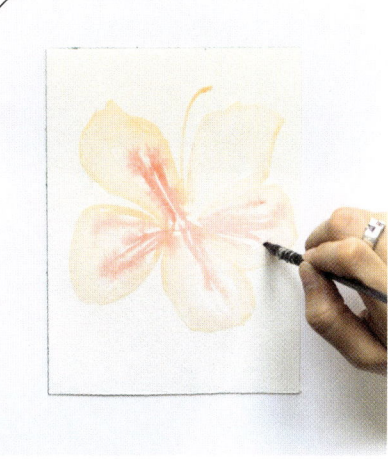

Using a darker solution (here it's pink), paint a set of lines running from the center of the flower to the middle of the petals. Deliberately leave lots of white spaces. Work fast, applying very little pressure to the brush.

4 /

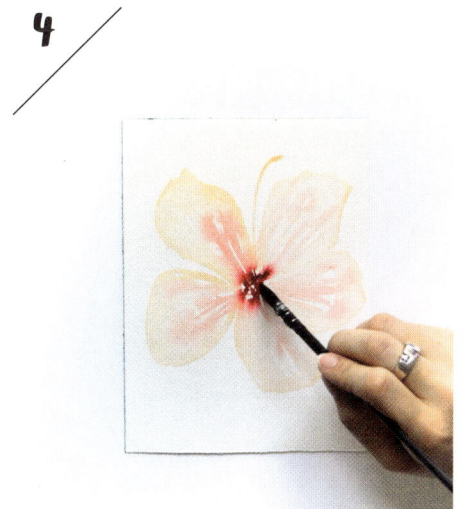

Make the most of the fact that everything is still wet to apply some highly concentrated solution to the very center of the flower. I use a mix of Opera Rose and Alizarin Crimson.

5 /

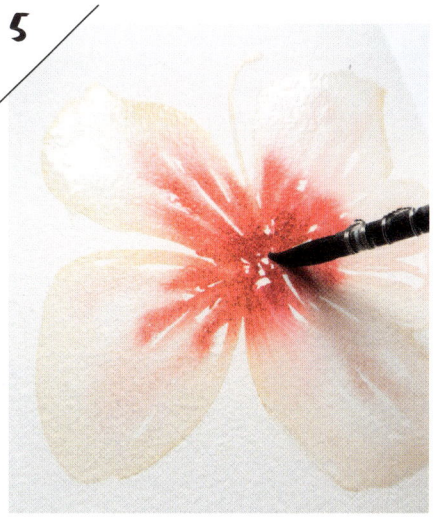

The dark red and pink pigments gently disperse, creating a lovely gradation effect. Add some just to the center, not touching the rest of the flower, and let the colors merge.

6 /

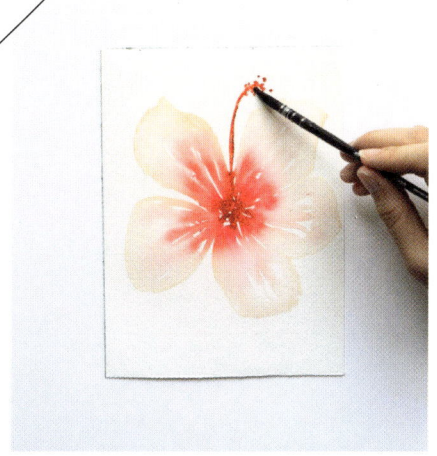

Paint the pistil (a long, curved stem) and the stamens (simple little dots) using the same concentrated solution.

BIRD OF *paradise*

BIRD OF PARADISE IS THE NAME GIVEN TO SPECIES WITHIN THE STRELITZIA GENUS. THE LEAVES OF THIS PLANT RESEMBLE THOSE OF A BANANA TREE AND THEIR STRIKING FLOWERS LOOK LIKE A BIRD'S HEAD. SEE HOW TO PAINT THEM IN JUST A FEW BRUSHSTROKES.

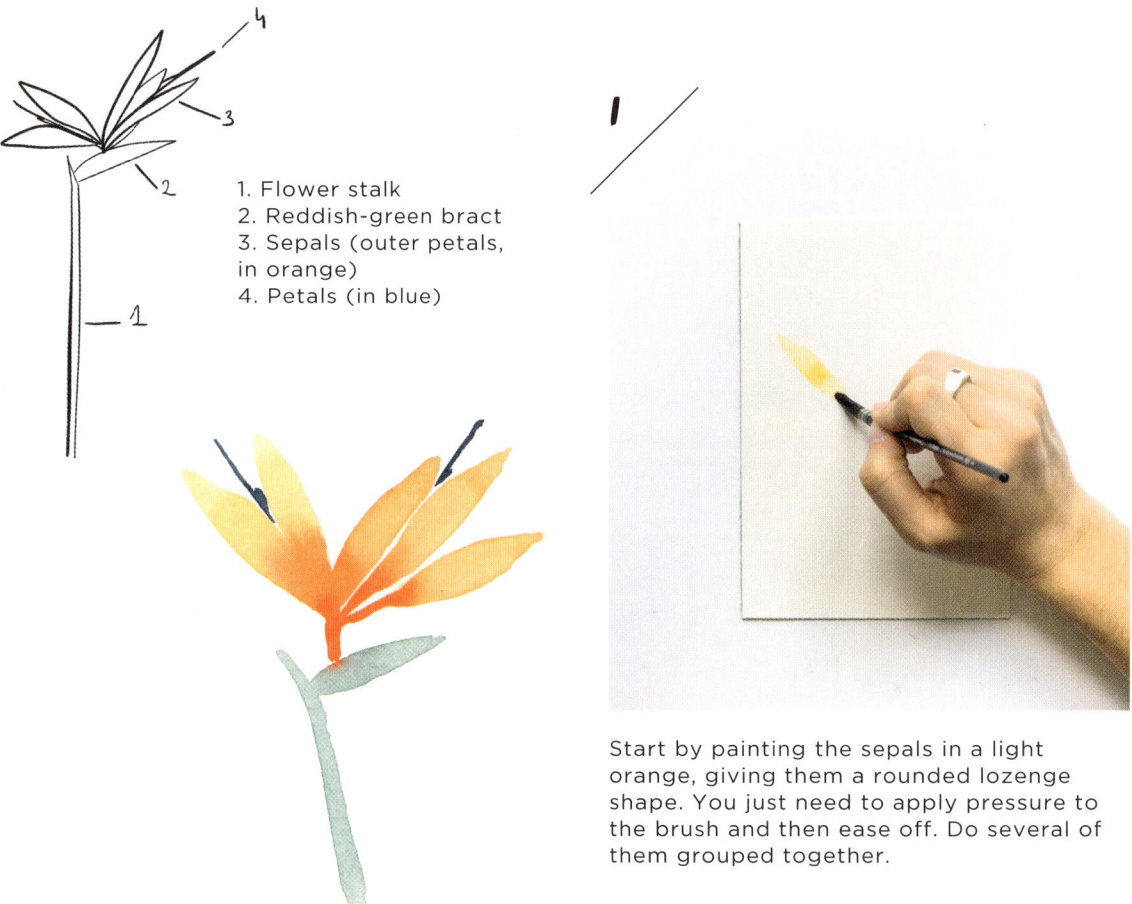

1. Flower stalk
2. Reddish-green bract
3. Sepals (outer petals, in orange)
4. Petals (in blue)

Start by painting the sepals in a light orange, giving them a rounded lozenge shape. You just need to apply pressure to the brush and then ease off. Do several of them grouped together.

2

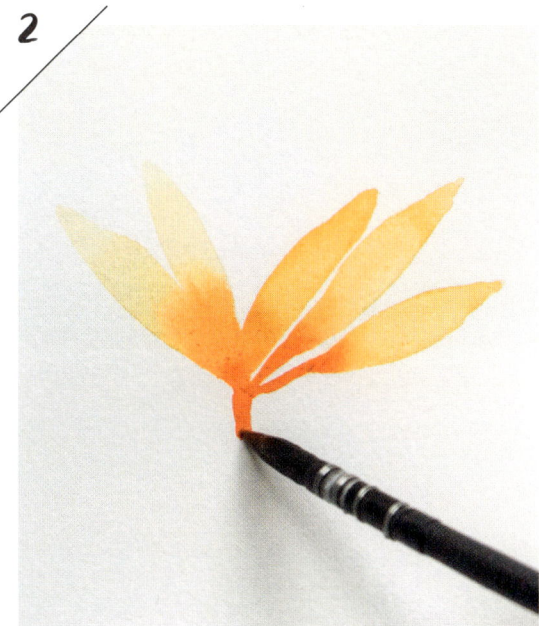

Using an orangy red color (French Vermilion shown here), paint the end of the sepals where they join together. The color will disperse to create beautiful color gradients.

3

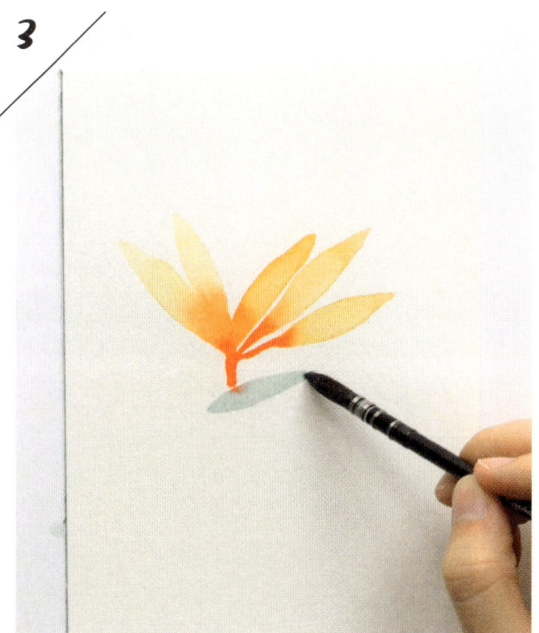

Now paint the bract, using a very light grey-green (here it is diluted Greenish Umber). It is in a virtually horizontal position and more or less the same shape as the sepals.

4

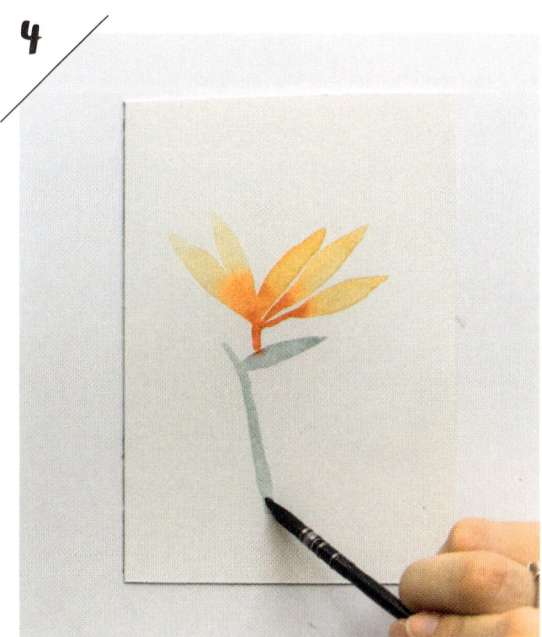

Continue using the same solution to paint the flower stalk as illustrated above.

5

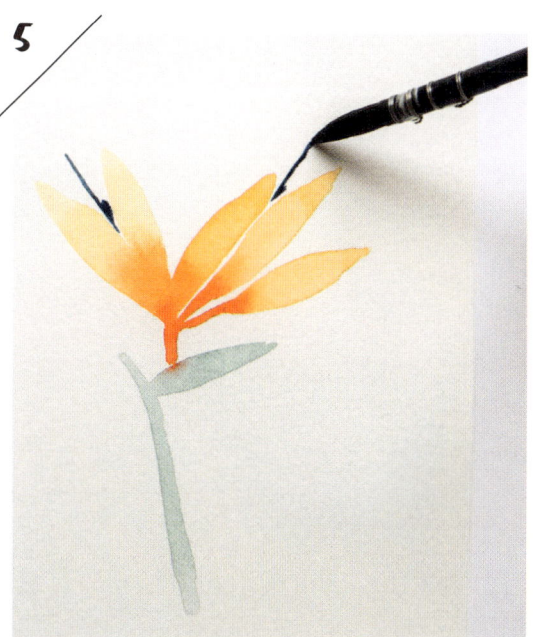

Finish off with bright blue petals (I used Indigo here). The base is wider than the tip. Press very gently on the tip of the brush to get this fine line.

Heliconia

THERE ARE DOZENS OF VARIETIES IN THE HELICONIA GENUS (ALSO KNOWN AS LOBSTER-CLAW OR PARROT FLOWER). THESE PLANTS ARE SIMILAR IN APPEARANCE TO A BIRD OF PARADISE BUT OFFER INTERESTING PICTORIAL VARIATIONS FOR EXPLORING IN WATERCOLORS.

HELICONIA PSITTACORUM OR PARROT'S BEAK

1. Bracts
2. Flowers

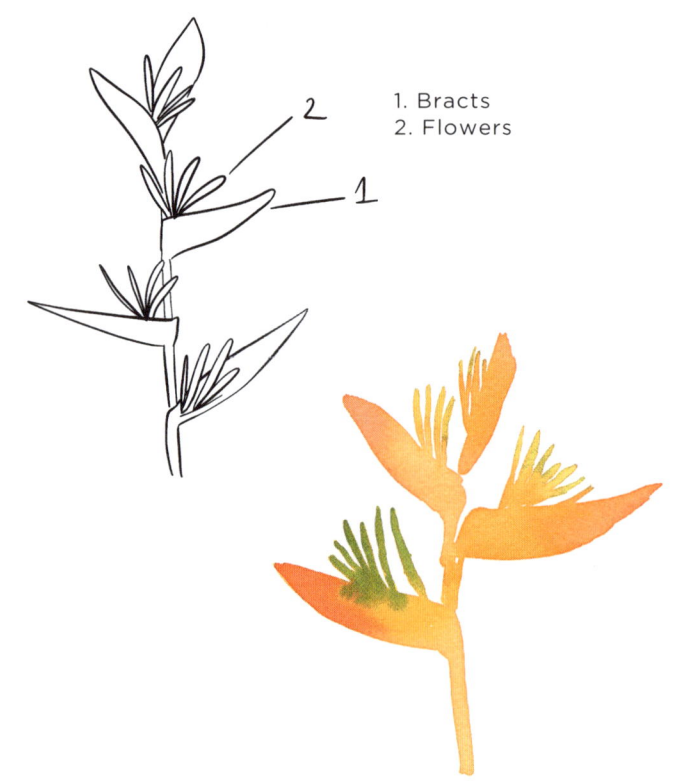

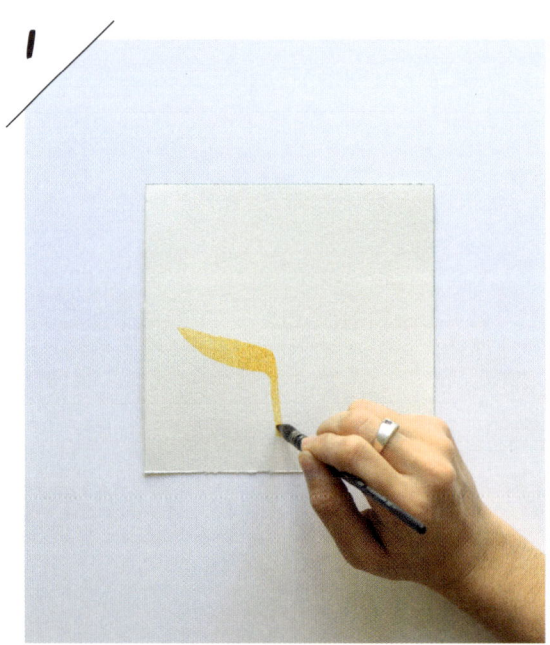

Using an orangy yellow solution (here it is Indian Yellow with a little Red Orange), paint the first bract and bottom of the flower stalk. Don't vary the color, just vary the amount of pressure on the brush: heavy for a thick line and light for a thin line.

2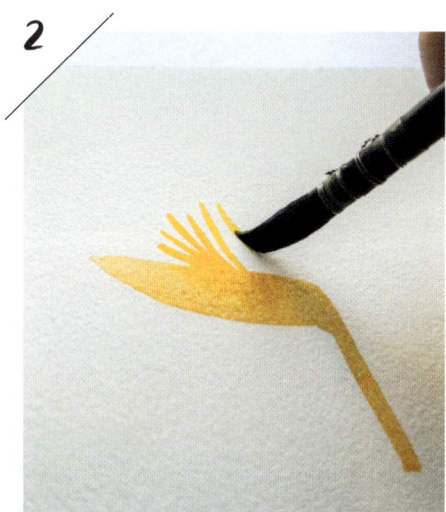

Using the same mix, paint the flowers, applying slight pressure to the tip of your brush.

3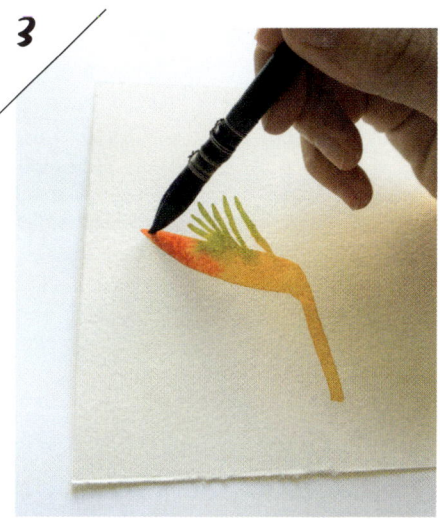

While everything is still wet, add some yellowish green to the ends of the flowers (Olive Green here) and orangy red to the end of the bract (French Vermilion shown here).

4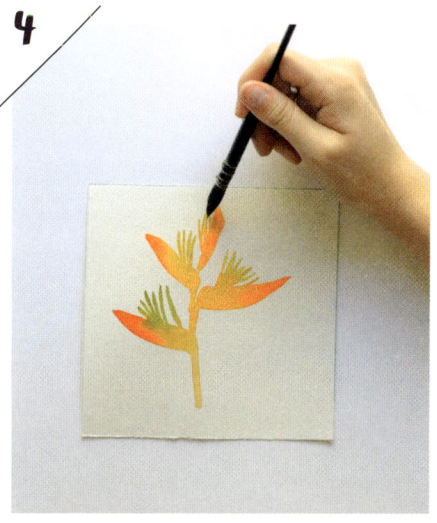

Repeat the process until you reach the top of the plant where the bracts are more vertical.

HELICONIA ROSTRATA OR LOBSTER-CLAW

Follow the same method to paint this variety of Heliconia, the flowers of which are virtually invisible, starting at the bottom and gradually adding pigment to create pretty color gradients. I used a French Vermilion base and added a greenish yellow mix. The bracts here are slightly less slender. There is another variety, Heliconia Peachy Pink, in mainly orange tones.

1. Bracts
2. Flowers

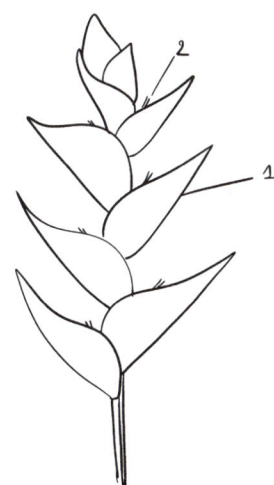

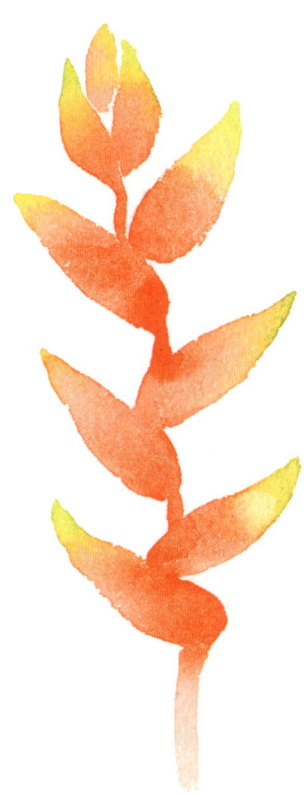

TORCH
ginger

THE TORCH GINGER FLOWER IS SO INCREDIBLE YOU'D THINK IT WAS ARTIFICIAL. ITS NUMEROUS SHADES OF RED ADD A MAGNIFICENT CONTRAST TO OUR VERDANT COMPOSITIONS THAT WE COULD NOT DO WITHOUT.

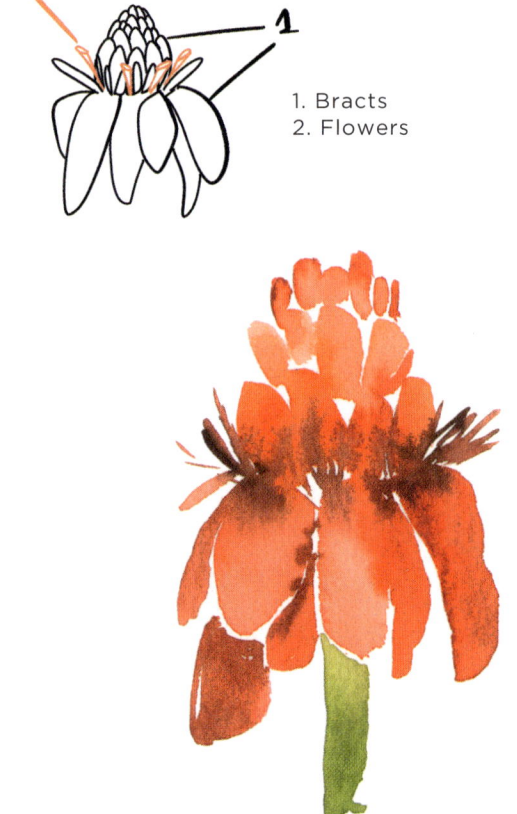

1. Bracts
2. Flowers

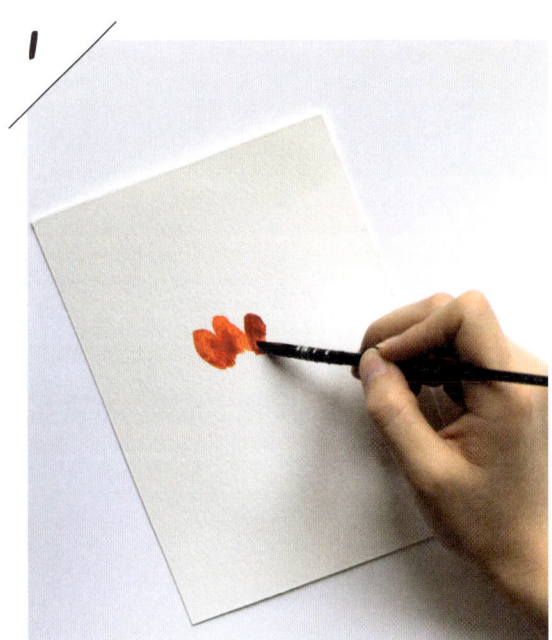

Start by painting several oval-shaped bracts in the center of the plant. I suggest you do not differentiate the flowers (see sketch), as they are very similar to the bracts, with the only difference being their yellow surround.

2 /

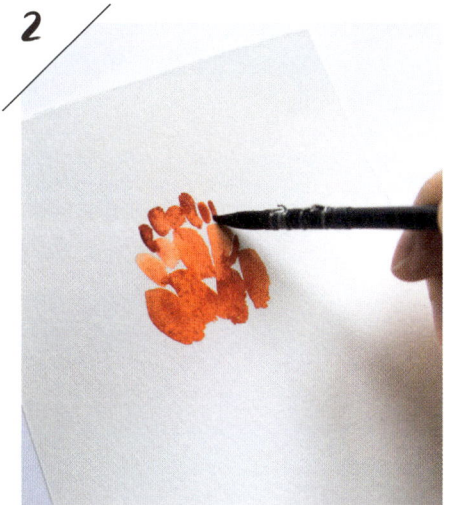

Continue painting bracts to represent the cone that forms the plant. Vary the concentration of red pigment (Alizarin Crimson + French Vermilion shown here).

3 /

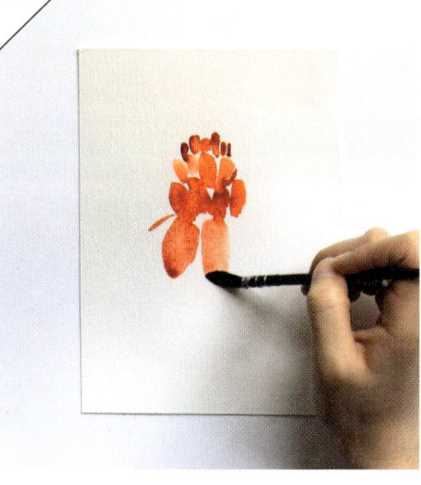

Paint the biggest bracts, hanging down, by pressing firmly on the brush. The bracts get smaller the nearer they are to the top of the cone.

4 /

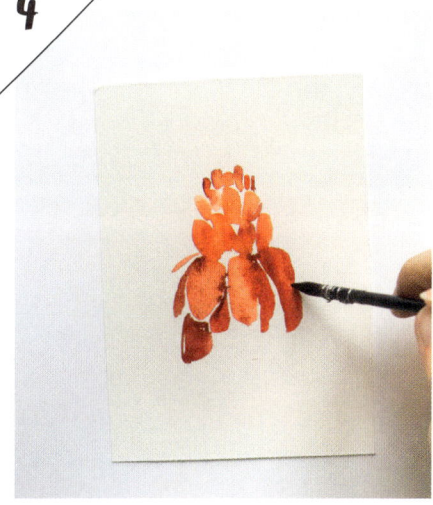

Once again, remember to vary the pigment concentration to make the plant interesting.

5 /

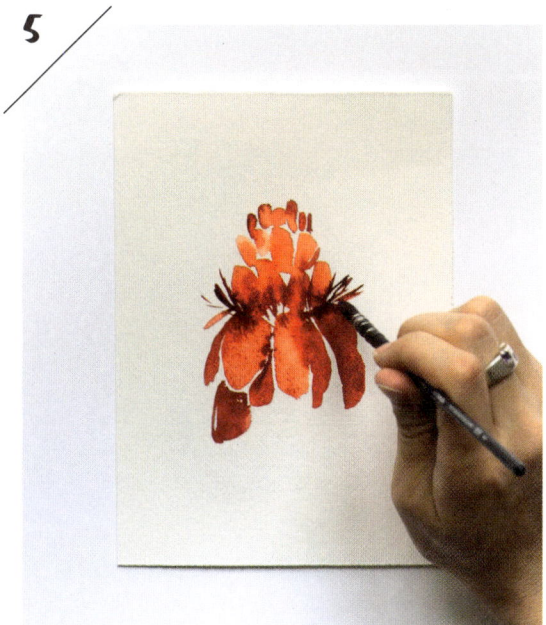

Using the tip of your brush, add the very fine bracts that point upwards, using a dark, concentrated mix (Alizarin Crimson + Raw Sepia shown here).

6 /

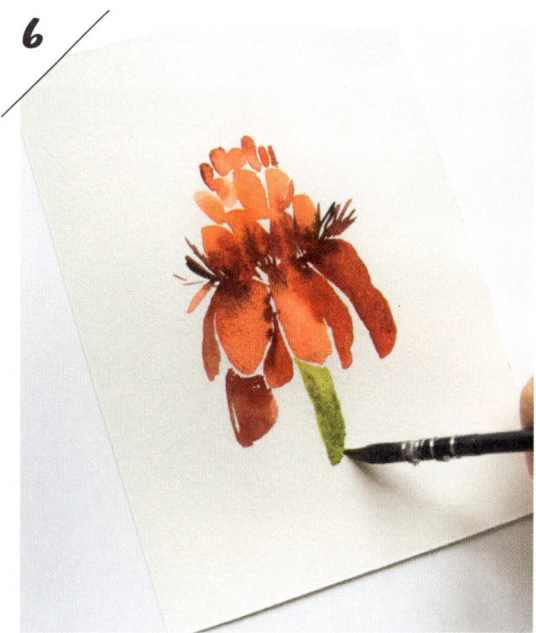

While the red pigments are merging and forming beautiful color gradients, paint the rather thick stem in a yellowish green (Olive Green shown here).

GINGER
flower

LIKE MOST OF THE PLANTS IN THIS CHAPTER, THERE ARE MANY GINGER FLOWER VARIETIES, INCLUDING ALPINIA PURPURATA (RED GINGER) AND ALPINIA ZERUMBET (SHELL GINGER). THESE FLOWERS GENERALLY FORM COLORFUL PINK, RED AND WHITE, CLUSTERS, IDEAL FOR FILLING OUR JUNGLE COMPOSITIONS.

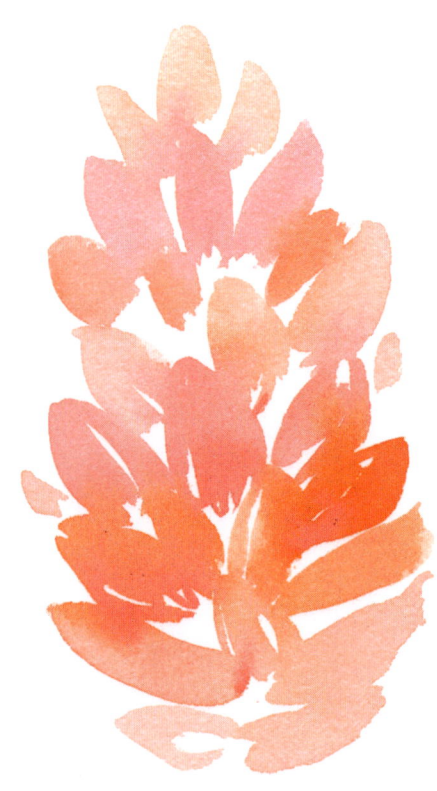

1

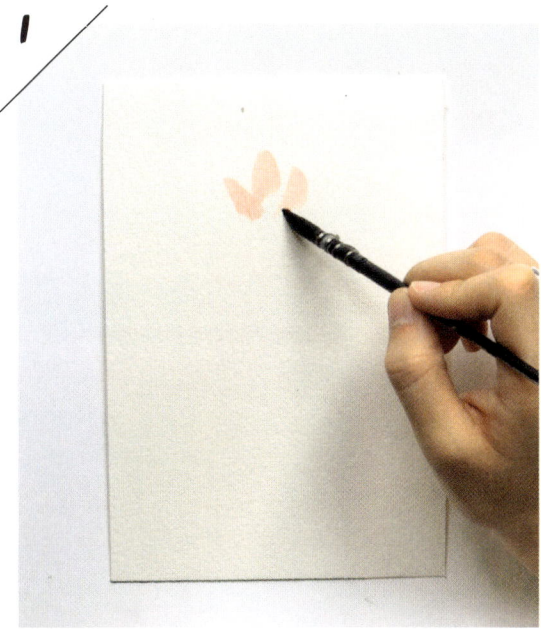

Start at the top of the plant, using a heavily diluted peach color (see page 23). Paint small oval shapes (the bracts of a red ginger flower). Leave white spaces between the shapes.

2

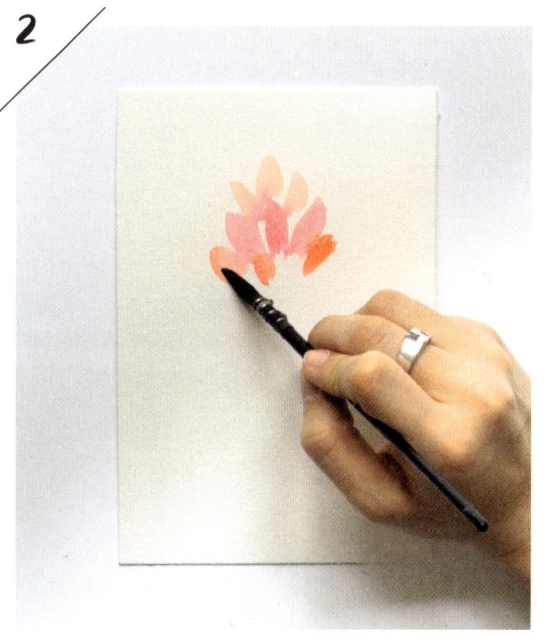

Continue painting more elongated shapes. Those in the center of the flower point upwards, while those on the side point sideways, as though enveloping the previous bracts.

3

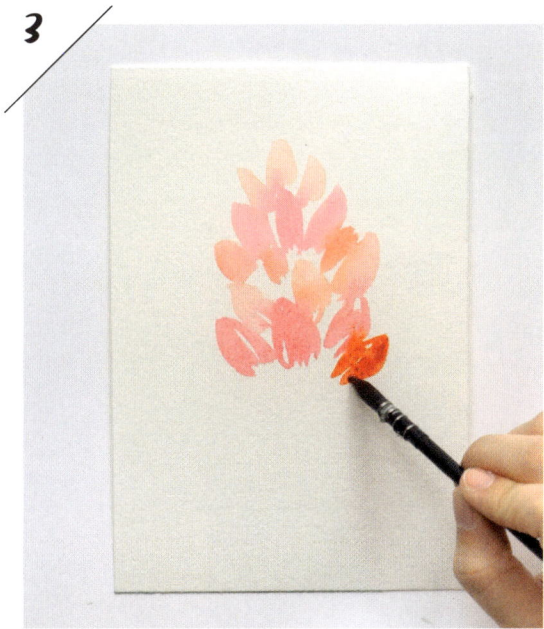

Continue painting some bigger bracts that widen out and are more pointed, using more concentrated pink, red or orangy solutions. Leave white gaps to give the cluster a more three-dimensional look.

4

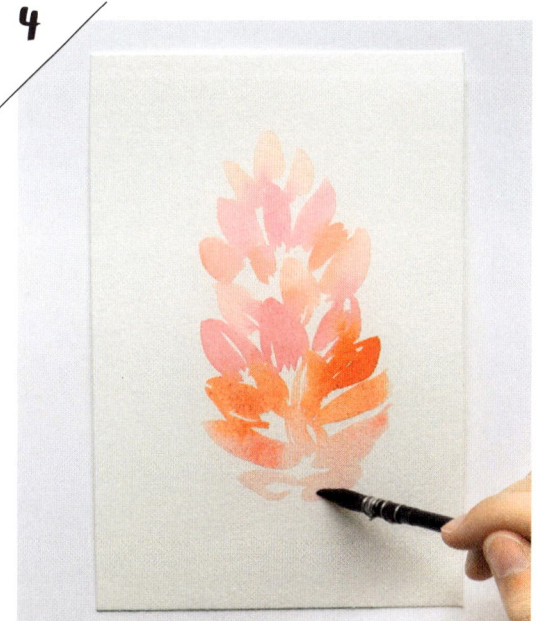

Finish off with smaller bracts, using a light peach solution again.

PINCUSHION
protea

THIS FLOWER SPECIES, WHOSE OFFICIAL NAME IS LEUCOSPERMUM CORDIFOLIUM, BUT IS COMMONLY KNOWN AS THE ORNAMENTAL PINCUSHION, HAS AN UNUSUAL, VERY STRIKING SHAPE THAT IS INTERESTING TO ADD TO YOUR TROPICAL COMPOSITIONS. THERE ARE ORANGY, RED AND ALSO YELLOW VARIETIES.

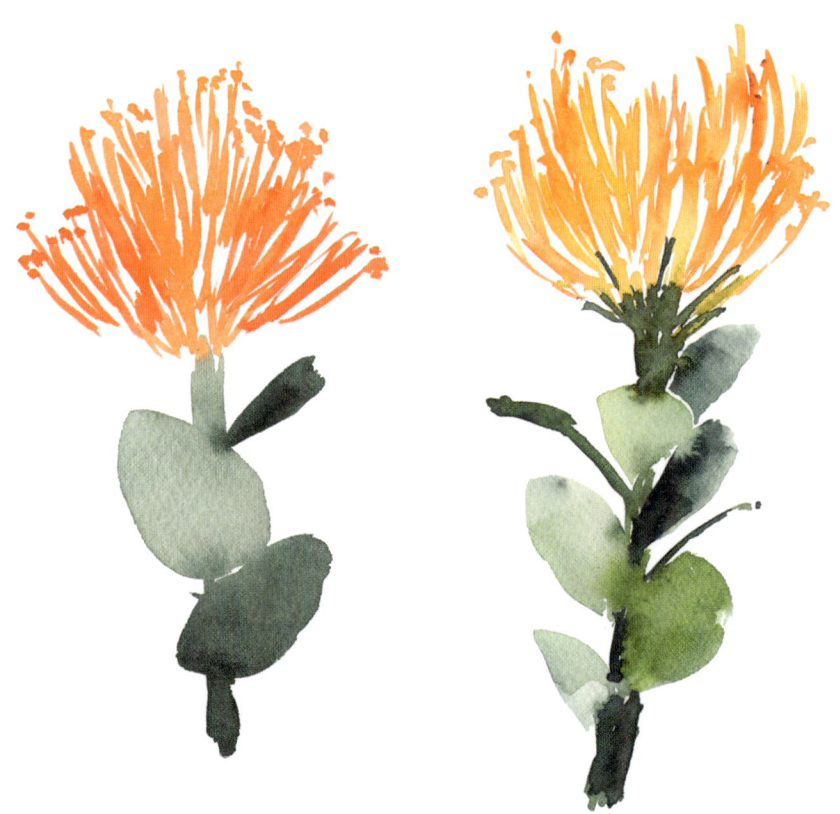

1

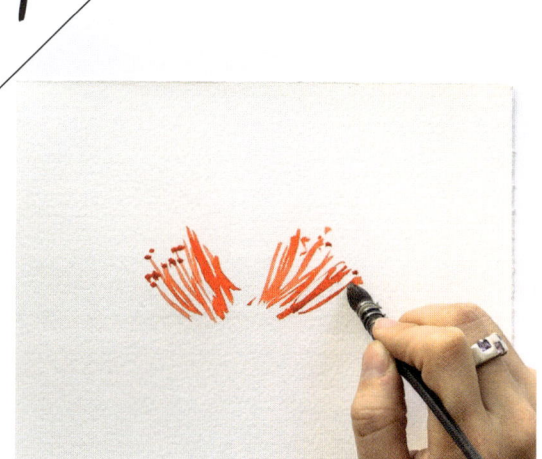

You're going to paint a red and orange pincushion. Start with a red solution to paint fine lines by pressing lightly on your brush. Add little dots to the tips.

2

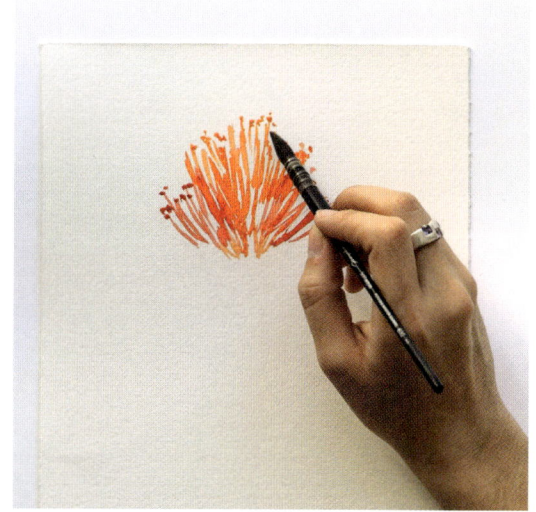

Add orange lines to the center of the flower. Feel free to paint some of these over the still-wet red lines so the colors mix together.

3

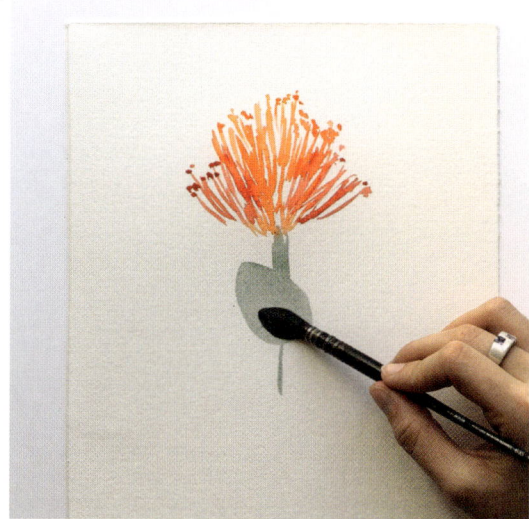

Now shape the thick stem using a lightly concentrated grey-green mix (Greenish Umber shown here). Paint a large oval leaf on this stem.

4

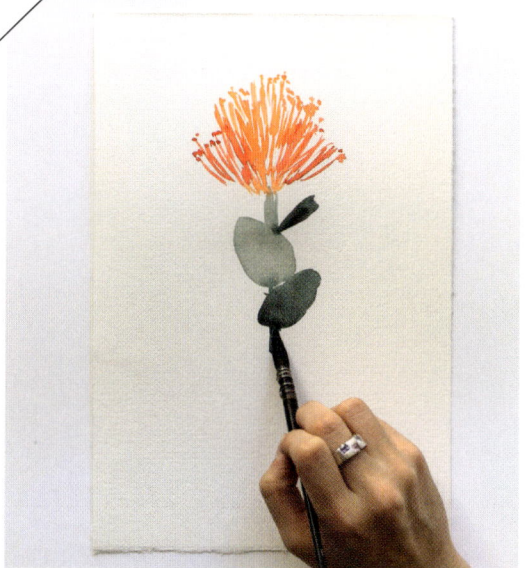

Add other oval leaves to the stem using a solution with a higher pigment concentration. Vary the angles of these leaves to create more of an overall three-dimensional effect.

Anthurium

UNLIKE THE OTHER PLANTS AND FLOWERS IN THIS
CHAPTER, THE ANTHURIUM HAS A SIMPLE SHAPE AND
IS OFTEN MONOCHROME. THIS SIMPLICITY WILL ADD A
LITTLE BREATHING SPACE TO YOUR COMPOSITIONS.

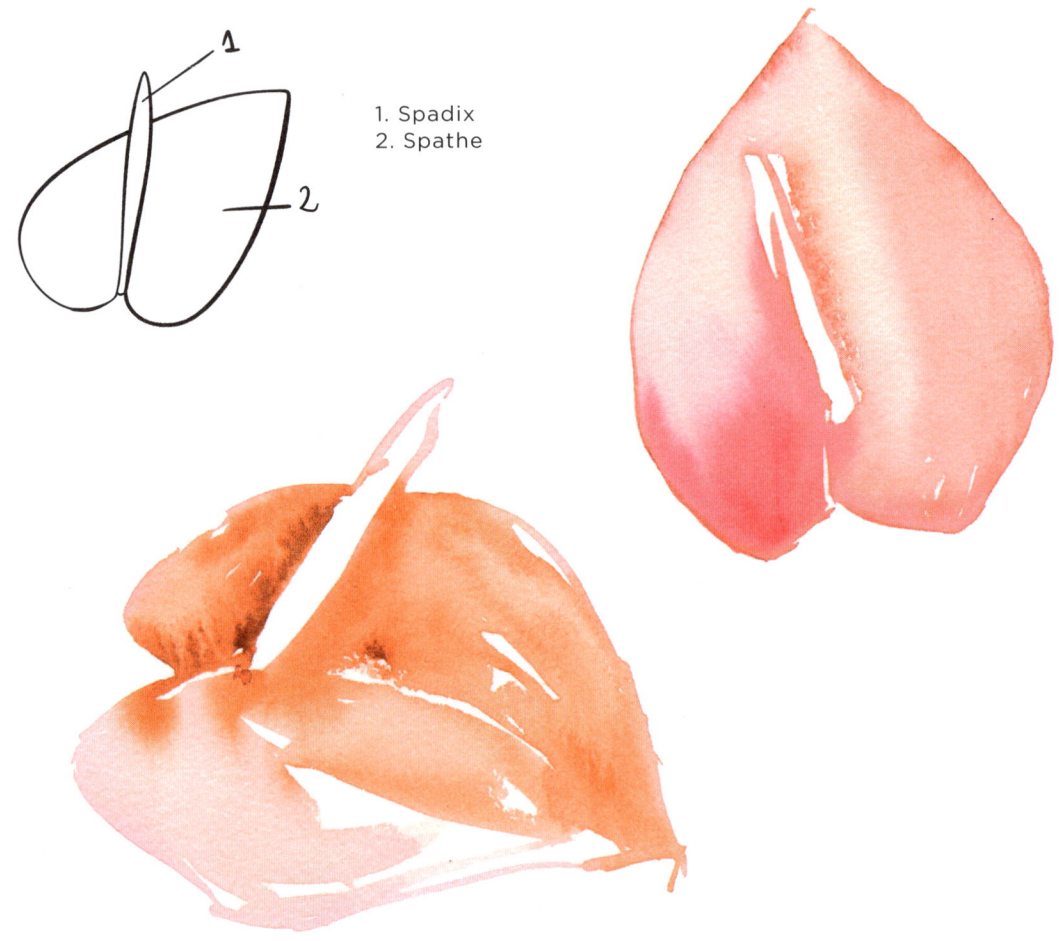

1. Spadix
2. Spathe

1 /

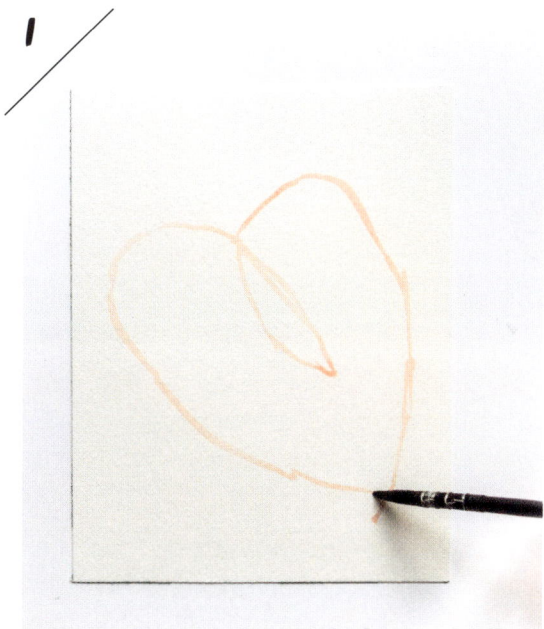

As with many plants in this book, start with the outline of the Anthurium, using a very light peach-colored solution (see page 23).

2 /

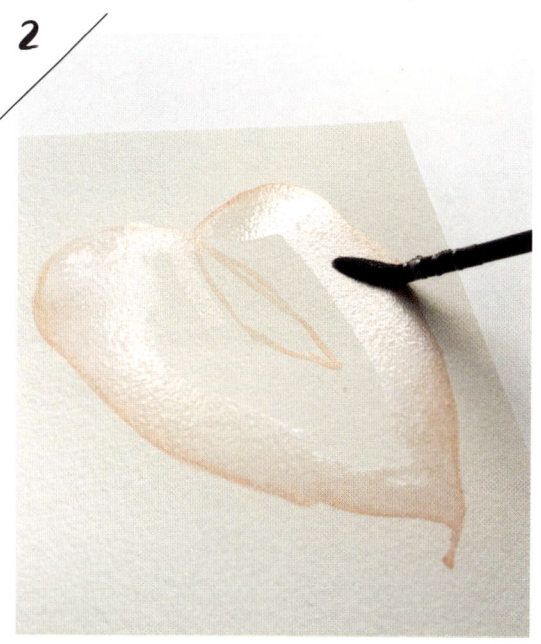

Thicken the outline of the spathe using this same solution. Two areas are created either side of the spadix. Cover one of them with highly transparent pigment, leaving some white spaces.

3 /

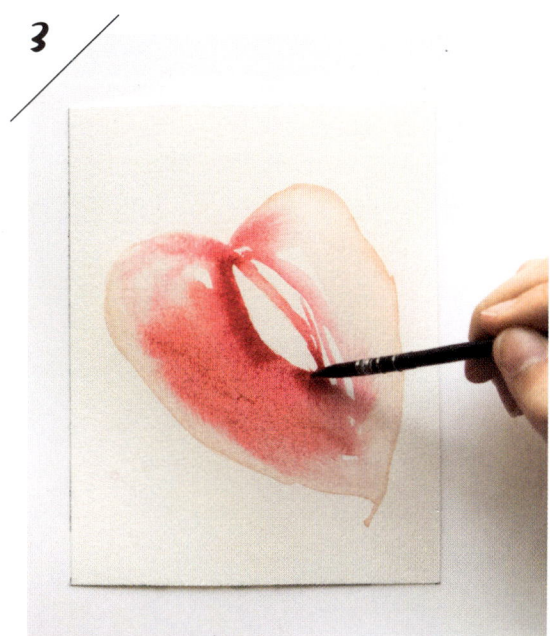

As a contrast, fill the second half with moderately concentrated and highly concentrated pigments, shown here in red and pink tones. Add the heaviest concentrations near to the spadix.

4 /

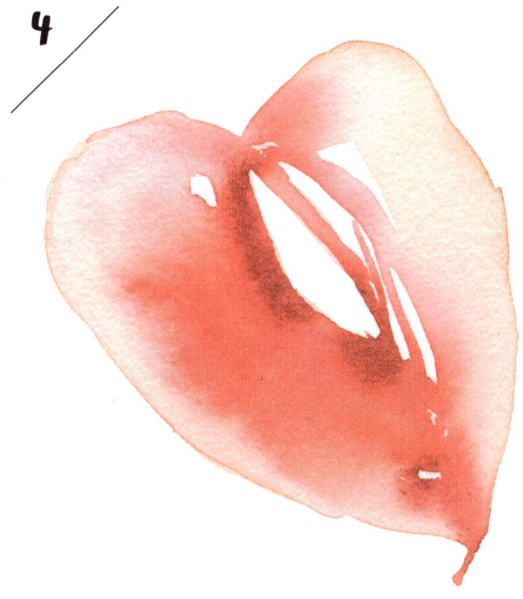

As the color of the flower is sufficiently dark, the spadix can be made out in negative form. If you paint light-colored Anthurium, feel free to paint the spadix in yellowish green tones, for example, once the spathe has dried.

TROPICAL
border

A COMPOSITION IN THE FORM OF A BORDER OR FRAME – JUST LIKE A PATTERN – IS PARTICULARLY SUITABLE FOR STATIONERY. YOU WILL USE MANY OF THE LEAVES AND FLOWERS SEEN IN PREVIOUS CHAPTERS FOR THIS PAINTING. I MAINLY CHOSE COOL GREENS AND THEREFORE BALANCED THEM UP WITH WARM-COLORED FLOWERS FOR THE SAKE OF HARMONY (SEE PAGE 25).

THE MAIN COLORS

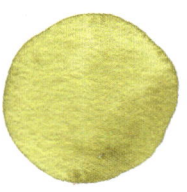  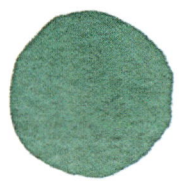 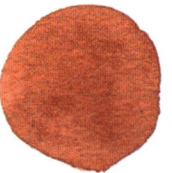

Brown Green   Greenish Umber   Dark blue-green (see page 23)   Alizarin Crimson

And also: orange, yellow and pink

Opposite: a Heliconia rostrata specimen that provided the inspiration for the colors in this painting.

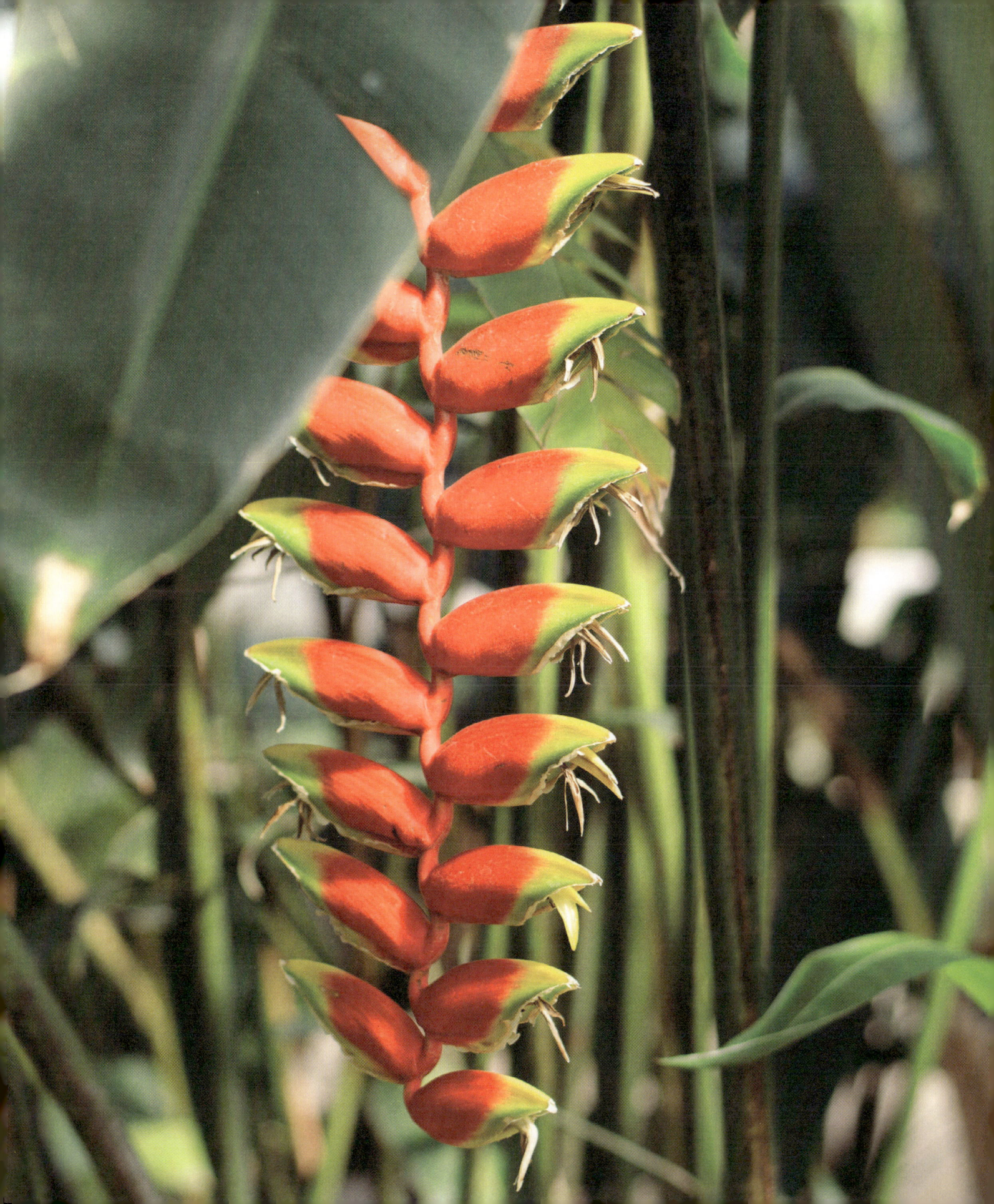

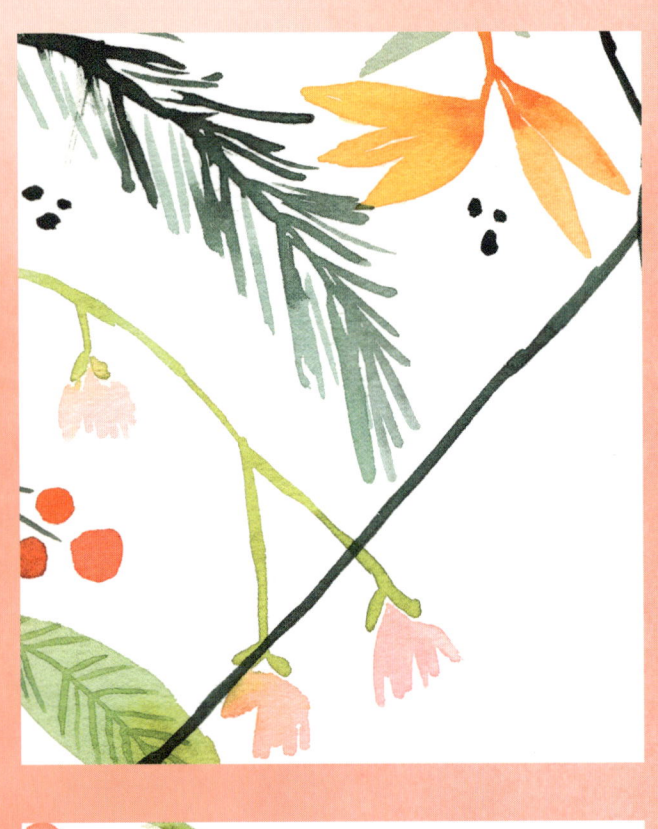
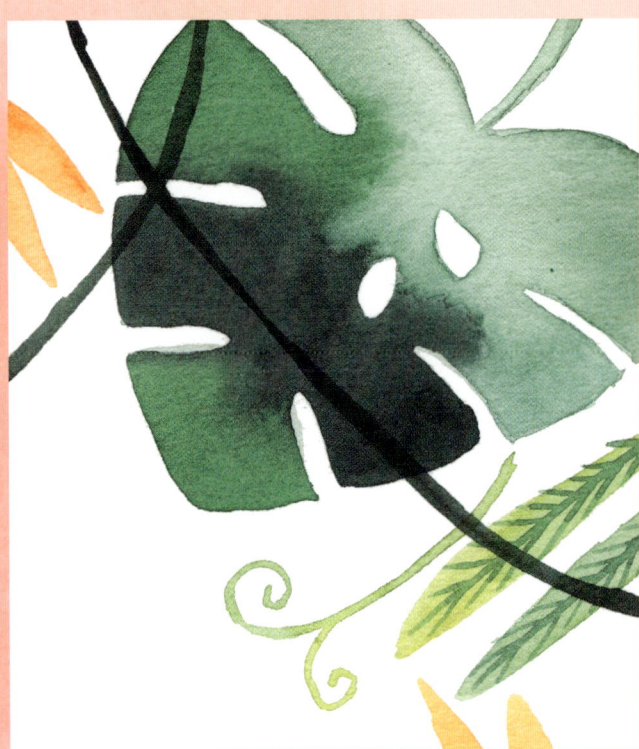
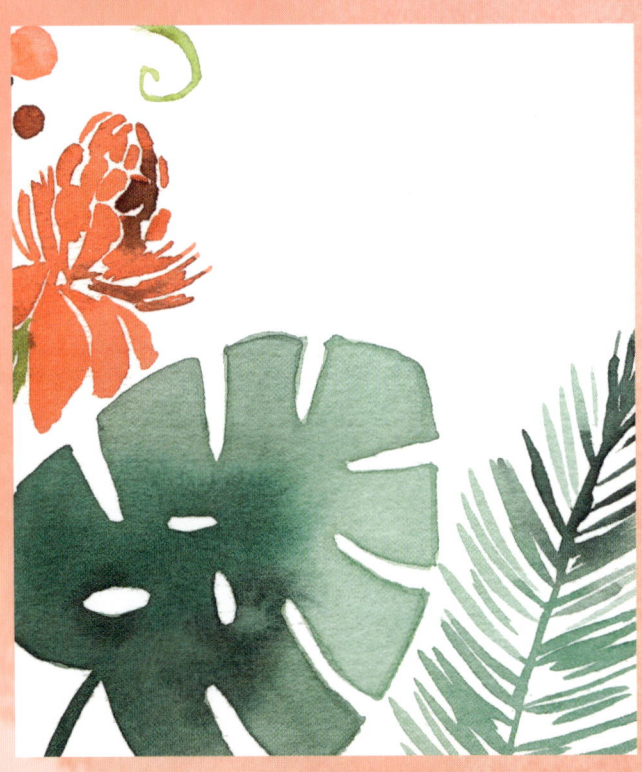
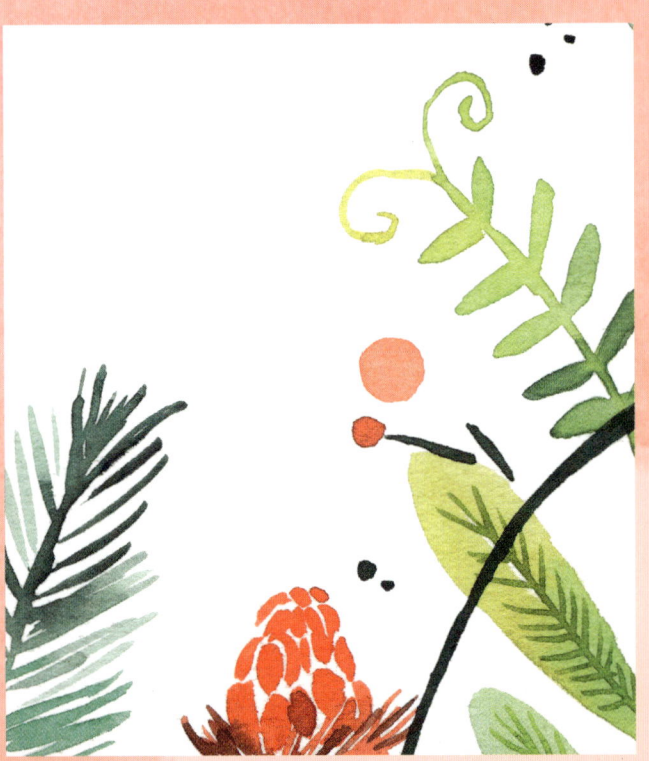

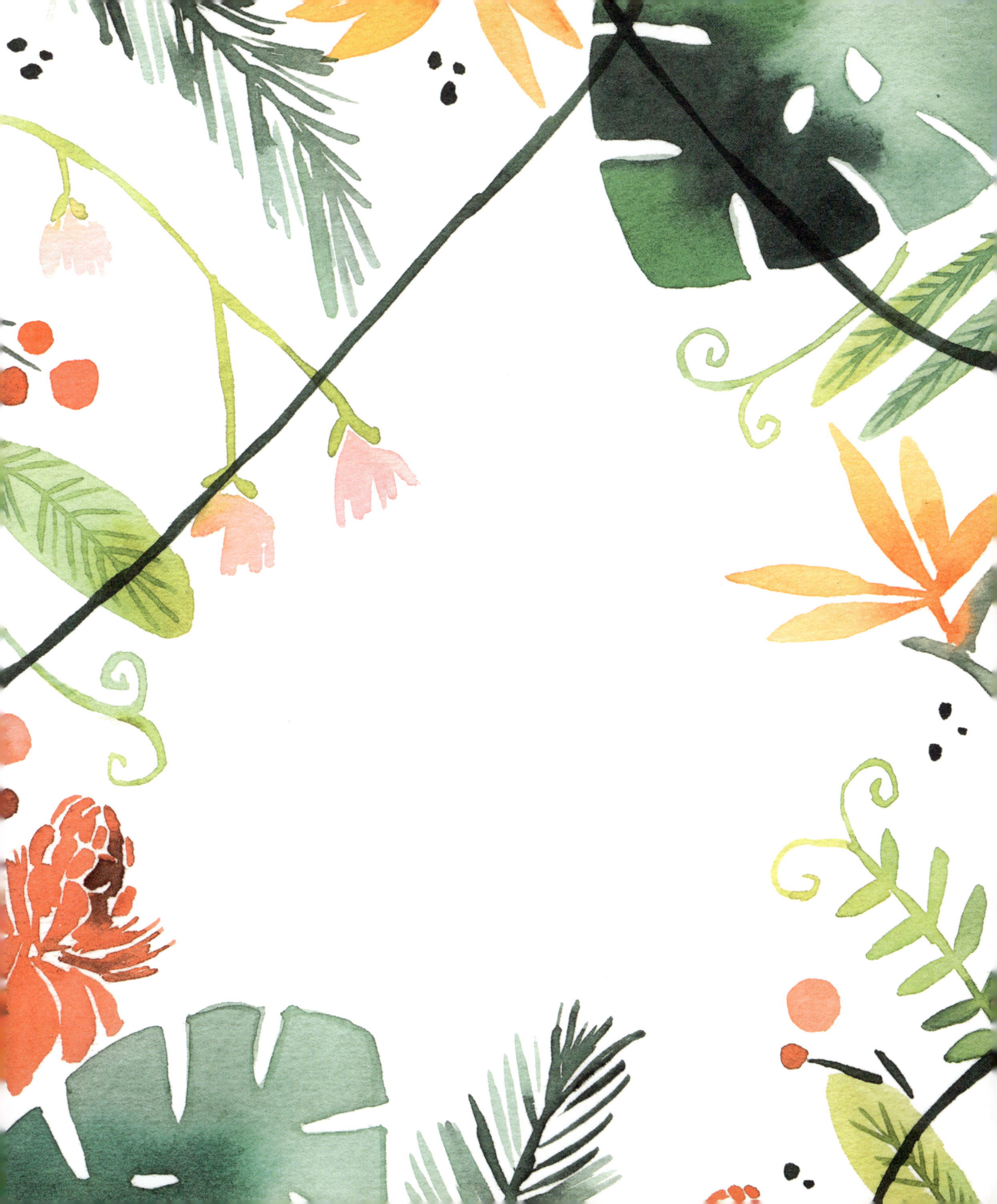

1 /

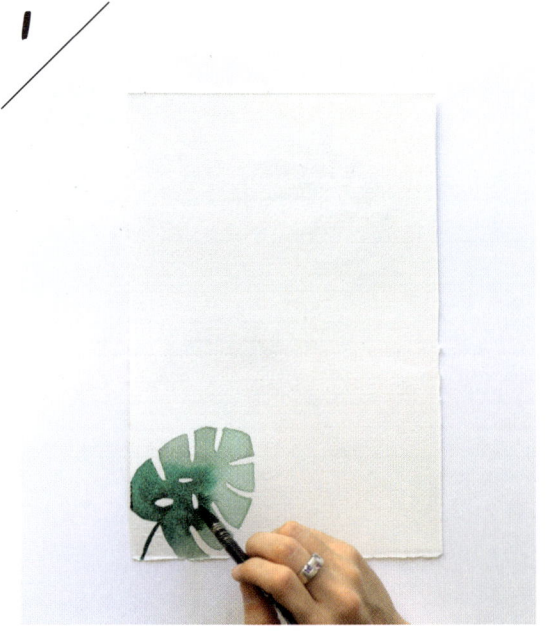

Start by painting a leaf from a Swiss cheese plant in the bottom left corner. Feel free to add several colors whilst the leaf is still wet (blue-green, Greenish Umber or Hooker's Green here).

2 /

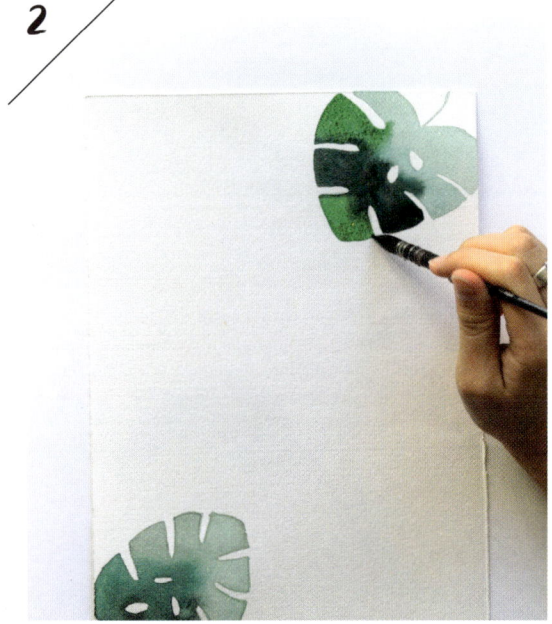

Paint a second Swiss cheese leaf in the top right corner. Use the same colors once again to create interesting blends before everything dries. Some parts of the leaf cannot be seen.

3 /

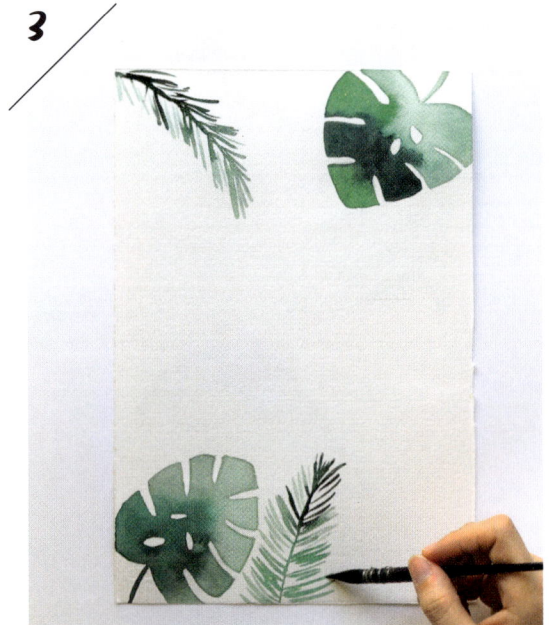

Now paint two slender palm leaves. Use a blue-green mix and vary this with a dark green to create a lovely contrast. Paint the palm leaf at the top as though hanging down slightly.

4 /

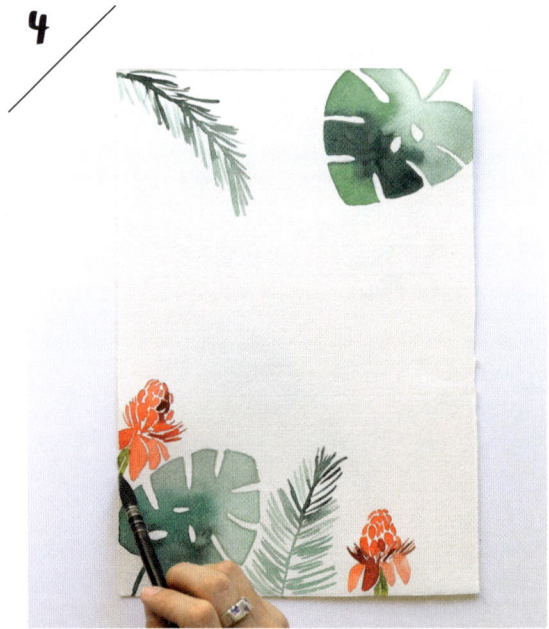

Add the first flowers: torch ginger. I decided to group them around the bottom left corner. Feel free to hide part of the one on the left.

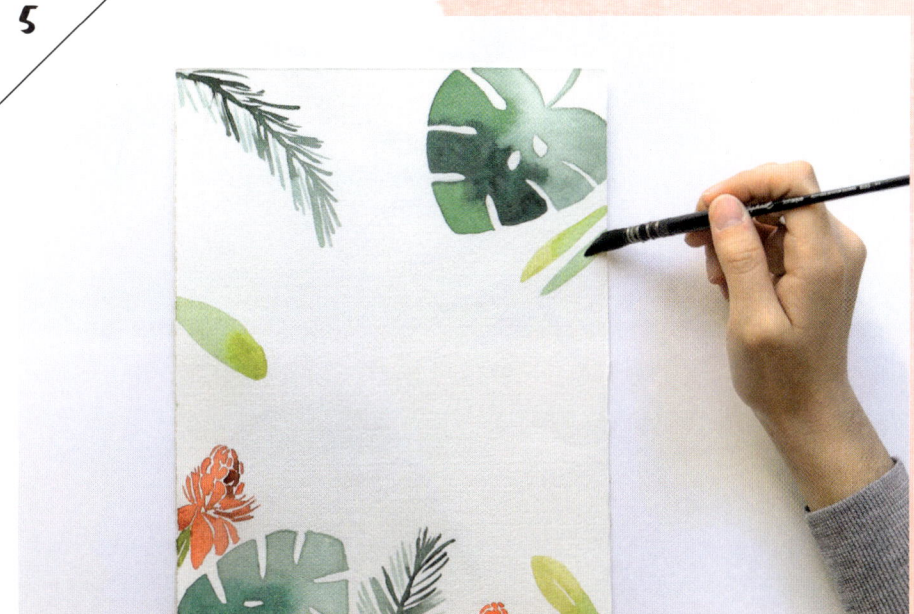

To emphasize the lush aspect of this plant border, add long, rounded leaves, as shown on page 58. I used several colors to paint these leaves, such as blue-green and a yellowish green (for example Brown Green). Vary the size of the leaves for greater dynamism.

6 /

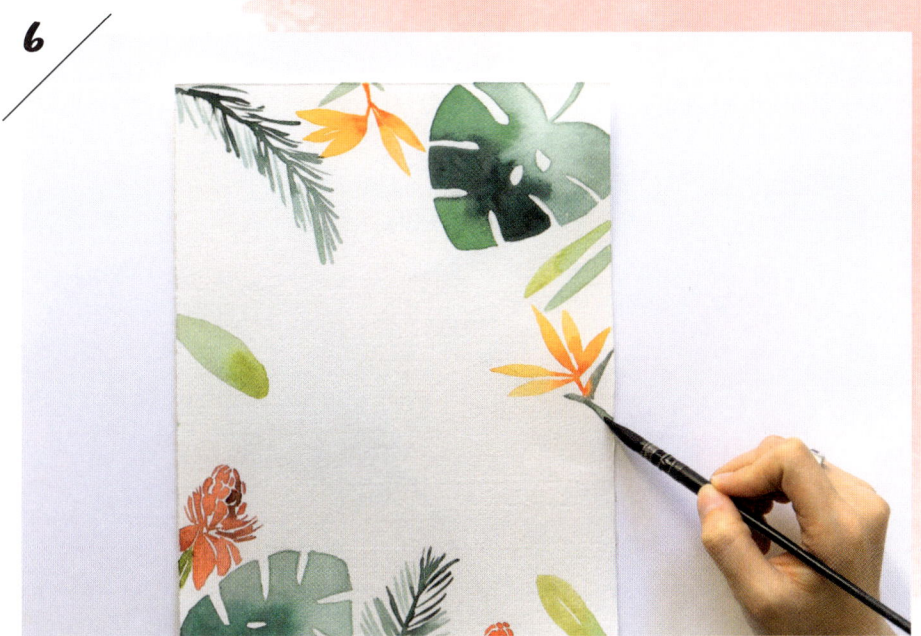

Now paint two bird of paradise flowers using a yellow and orange mix (Indian Yellow and Red Orange shown here). Once again, hide some parts of the flowers to emphasize the border effect.

1 /

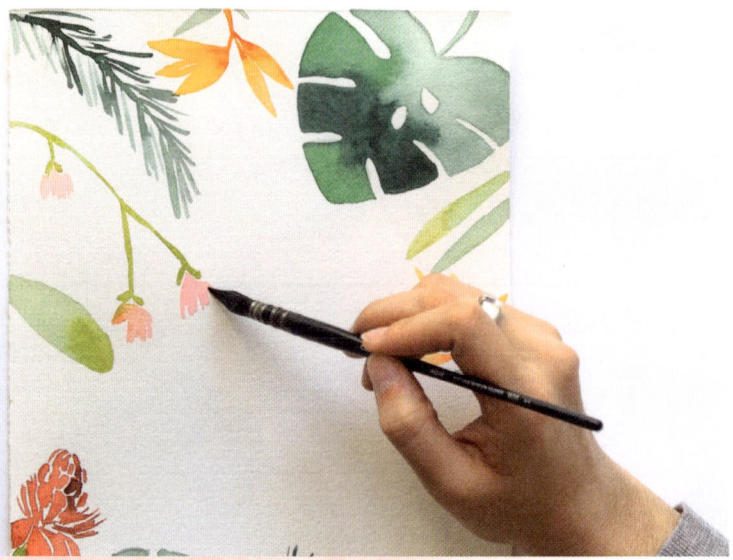

Paint a plant top left with some fairly simple little peachy-colored flowers. The stem is painted in a yellowish green mix (Brown Green shown here).

8 /

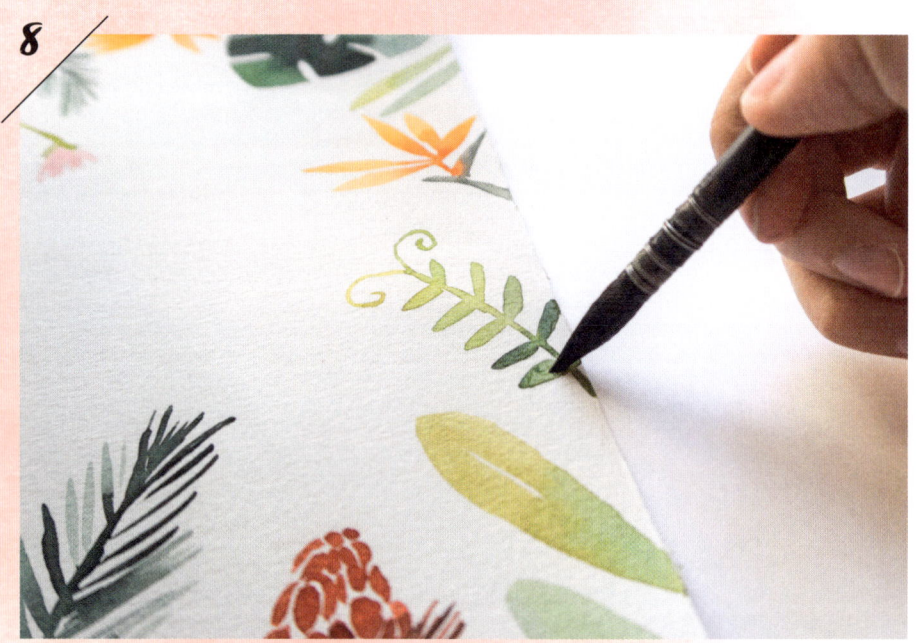

On the right-hand side, add a little stem using several shades of green: Olive Green and Green Yellow (Brown Green). Add spirals, too, to the tip of the stem to emphasize the sense of lushness.

9 /

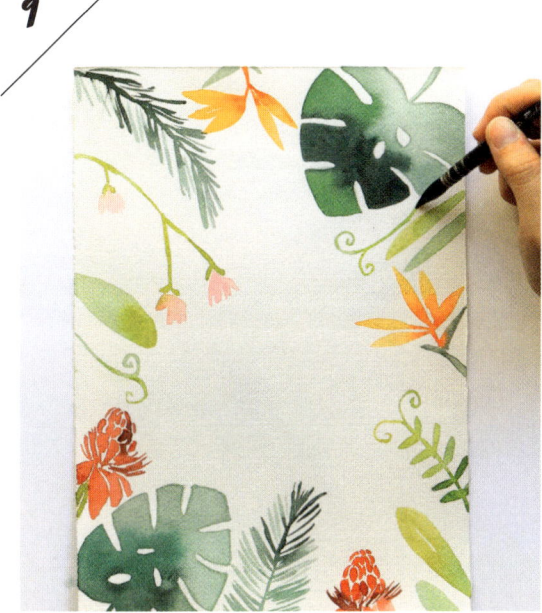

In empty spaces, continue adding spirals to the tips of thin stems, in a yellowish green mix.

10 /

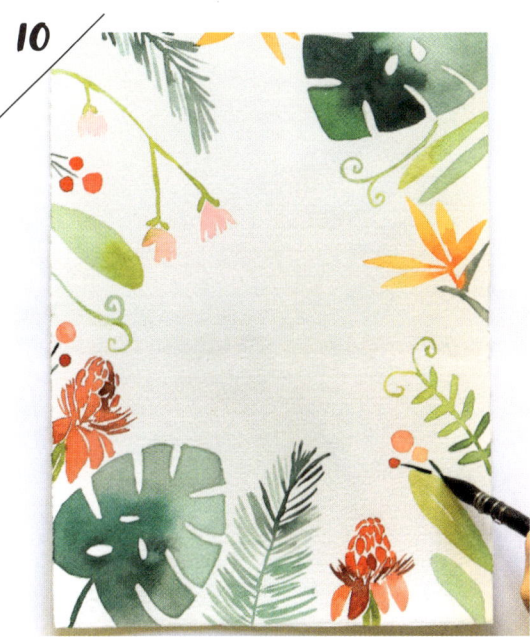

Add small round fruits in red tones. Paint stems heading from the outer edge towards the center in a very dark green mix.

11 /

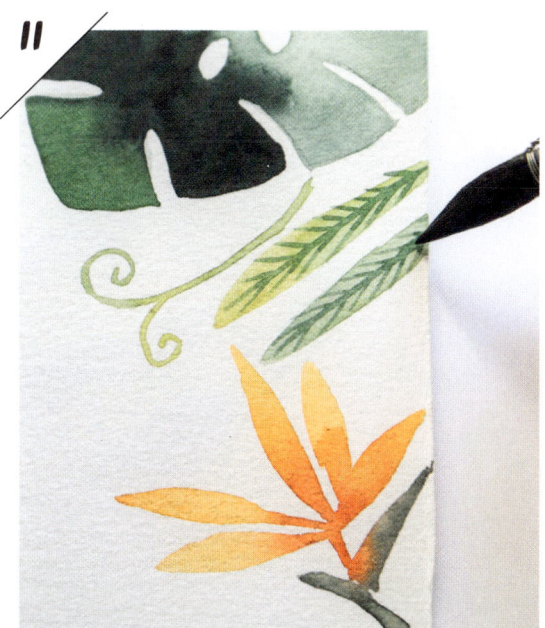

When the rounded leaves are dry, add veins in a concentrated blue-green mix.

12 /

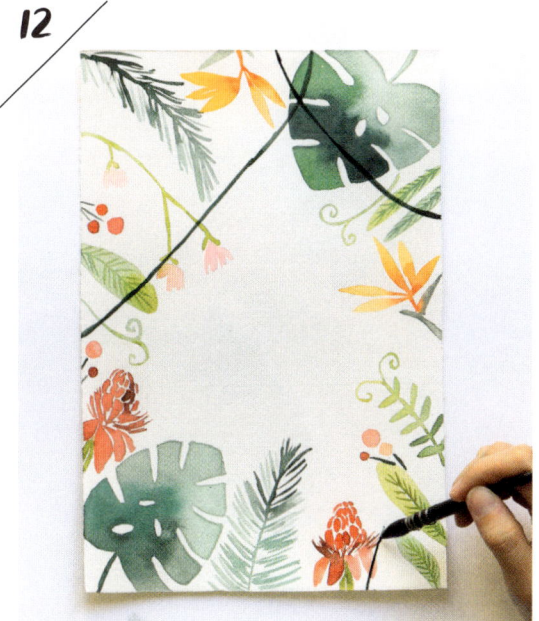

To finish off, once everything is dry, paint various vines, especially at the top of the frame, using a dark green mix.

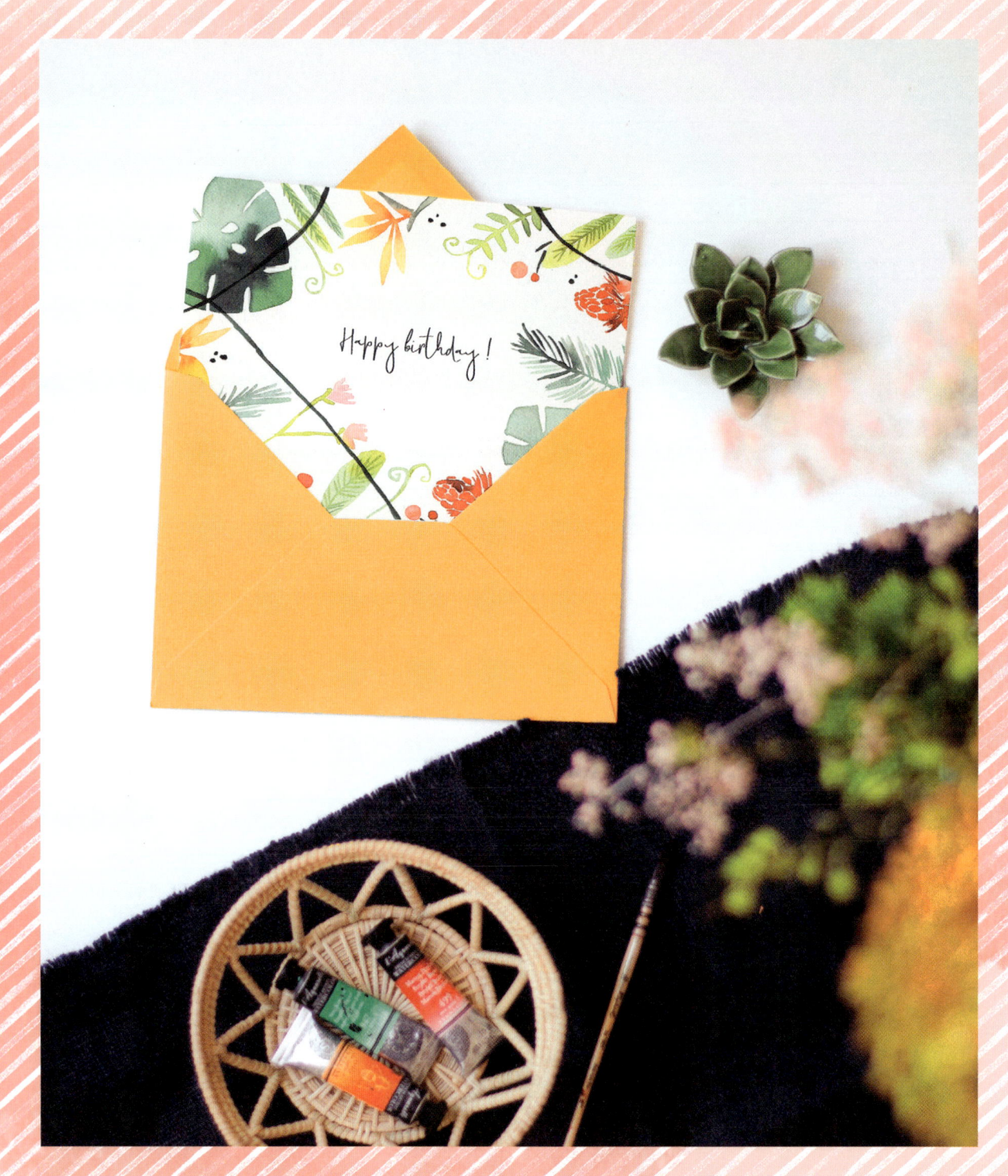

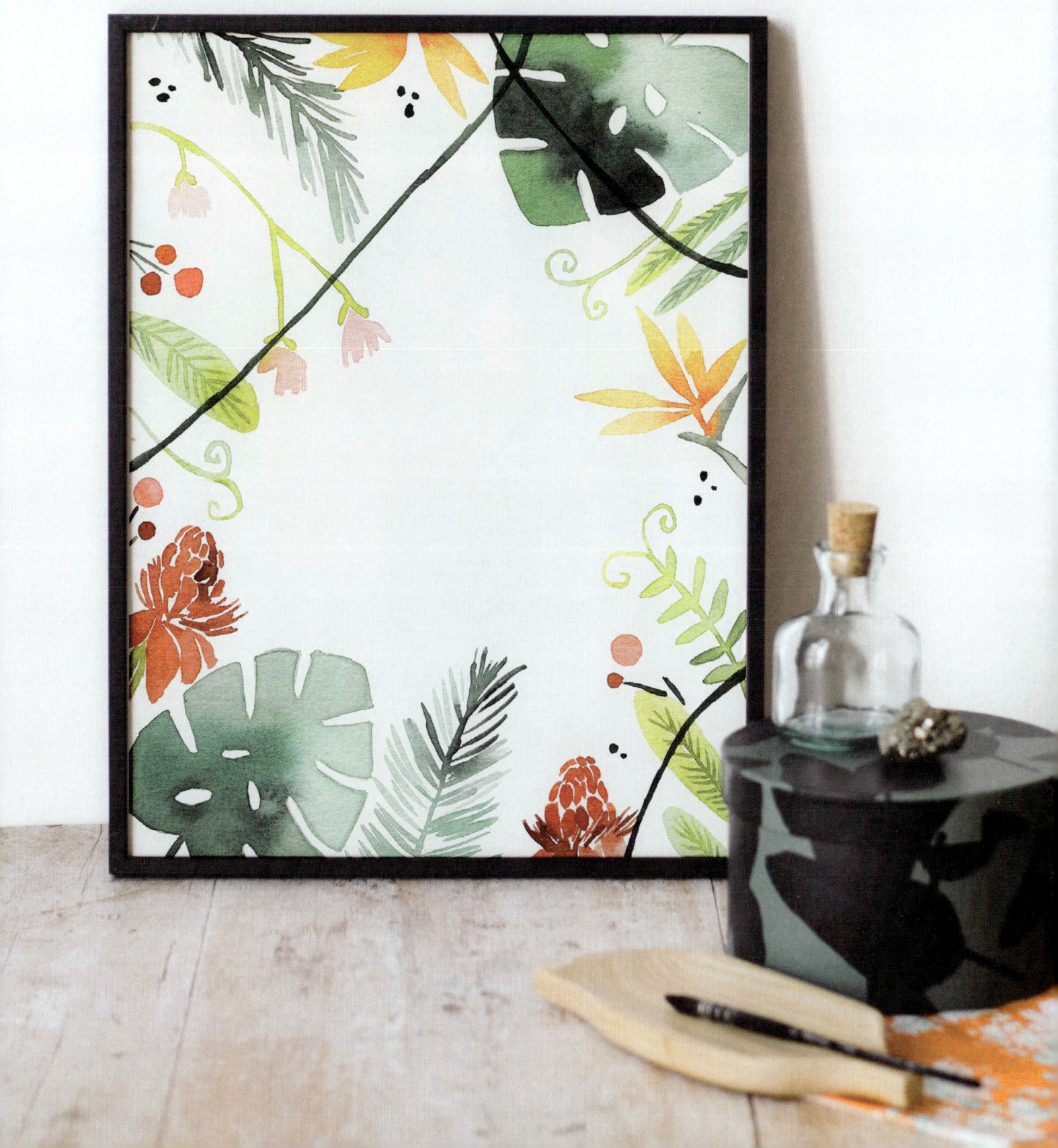

Bouquet

TROPICAL FLOWERS AND FOLIAGE, WITH THEIR MAGNIFICENT SHAPES AND COLORS, MAKE BEAUTIFUL BOUQUETS. FOR THIS COMPOSITION, BE PRECISE. THE OBJECTIVE IS TO PAINT DIFFERENT ELEMENTS CLOSE TO ONE ANOTHER TO GIVE THE ILLUSION OF VOLUME. IF NECESSARY, REPEAT EXERCISE 1 ON PAGE 36 TO BE SURE OF YOUR BRUSHWORK BEFORE GETTING STARTED!

THE MAIN COLORS

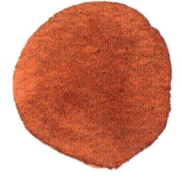

Alizarin Crimson

Peach
(see page 23)

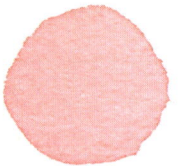

Cool pink
(see page 23)

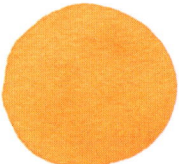

Red Orange

Light green
(see page 23)

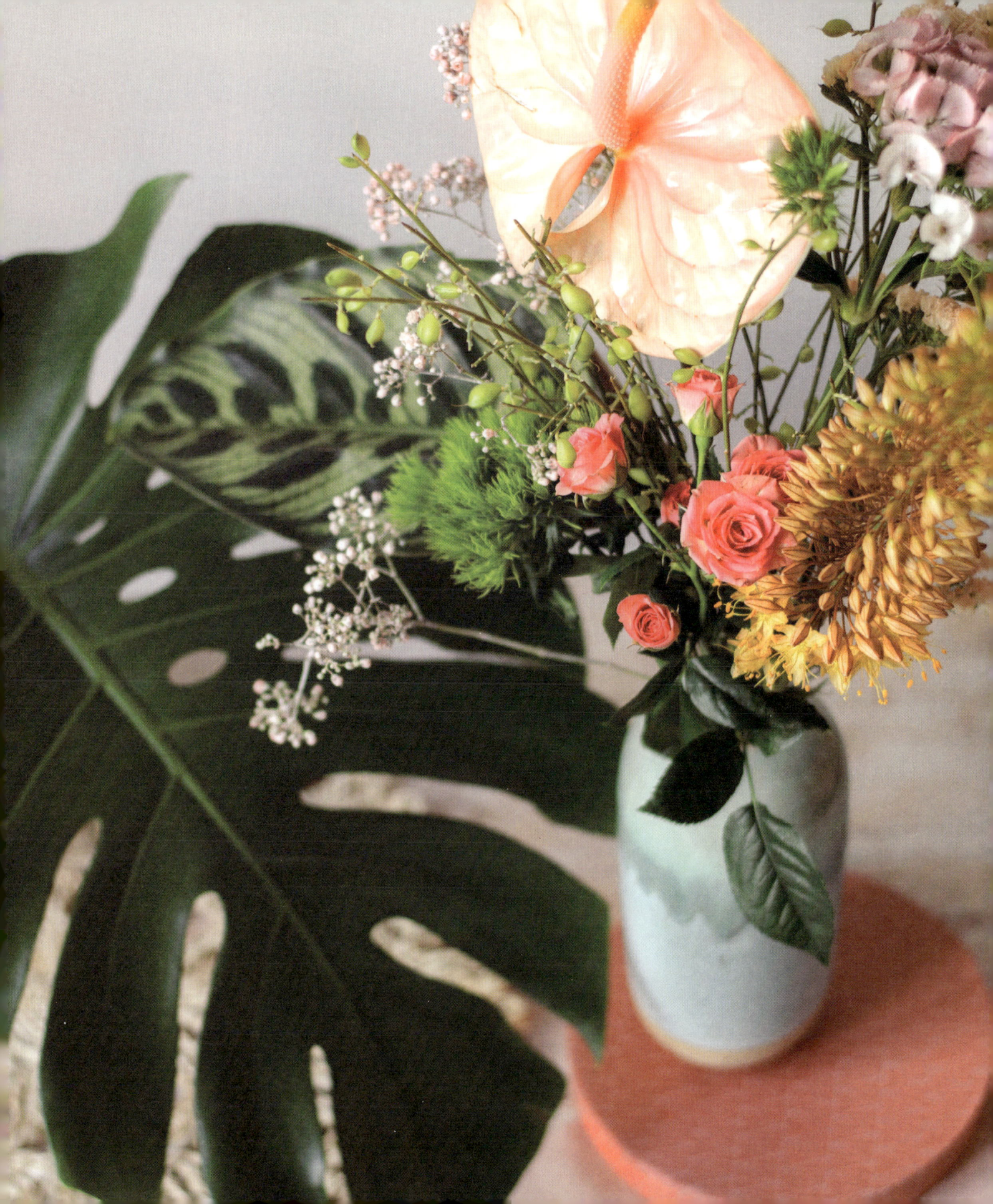

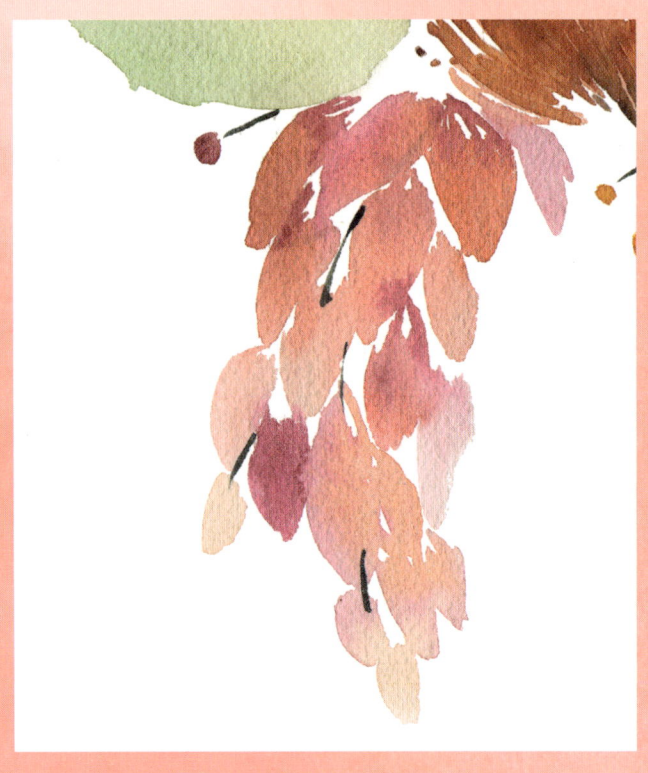
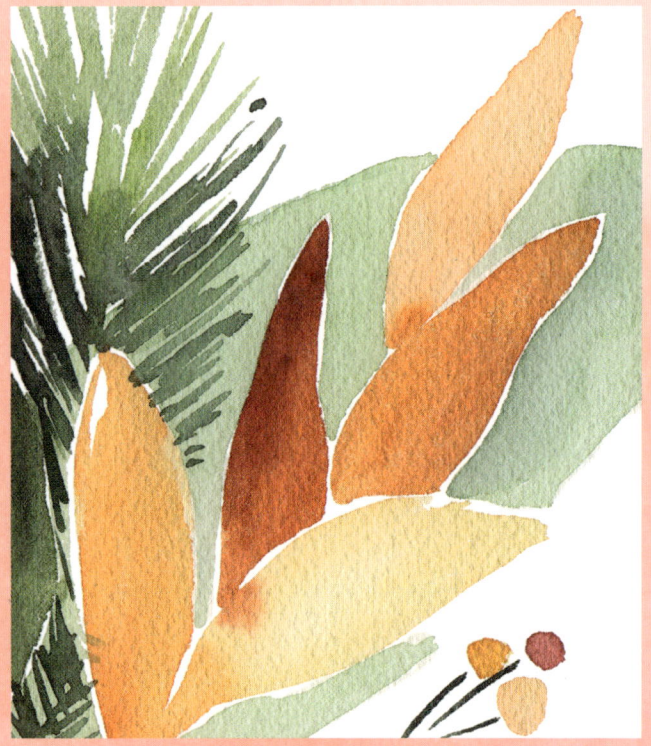
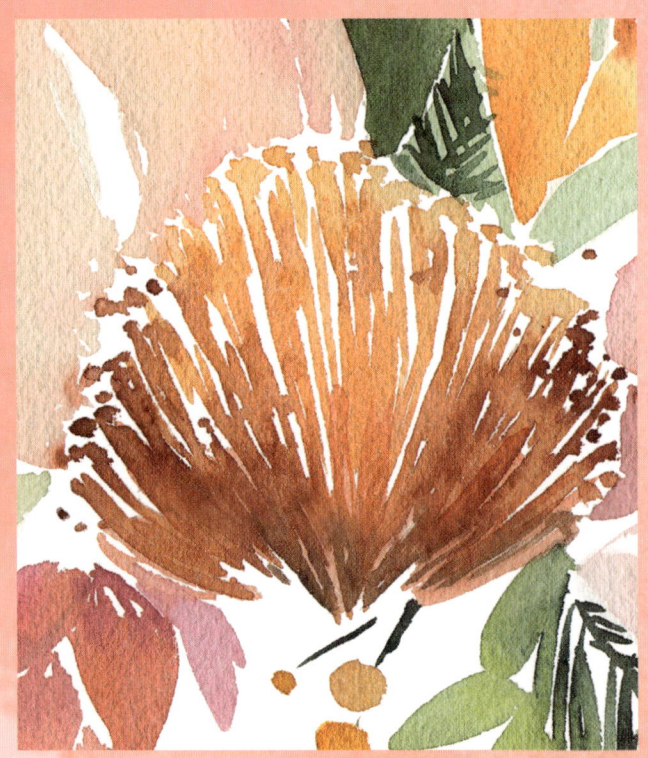
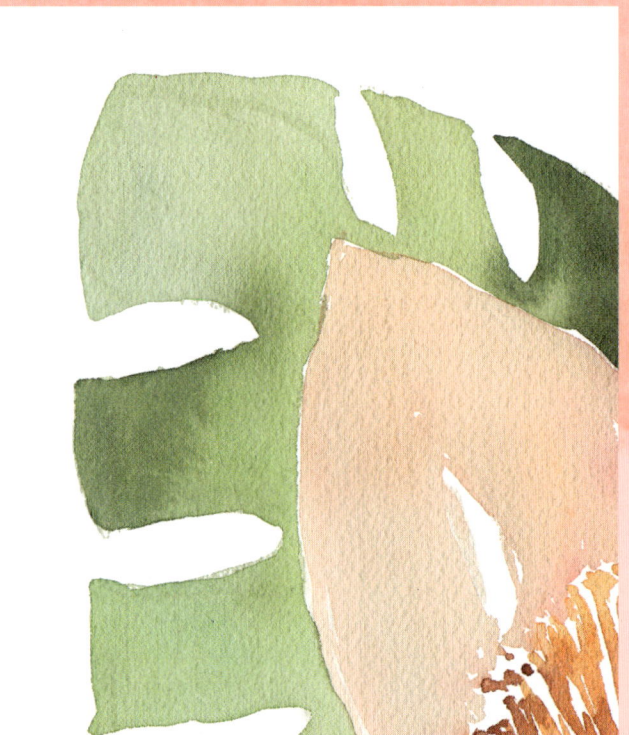

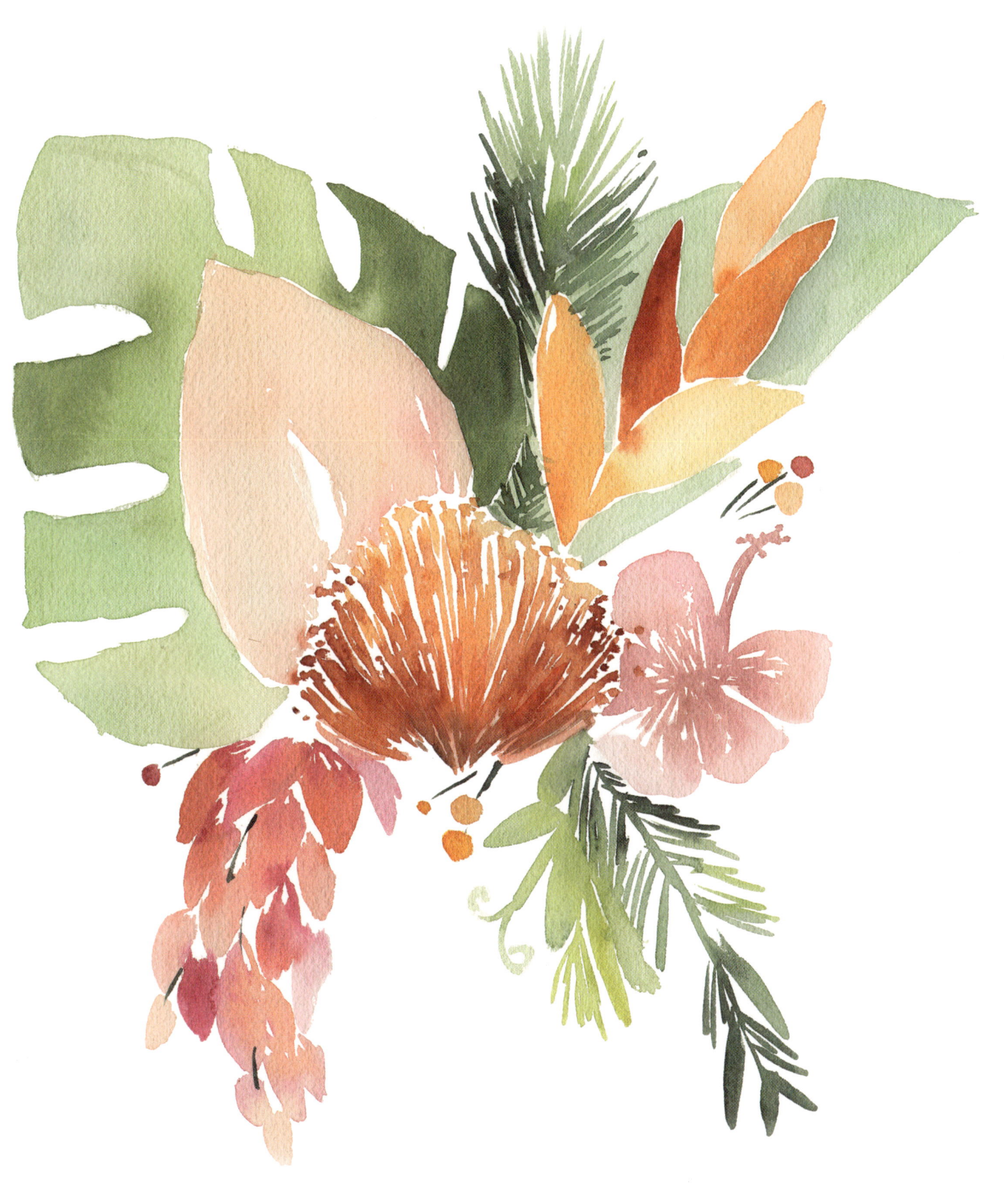

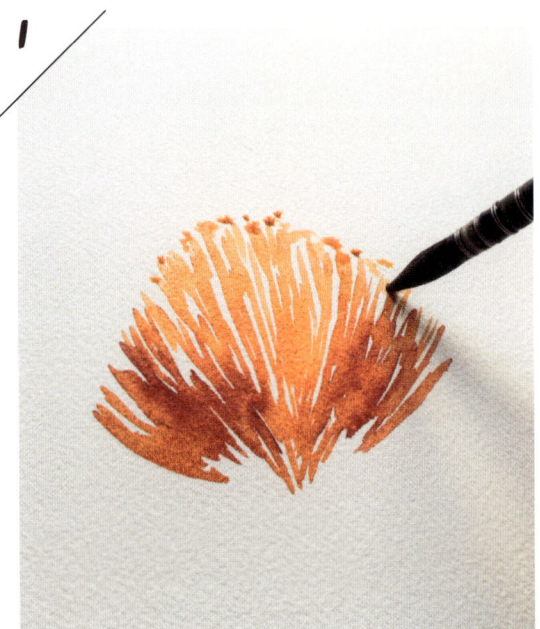

1

Start with an ornamental pincushion flower in the center of the bouquet. Use red and orange, as shown in the tutorial on page 96.

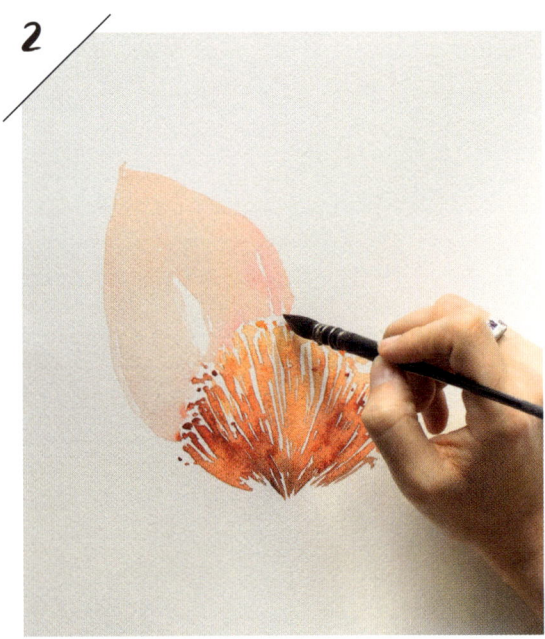

2

Then paint the peachy-colored Anthurium behind the pincushion, painting as close to it as possible, as detailed on page 98. Make sure the pincushion flower is fully dry to avoid any smudging.

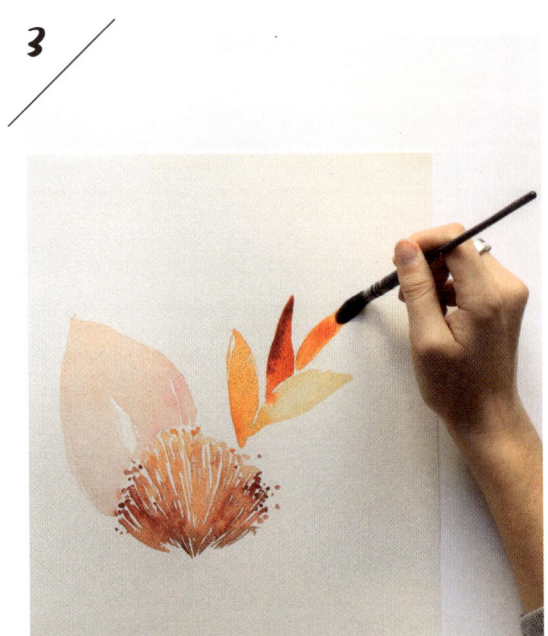

3

On the right-hand side of the bouquet, paint a Heliconia in light and dark orangy shades. I decided to do a variety without flowers as the composition was already visually complex with the pincushion flower.

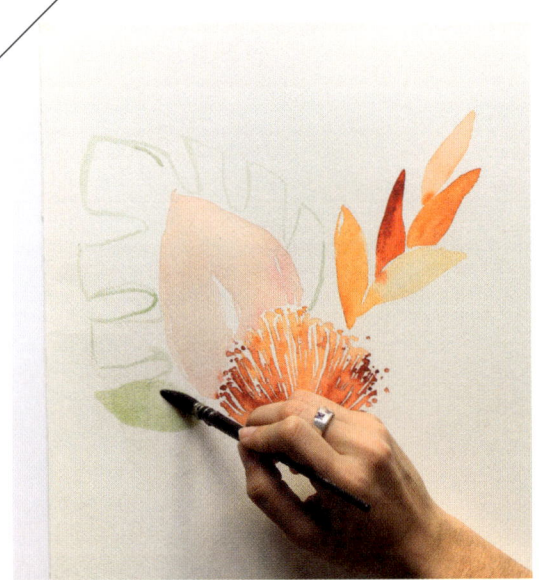

4

Behind the Anthurium, paint a large Swiss cheese plant leaf. The size of these leaves is really very impressive, so feel free to play with scale when you depict them. Start with the outline, in a light green solution.

5

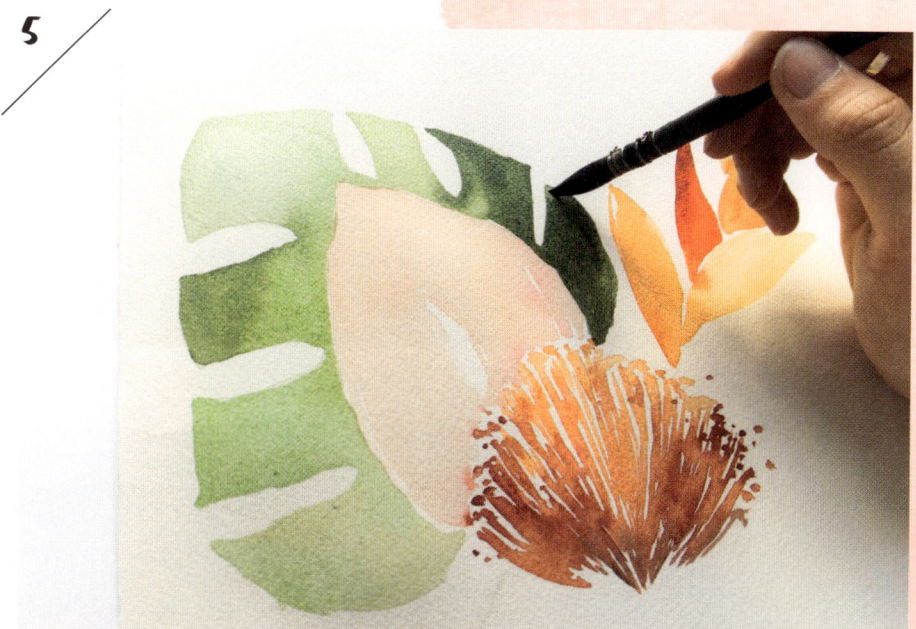

Continue filling in the Swiss cheese leaf, then vary the tones, using light green and the wet-in-wet technique. For darker areas, I used Olive Green and a little Greenish Umber.

6

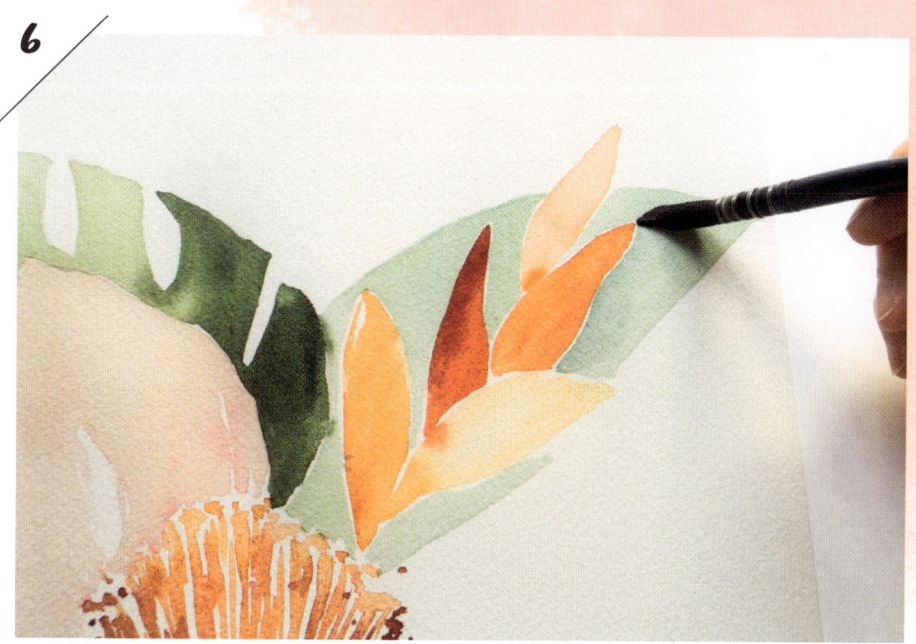

Paint a long banana leaf behind the Heliconia, using a light green mix. Keep its shape simple as it is in the background, so there is no need to add any details. Pay particular attention to the precision of your brushstrokes and the amount of water used so as to get an evenly colored area.

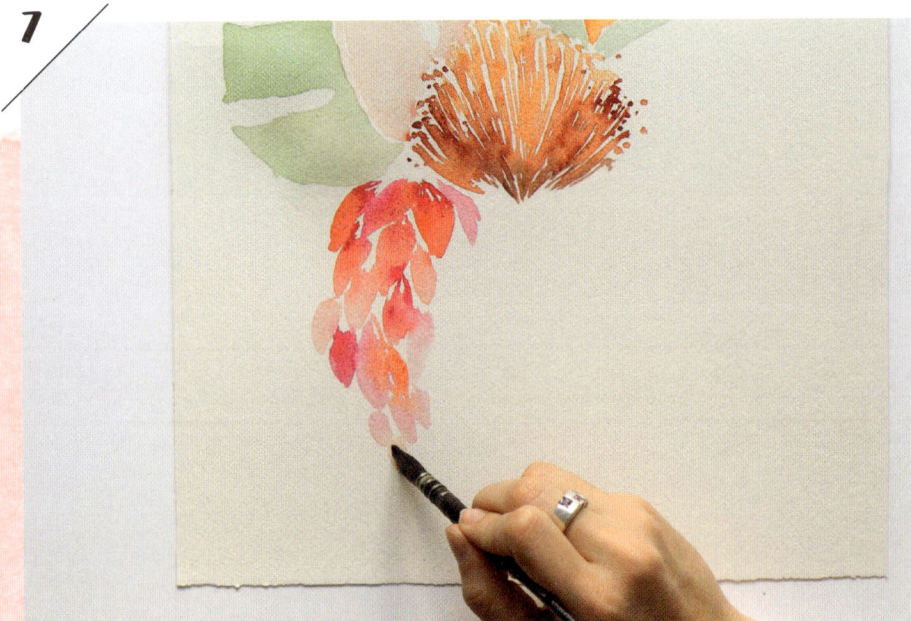

7

Paint a ginger flower hanging down from the left corner of the bouquet. Use a number of shades and mixes of pinks, reds and a few touches of different shades of orange. Use the colors already used for the previous flowers.

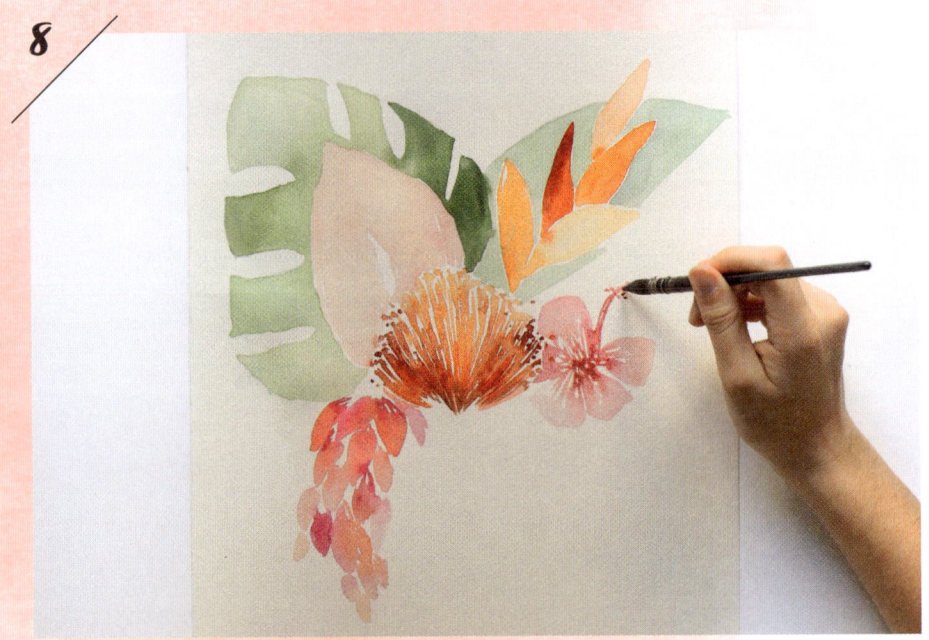

Add a final flower, a hibiscus, in a cooler pink mix (see page 86). Don't forget to add more concentrated pigment to the heart of the flower.

9 /

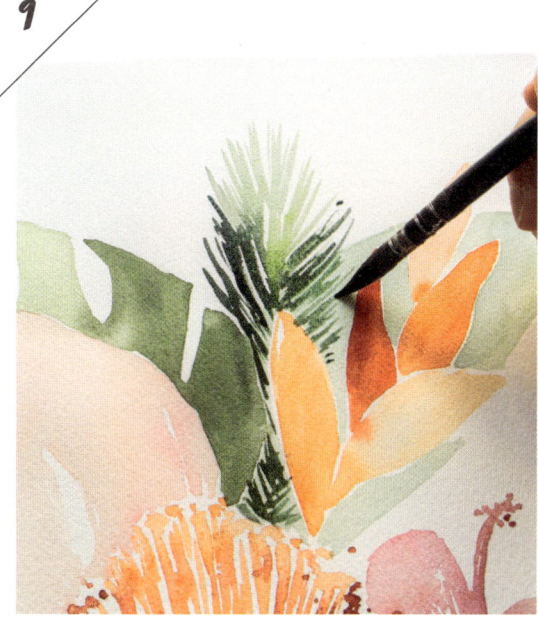

When the whole thing is dry, paint a palm leaf behind the Heliconia and Swiss cheese leaf. Use several shades of green, including dark green in particular, as shown here with Greenish Umber.

10 /

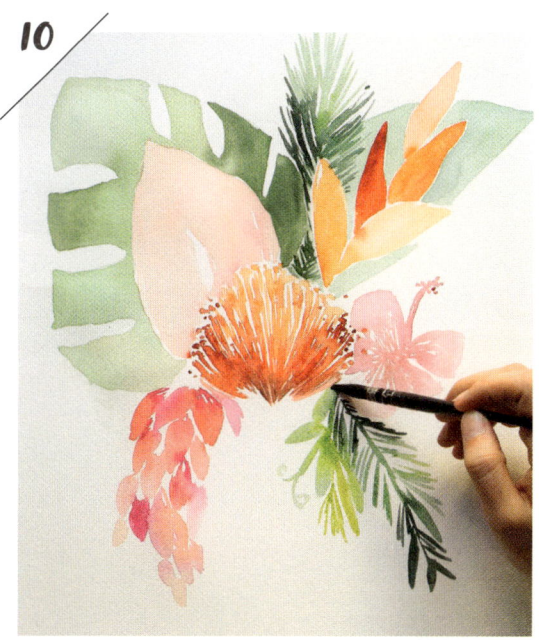

Now add another palm leaf to the bottom right part of the bouquet, varying the thickness of the leaflets. Add little jungle plant elements to the left in yellowish green tones.

11 /

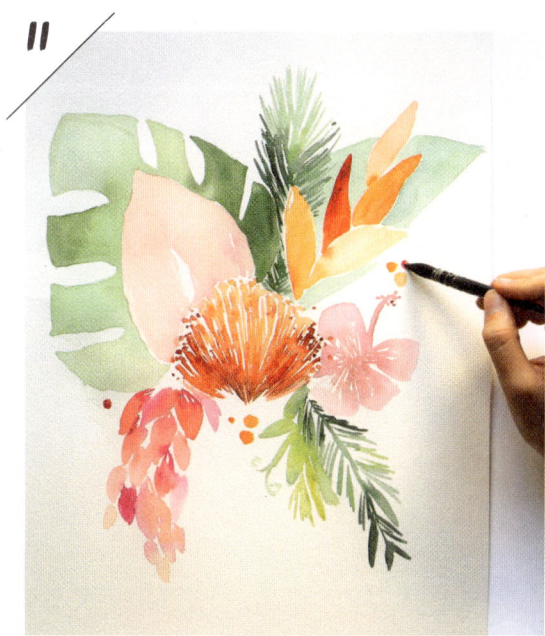

Add little dots (fruits) to the composition in the same orangy red tones.

12 /

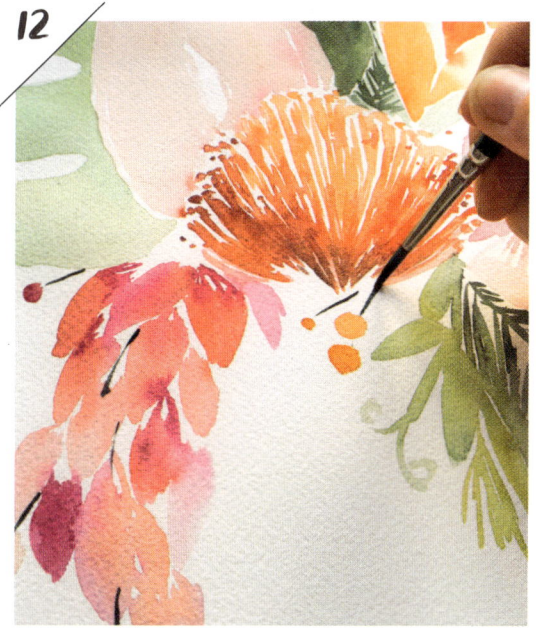

Paint the stems of these little fruits in a very dark solution. Also add a few dark-colored details to the ginger flower.

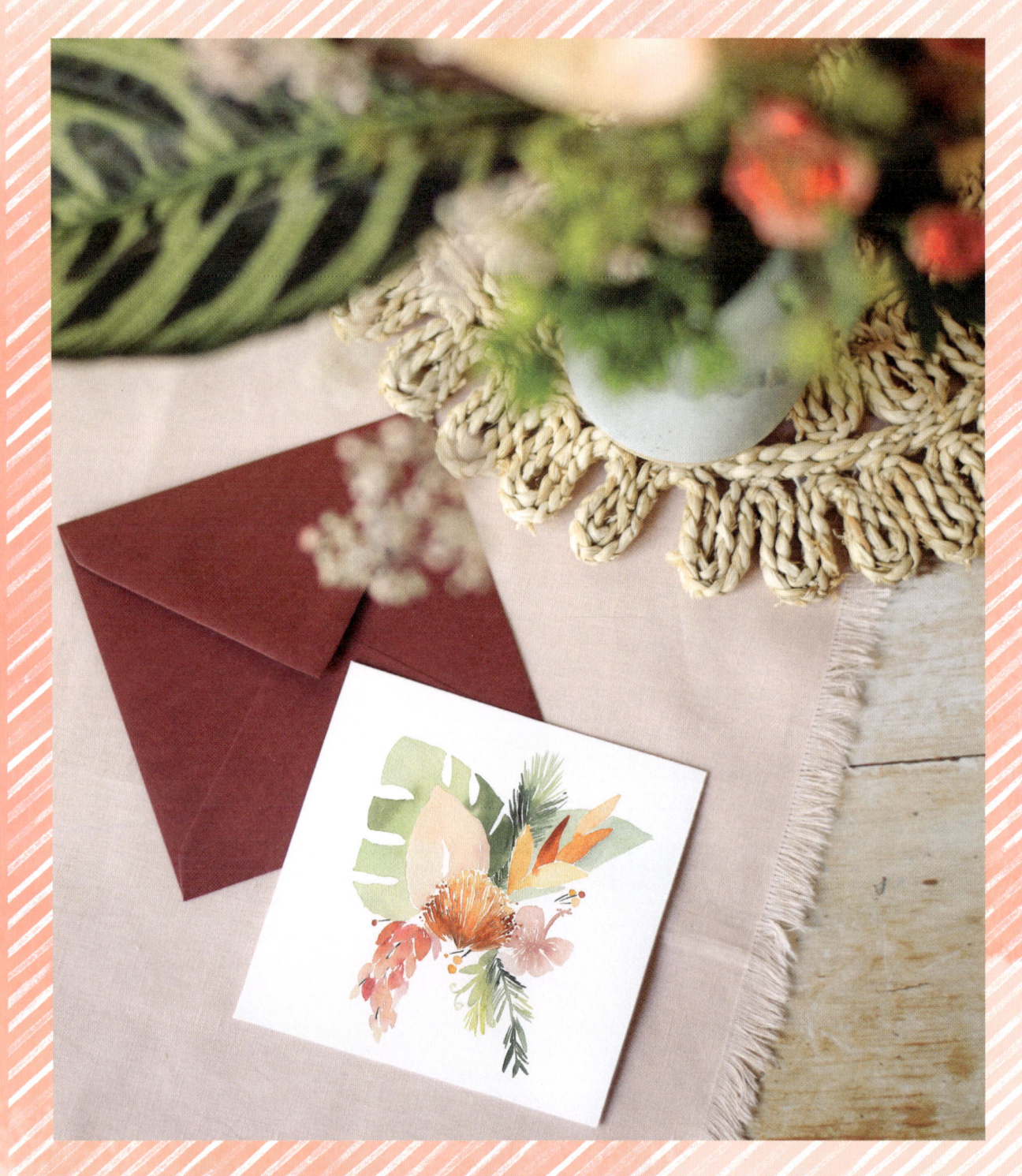

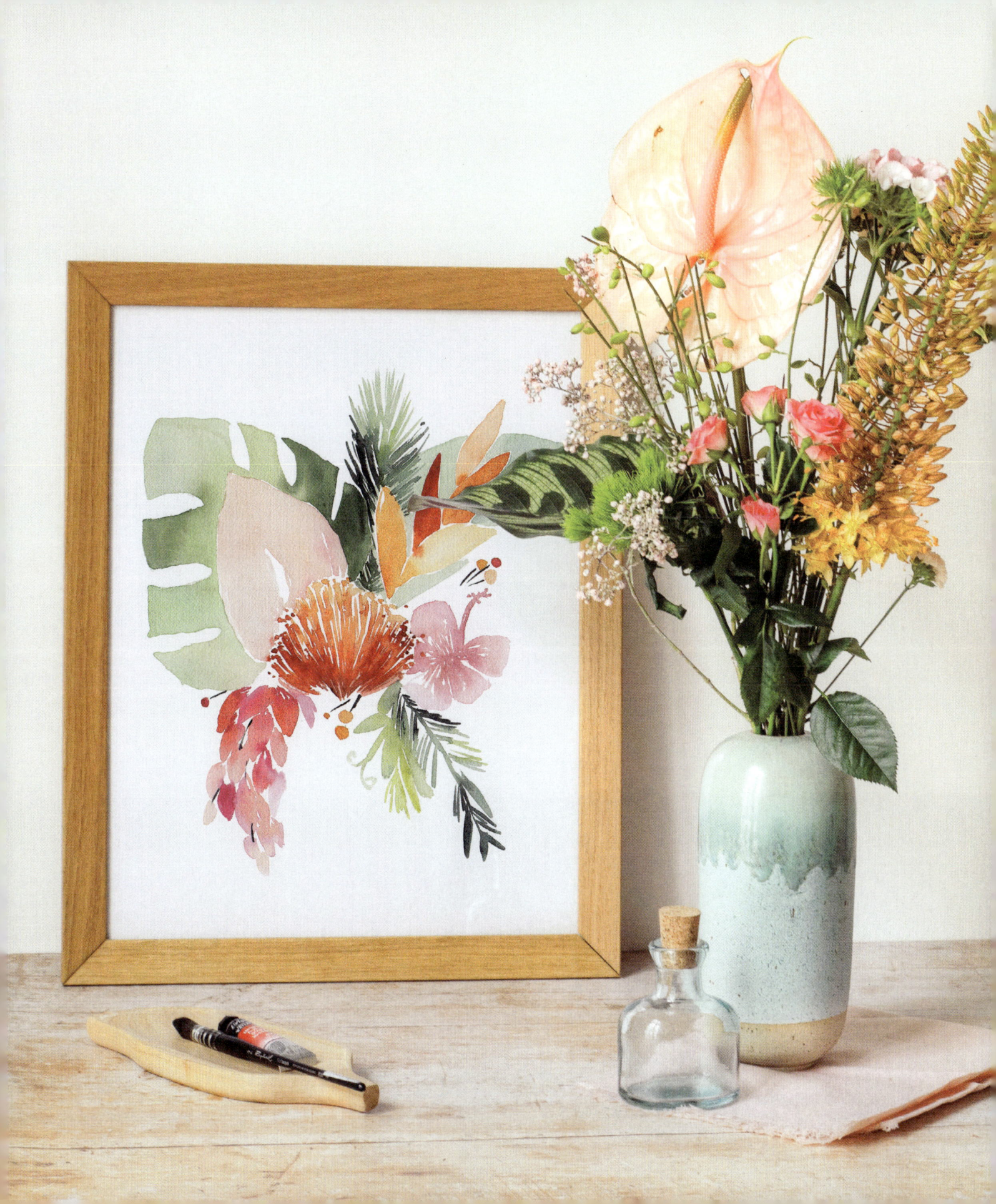

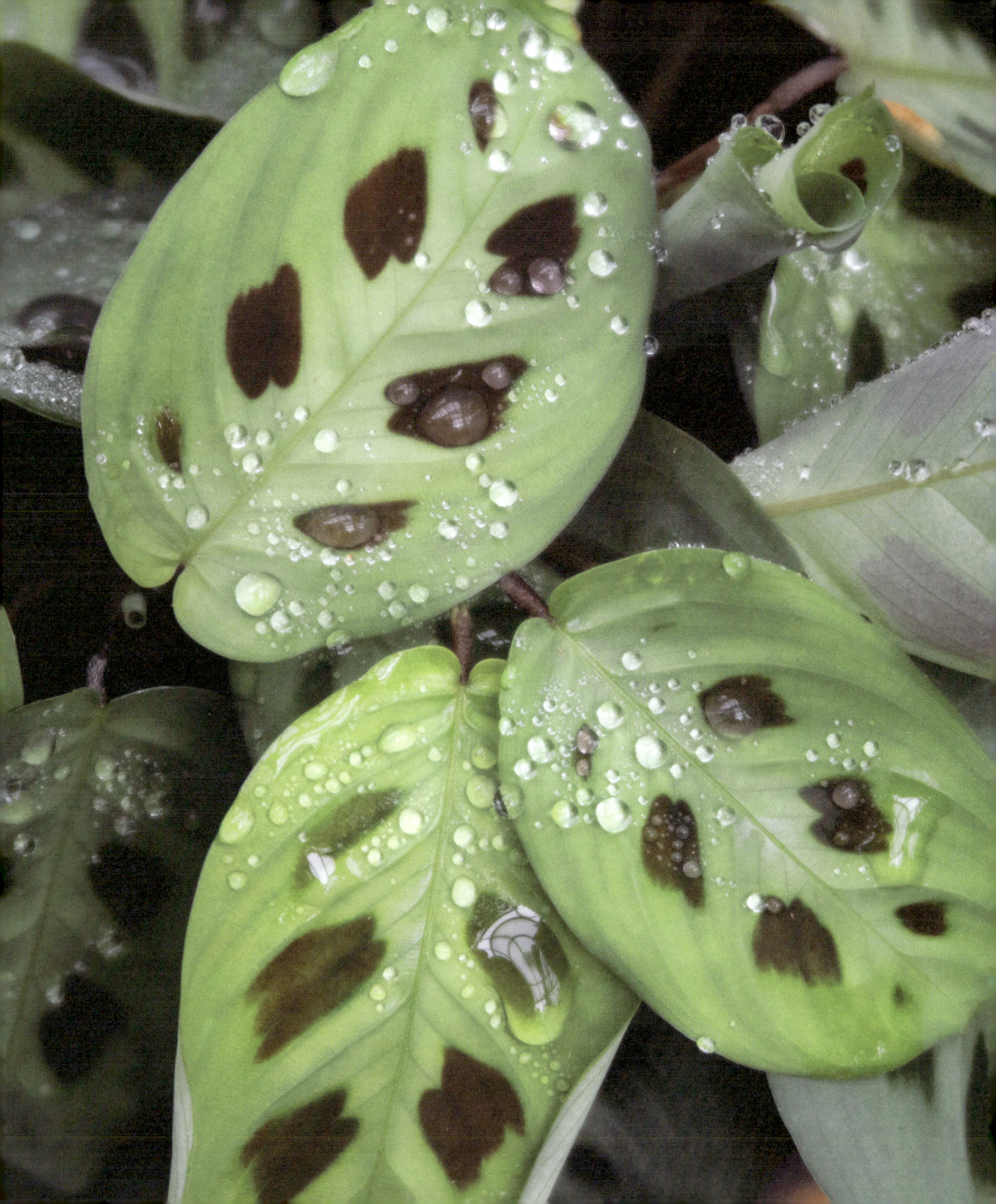

CHAPTER 04

Urban jungle plants

IN THIS FINAL CHAPTER, WE WILL FOCUS ON TROPICAL PLANTS AS A READY FEATURE IN OUR HOMES, HELPING TO CREATE A MINI URBAN JUNGLE. THESE PLANTS WILL ALLOW YOU TO EXPERIMENT WITH THE NUMEROUS TECHNIQUES SHOWN IN CHAPTER 1. COMBINE THEM WITH OTHER VEGETATION TO CREATE UNIQUE COMPOSITIONS.

VARIEGATED
plants

LICUALA GRANDIS OR RUFFLED FAN PALM

1 /

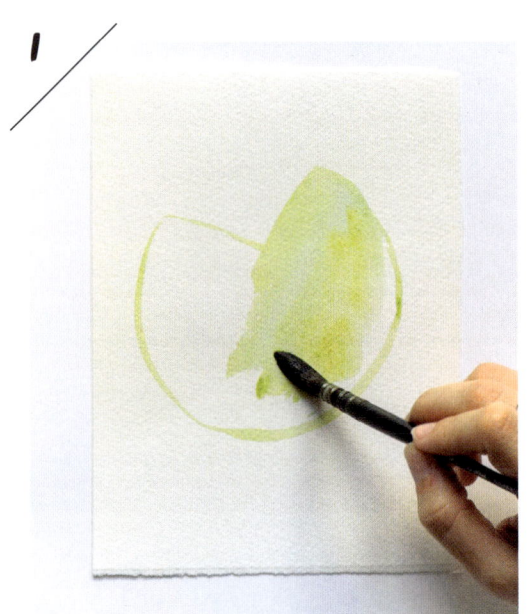

2 /

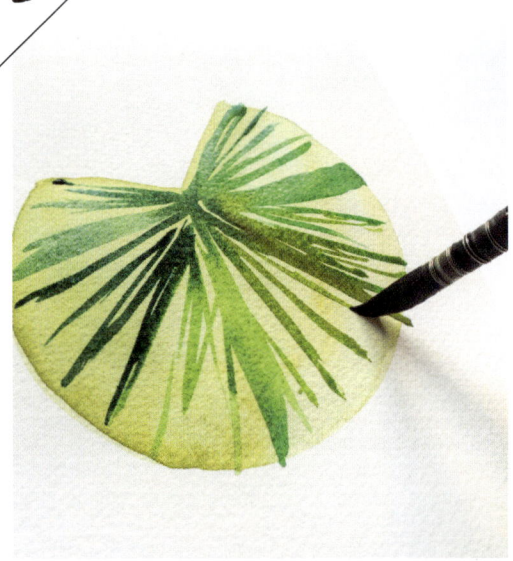

When painting a fan-shaped palmate leaf, my method is very different from that used for the pinnate palm leaves seen in chapter 2. Start by painting an incomplete circle in a yellowish green shade, as shown above.

When it has dried, paint the leaf details using a mix of colors (Hooker's Green and Olive Green shown here). Vary the thickness of the strokes and paint quickly for a more random effect.

CALATHEA INSIGNIS

1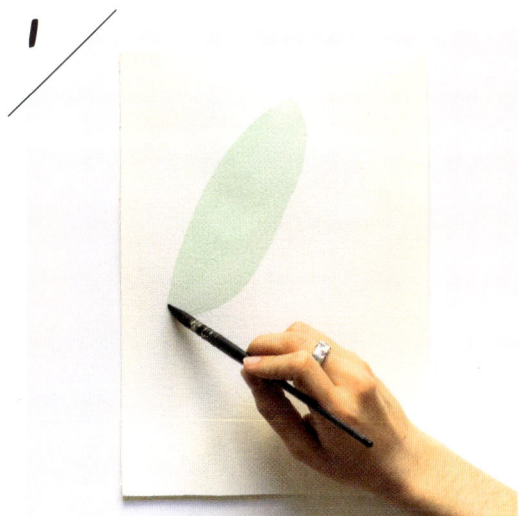

Start with a wide shape using a light green solution (see page 23). Make sure you use the right amount of water so as not to create a halo effect (see page 18).

2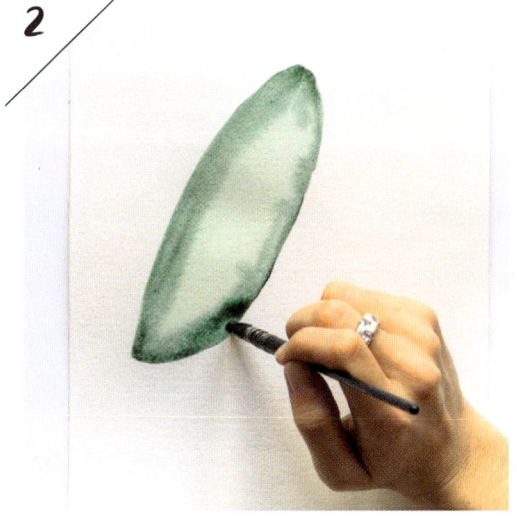

Using the wet-in-wet technique, add dark green round the edge of the leaf (Greenish Umber shown here).

3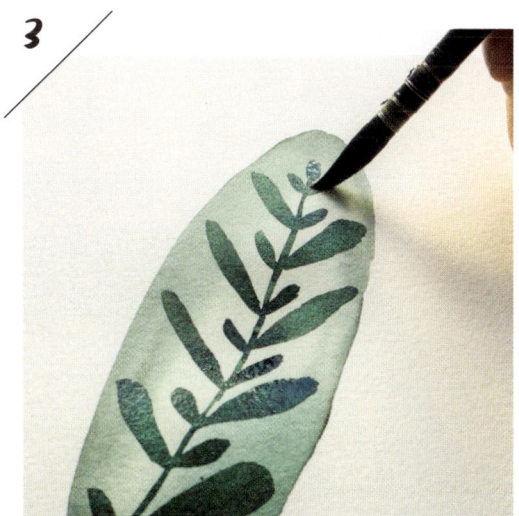

Wait for the leaf to dry and then use a dark green solution to paint a pattern of alternating small and large leaves on the leaf.

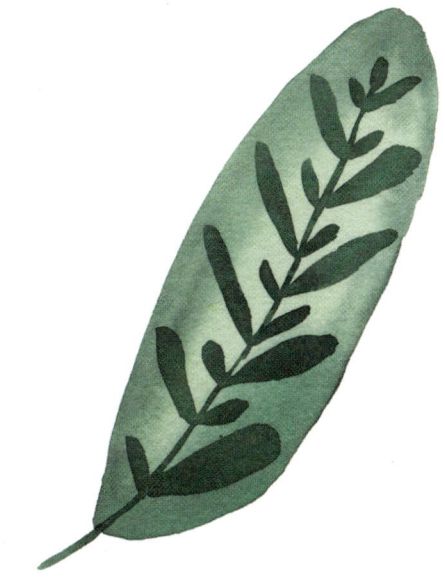

1

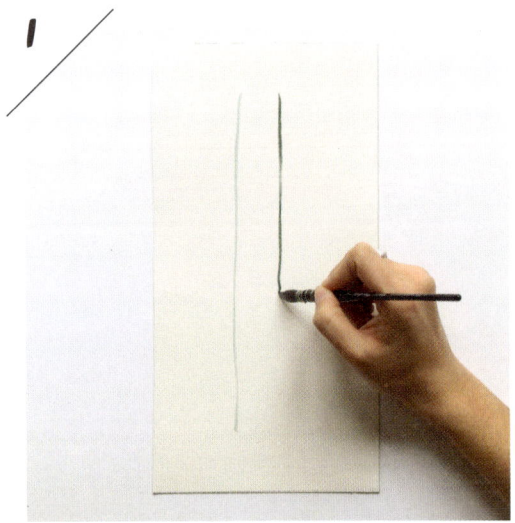

Start by painting very upright stems in a grey-green solution (Greenish Umber shown here). This vine-like plant will add a touch of delicacy to your compositions.

2

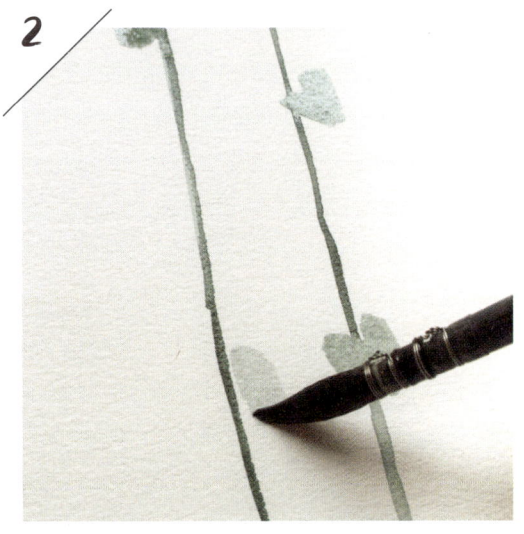

To paint heart-shaped leaves, I recommend you start on one side with this oval shape. The top is attached directly to the stem.

3

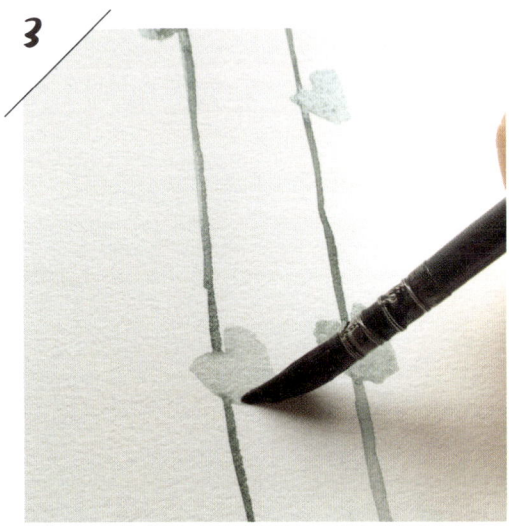

Then add another oval to complete the heart shape and finish with the tip. The hearts are often attached to the stem in pairs.

4

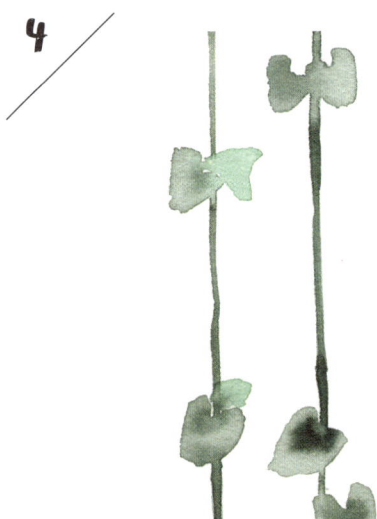

Feel free to add concentrated pigments to the stem, as well as little touches of color, but overall this plant is rather grey-green in color.

ALOCASIA AMAZONICA OR AMAZONIAN ELEPHANT'S EAR

1

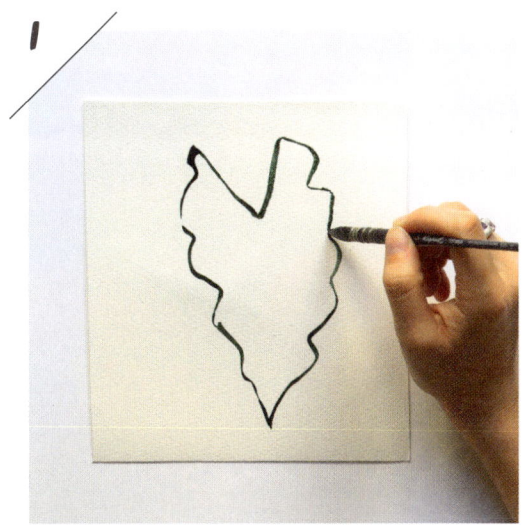

For this lovely impressive leaf, start with the wavy outline using dark green (I used Greenish Umber here - one of my favorite greens, as you will have gathered).

2

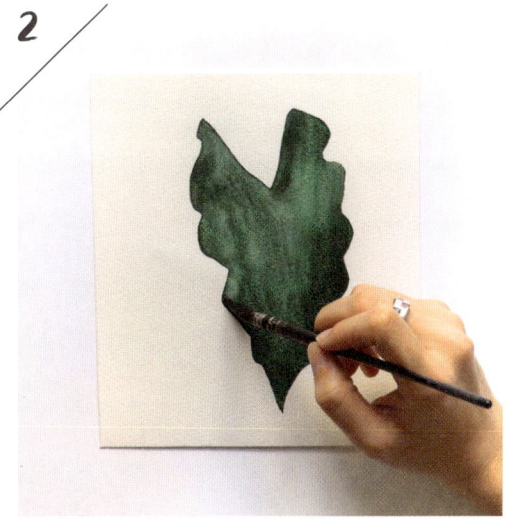

Fill in the leaf evenly and leave it until almost dry, remembering to keep a check on it.

3

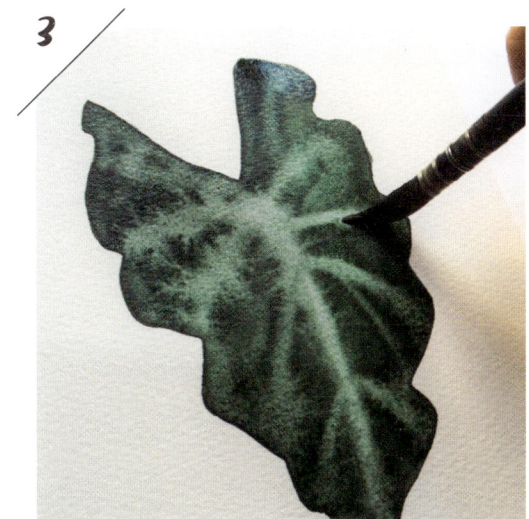

When the whole thing is almost dry, add some water to create furrows in the leaf (the veins), as shown on page 28.

4

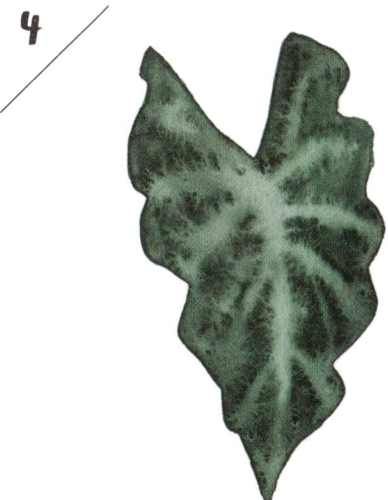

The water spreads through the dark pigments to create these magnificently striking starry patterns.

PEPEROMIA ARGYREIA OR WATERMELON BEGONIA

1 /

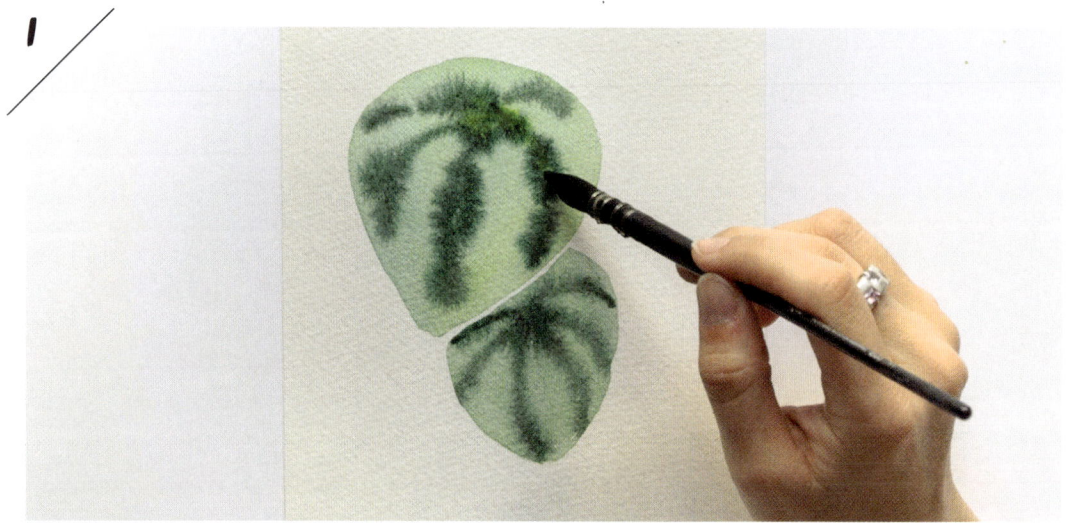

To paint this peperomia with its watermelon-like appearance, start with the shape of the leaf, which is rounded overall but with a more pointed area. Here I used a light green (see page 23). Using the wet-in-wet technique, add dark green lines (Greenish Umber), starting them all from the same central point.

2 /

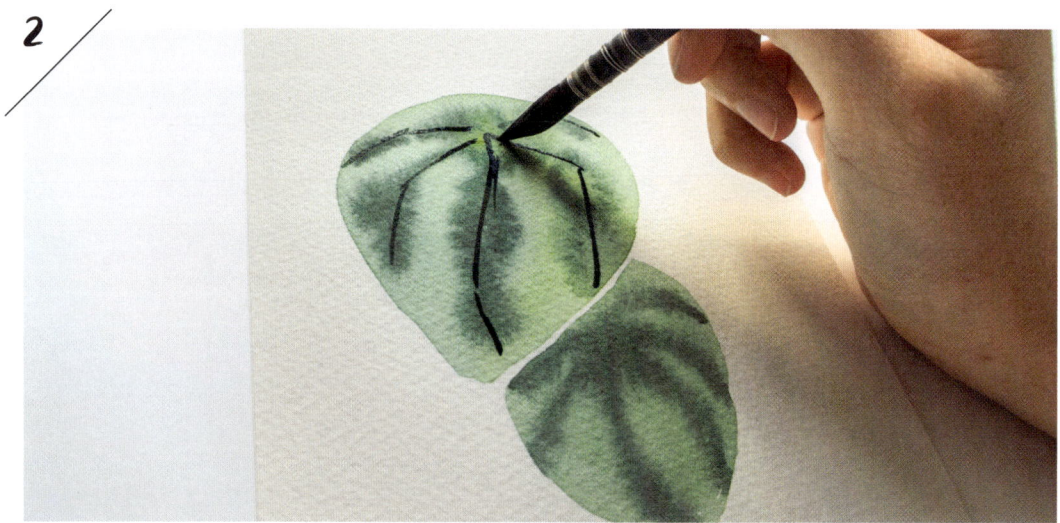

Once everything has dried, paint lines in a more concentrated solution, using the tip of the brush. This adds contrast to your leaves.

1

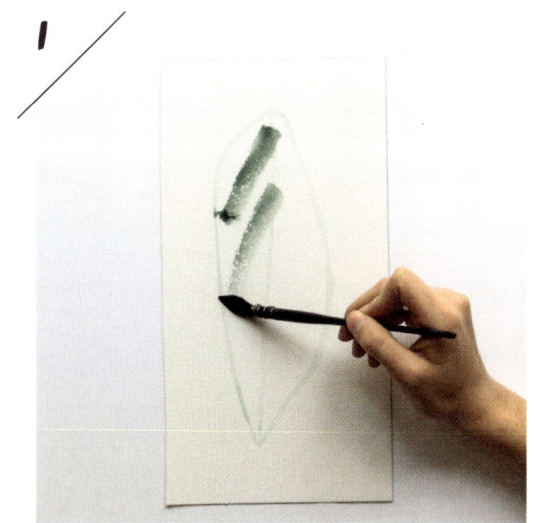

Start by painting your guide: the outline of the leaf, in a light green solution, as well as the central vein. Take a grey-green solution and press the brush flat (see page 37) to paint broad textured lines running from the center to the edge.

2

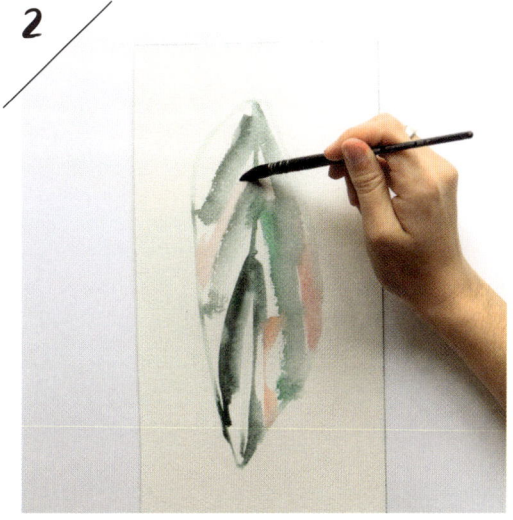

Continue these highly textured lines in different colors (shown here in grey-green, Emerald Green and pink) and of varying lengths. Leave white spaces between the lines to make them stand out.

3

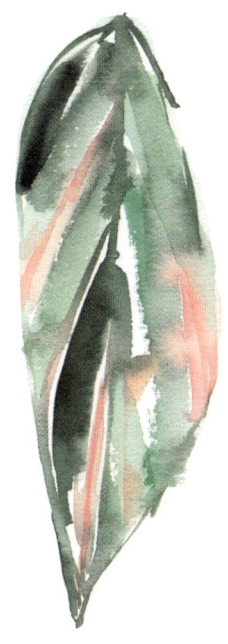

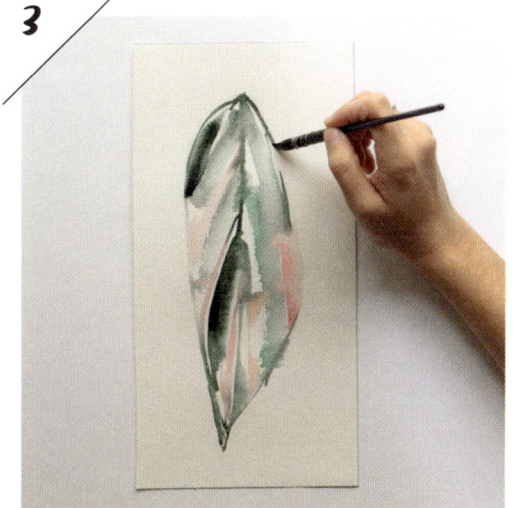

Add some contrast with finer lines and a highly concentrated solution (Greenish Umber shown here). Go back over a few areas with the same solution; be careful not to go over everything, so as to retain the lovely initial texture.

Pilea

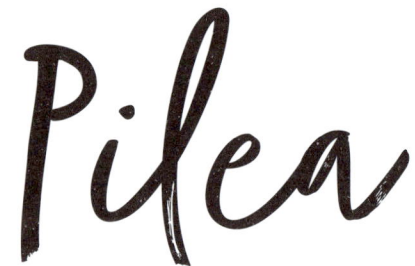

WE MUSTN'T FORGET THE PILEA PEPEROMIOIDES, OR CHINESE MONEY PLANT, ALSO KNOWN AS A MISSIONARY PLANT, ONE OF THE MOST POPULAR PLANTS FOR CREATING A JUNGLE MOOD IN THE HOME. SEE HOW TO PAINT IT BY LAYERING WATERCOLORS.

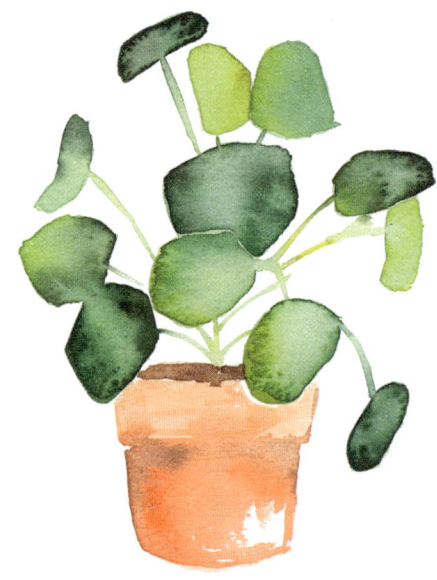

THE MAIN COLORS

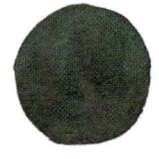
Greenish Umber

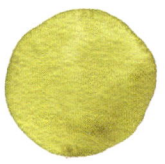
Brown Green

Burnt Sienna

Light green
(see page 23)

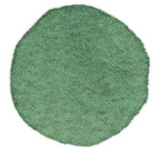
Dark blue-green
(see page 23)

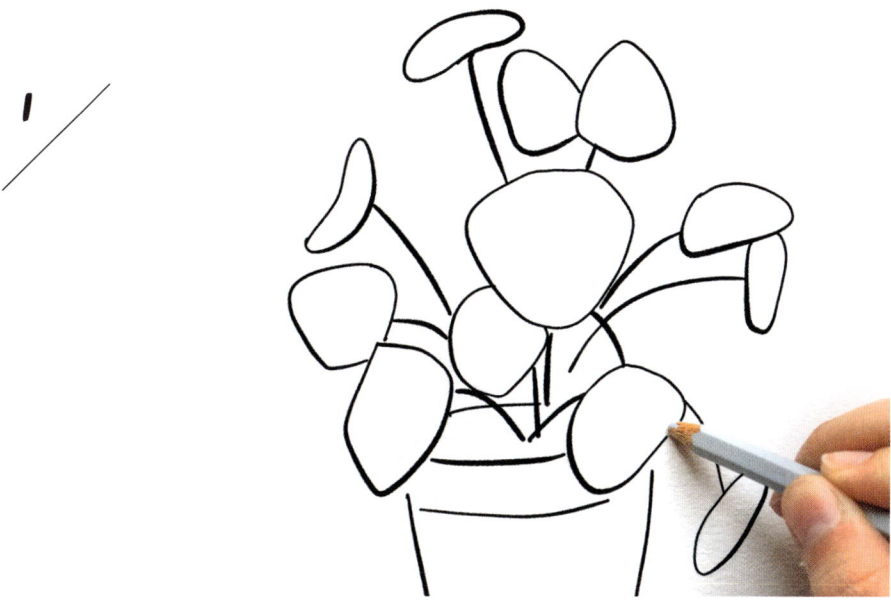

1

Start by doing a light sketch using a drawing pencil or watercolor pencil. Use the suggestion above to help you (deliberately accentuated). Remember that the leaves are rounded but not perfectly, and are often slightly pointed at the bottom. The stalk is attached not to the middle but more to the top of the leaf. The stalks fan out around the main stem. For leaves pointing backwards, paint them as a sausage shape.

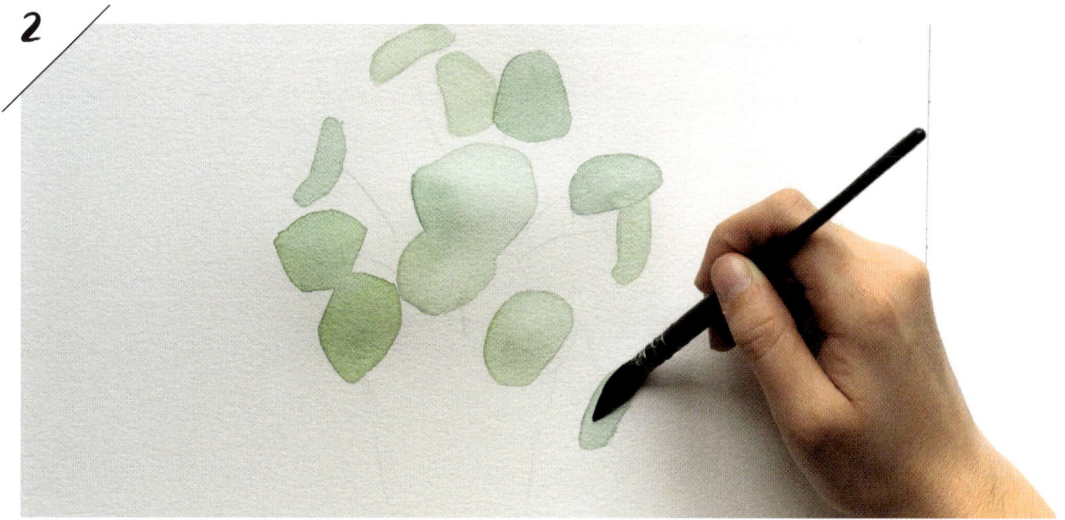

2

Start by painting all the leaves in a light green solution. Feel free to vary the mix slightly to add interest. Wait for everything to dry properly (use a blow-dryer to speed up the process).

3 /

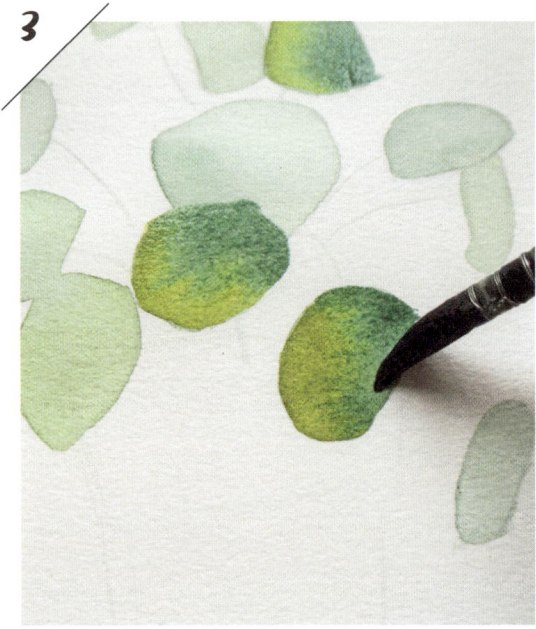

Go over some leaves to create color gradients (Brown Green and blue-green).

4 /

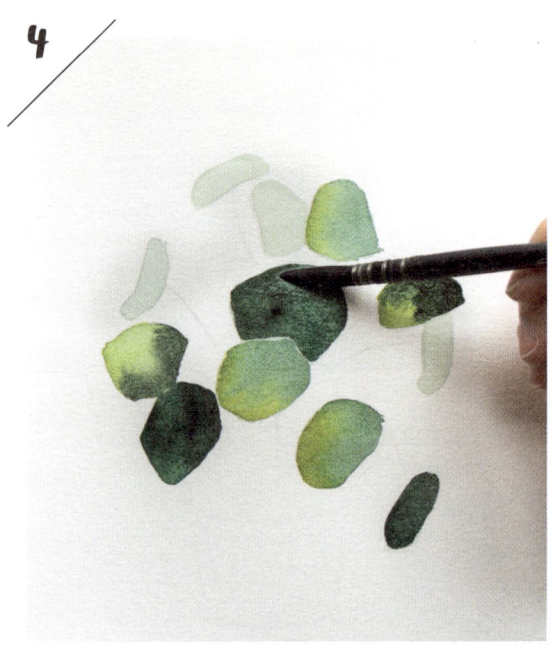

Go over other leaves with a dark green.

5 /

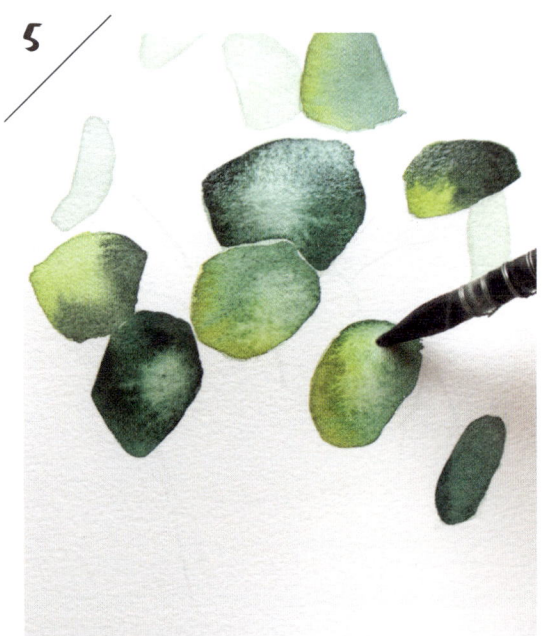

While everything is in the process of drying but not yet completely dry, add little drops of water to the leaves. This will reveal the light green of the lower layer and create lovely effects.

6 /

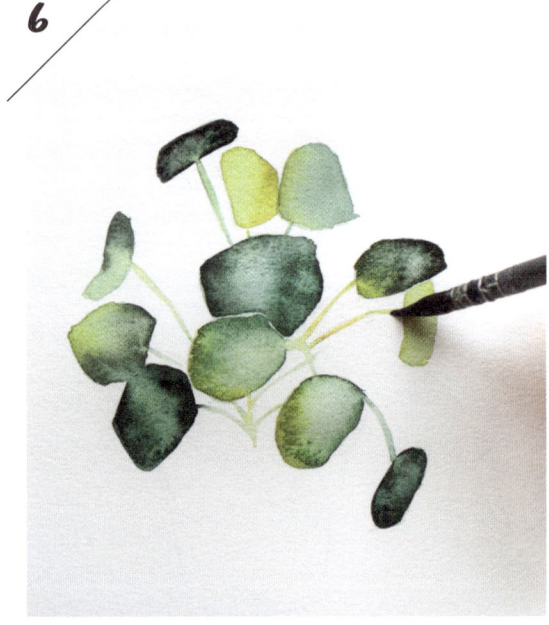

Add the remaining leaves using a yellowish green mix and paint the stems in light colors.

7

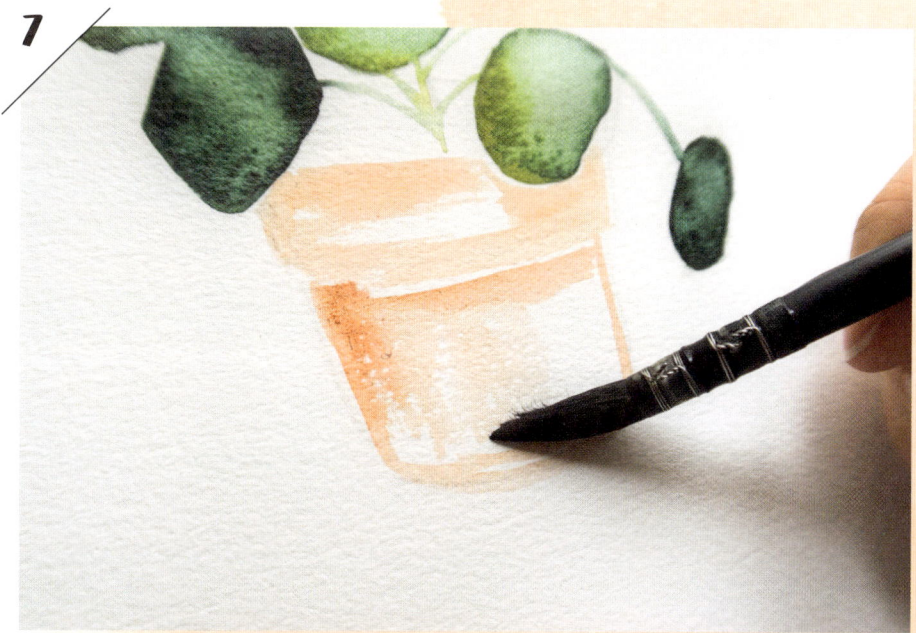

Use an orangy brown mix (Burnt Sienna shown here) to paint the terracotta pot. Use the side of your brush to create texture with the grain of the paper.

8

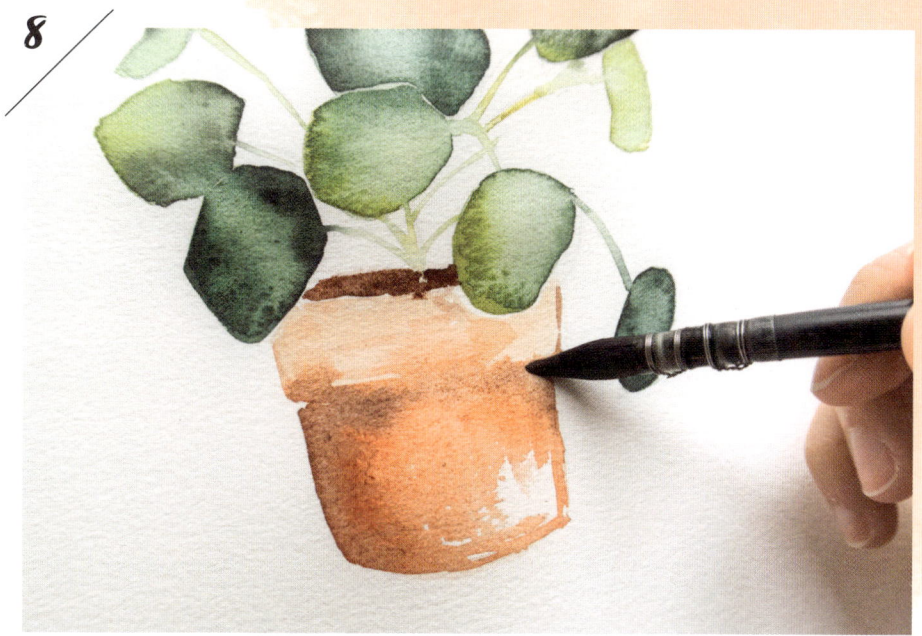

Whilst keeping some white spaces, add slightly more concentrated pigment to form shadows on the pot to give it greater volume. Paint a fine dark brown line for the soil.

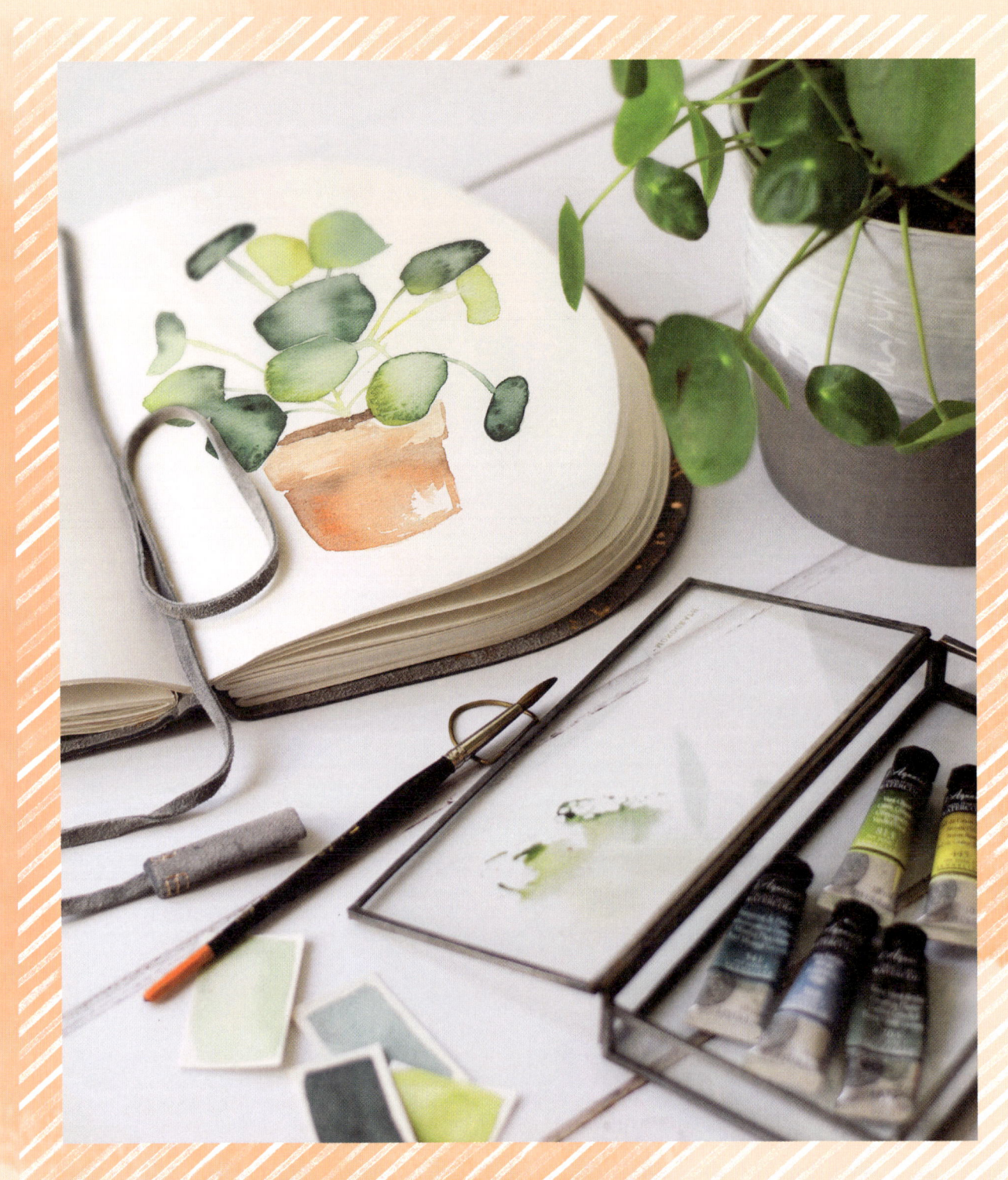

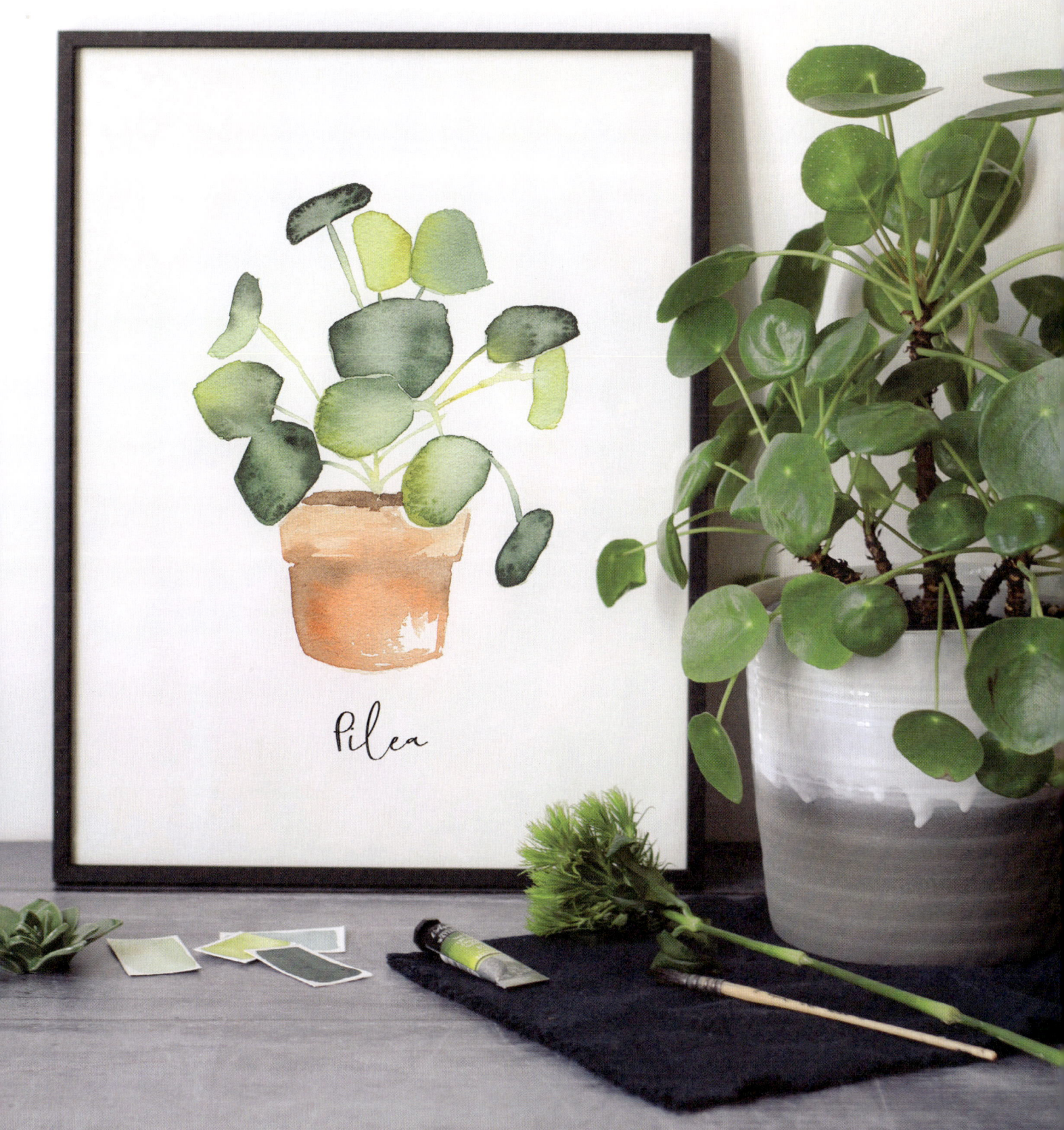

Caladium

WITH ITS WONDERFUL PINK AND GREEN COLOR GRADIENTS, CALADIUM FOLIAGE IS ALMOST LIKE A NATURAL WATERCOLOR. IF, LIKE ME, YOU ARE ENTRANCED BY THESE BEAUTIFUL TROPICAL COLORS, I SUGGEST YOU TRY THE FOLLOWING PAINTING WHICH REALLY SHOWS THEM OFF.

THE MAIN COLORS

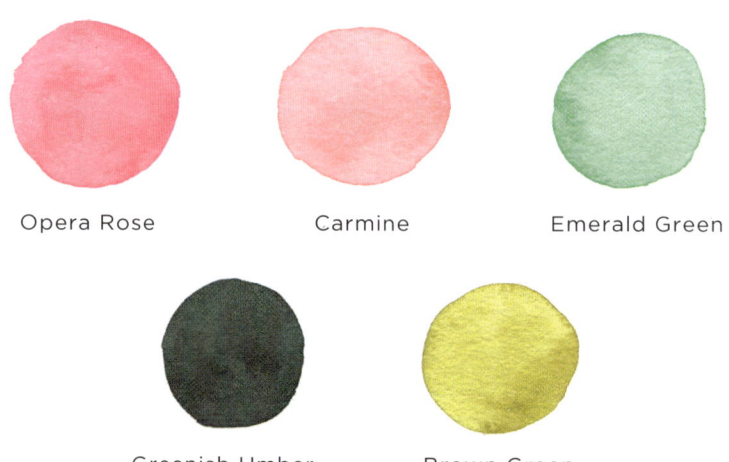

Opera Rose   Carmine   Emerald Green

Greenish Umber   Brown Green

Remember

- Use masking tape to create a frame; press it against your clothing first before sticking it down, so as to reduce its adhesiveness and prevent it tearing the paper.
- Keep large sections of the leaves hidden.
- Let the colors merge, don't touch them any more than necessary.

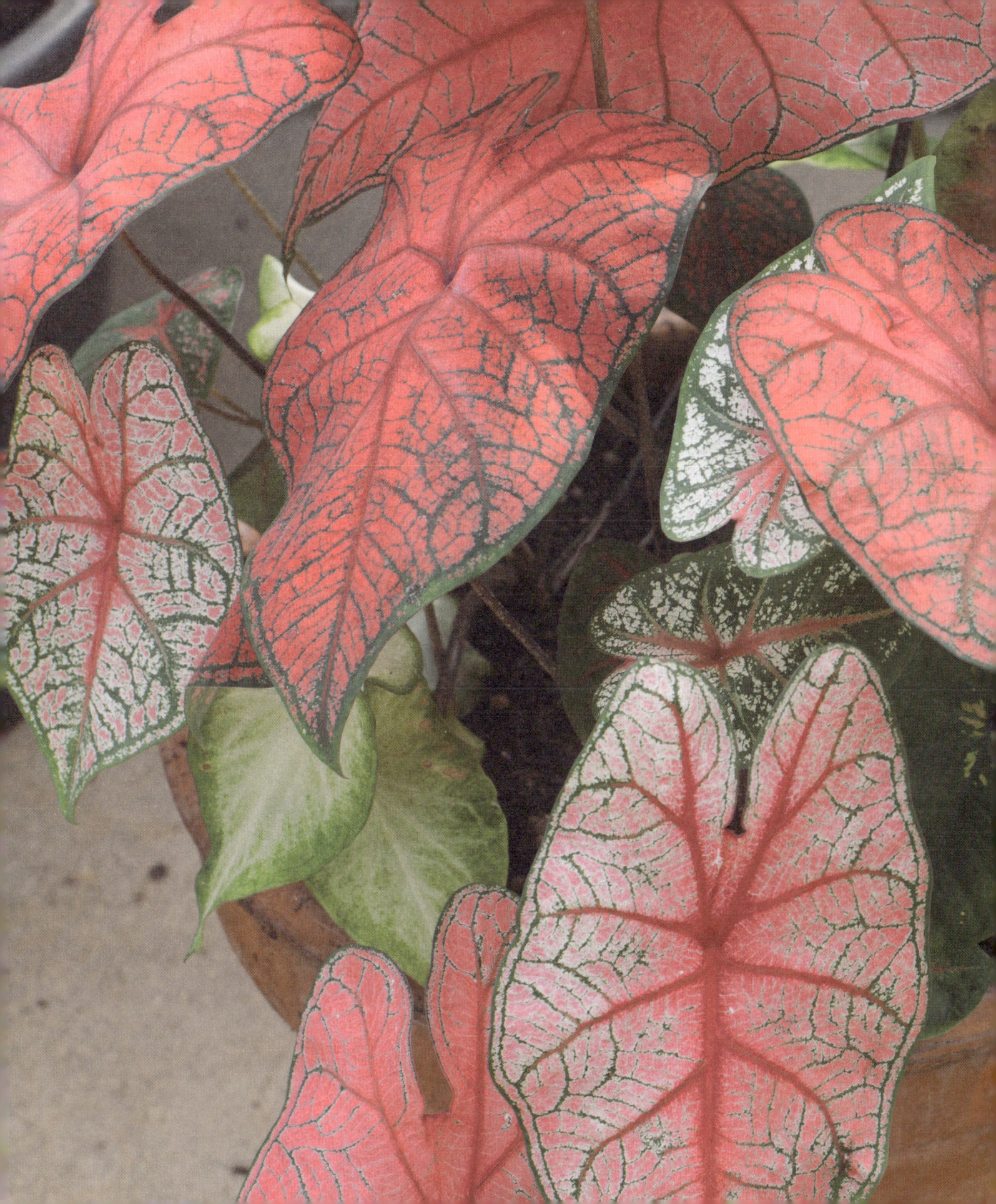

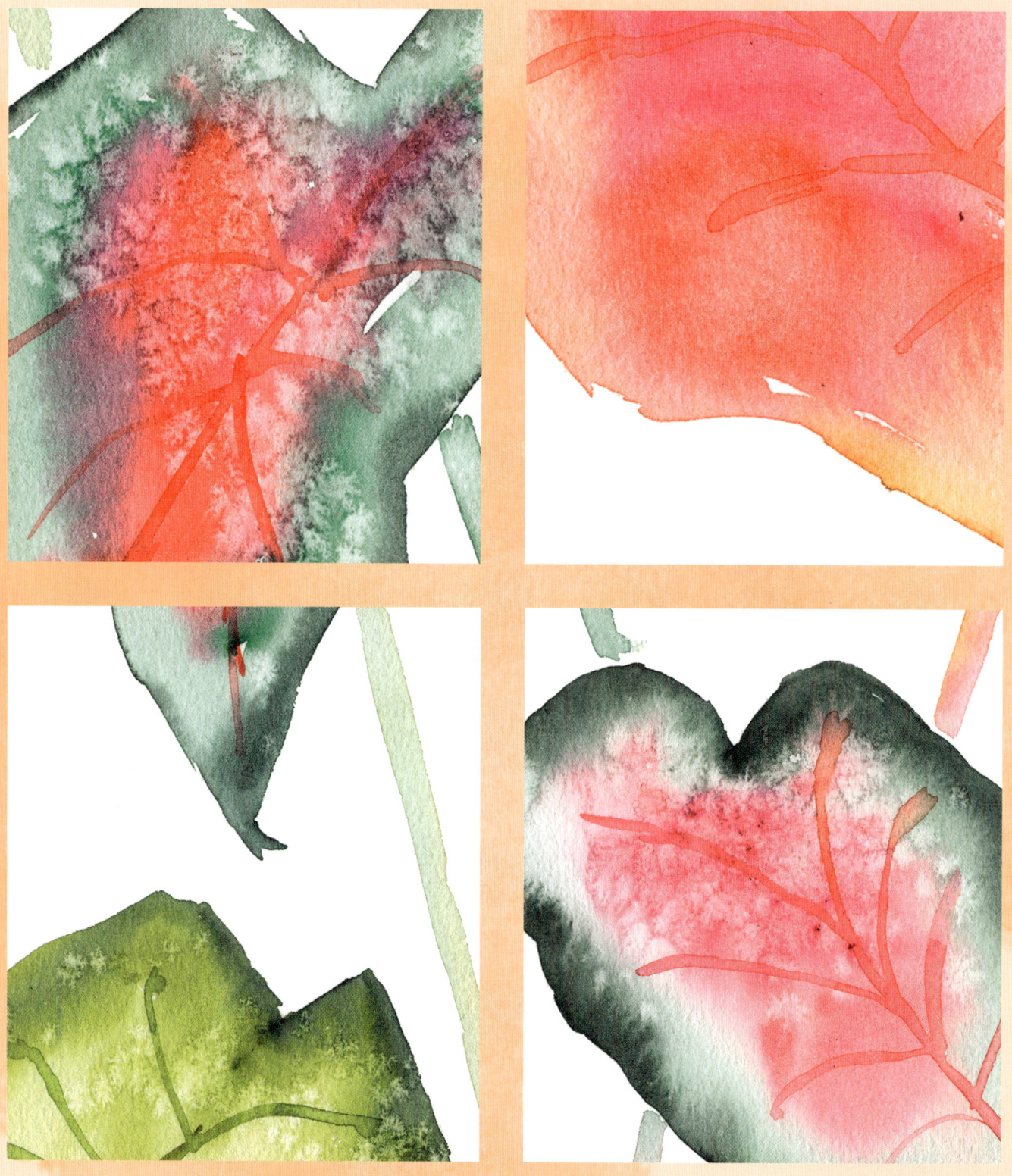

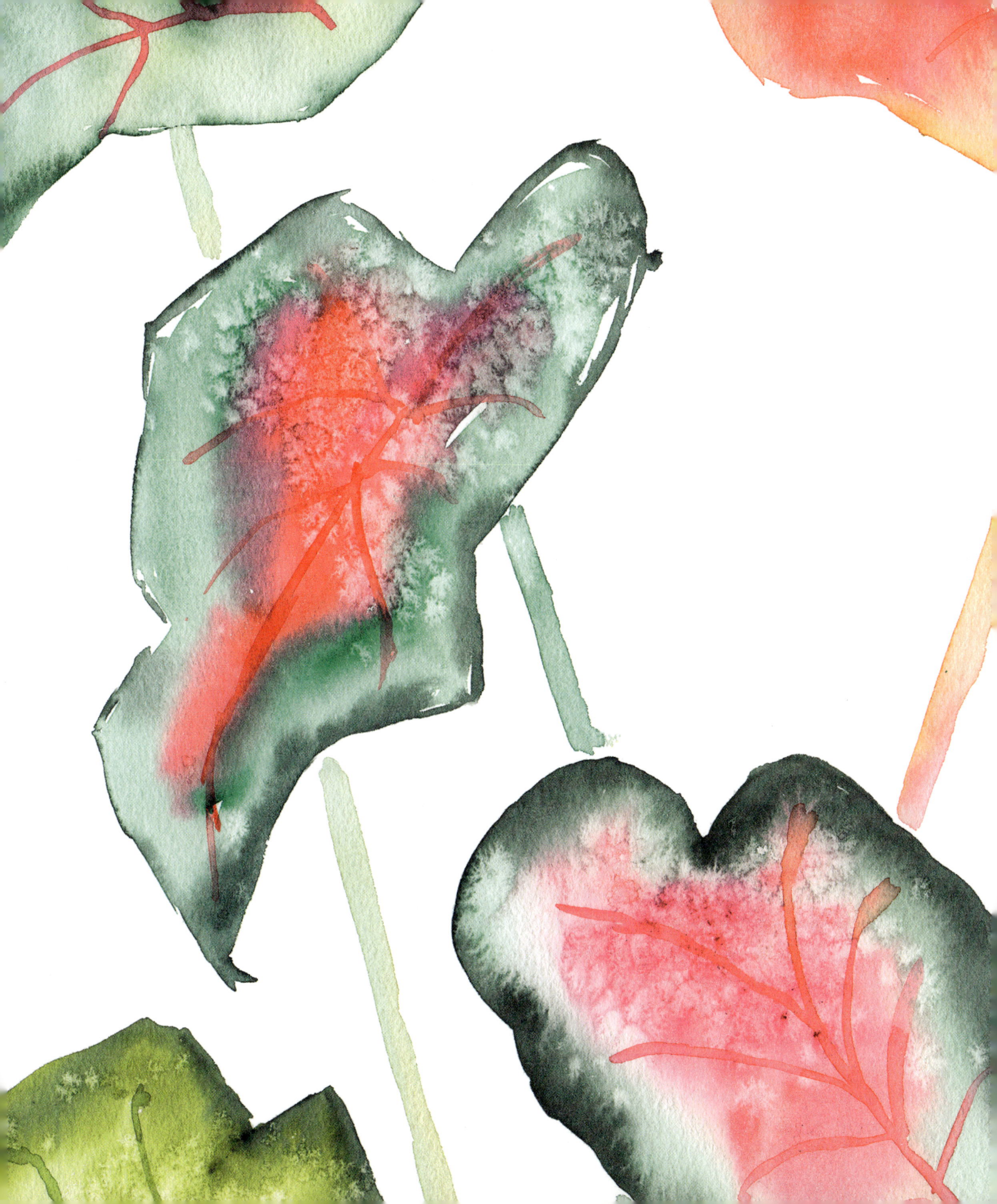

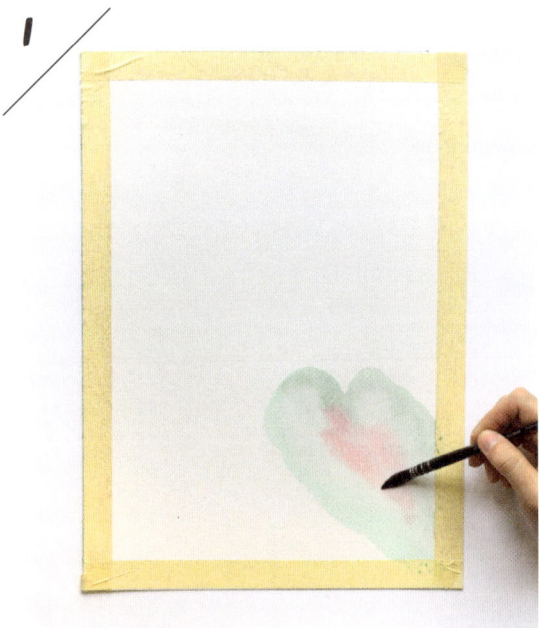

1

Having arranged four strips of masking tape to protect the edges of your painting, start with the first leaf in the bottom right corner. Use a light Emerald Green solution for the outlines and Opera Rose for the center.

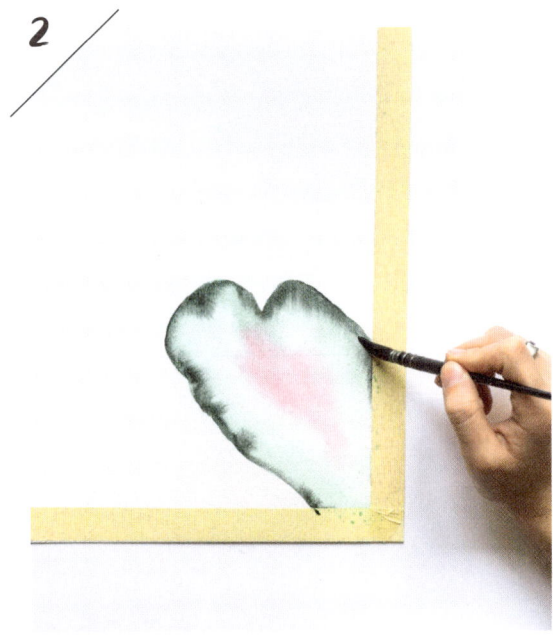

2

Use the wet-in-wet technique for the edge of the leaf, adding a dark green (Greenish Umber shown here). Notice that part of the leaf is concealed to emphasize the chosen framing effect.

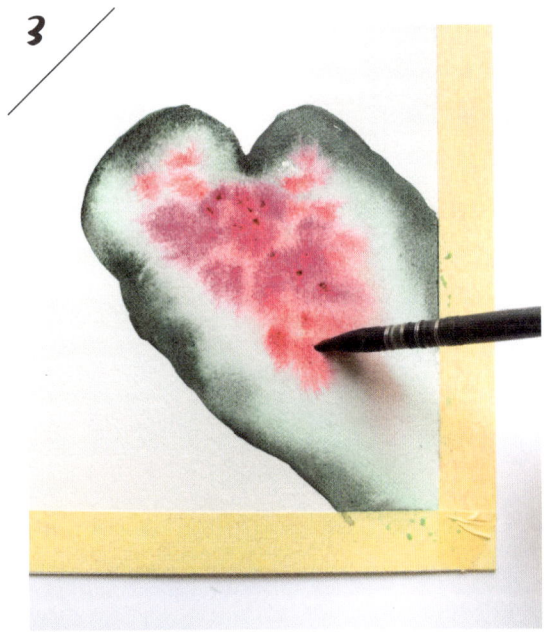

3

Continue painting wet-in-wet, tapping the heart of the leaf with concentrated Opera Rose.

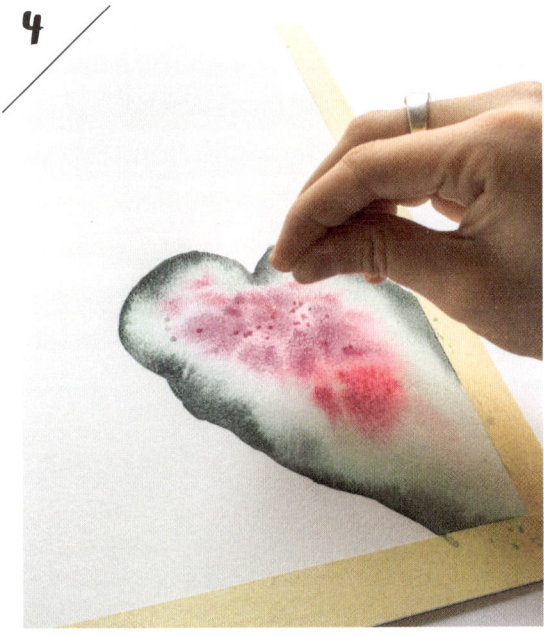

4

Now sprinkle coarse salt crystals on the central area while everything is still wet.

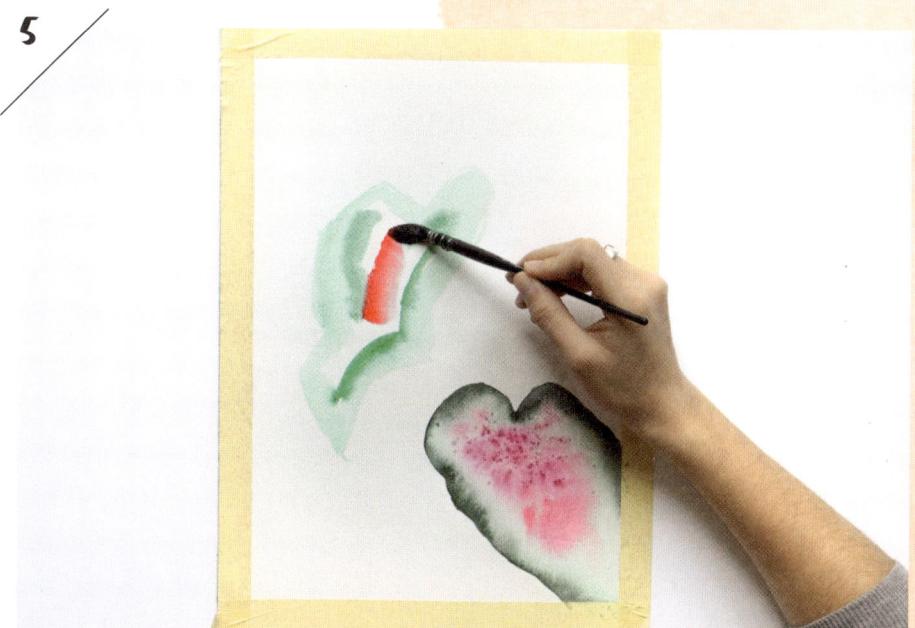

5

Move on to a second leaf in the center of the page. Once again, paint thick outlines in Emerald Green and then the inner part of the leaf, this time with Carmine (or a slightly more concentrated redder shade than the pink you used previously).

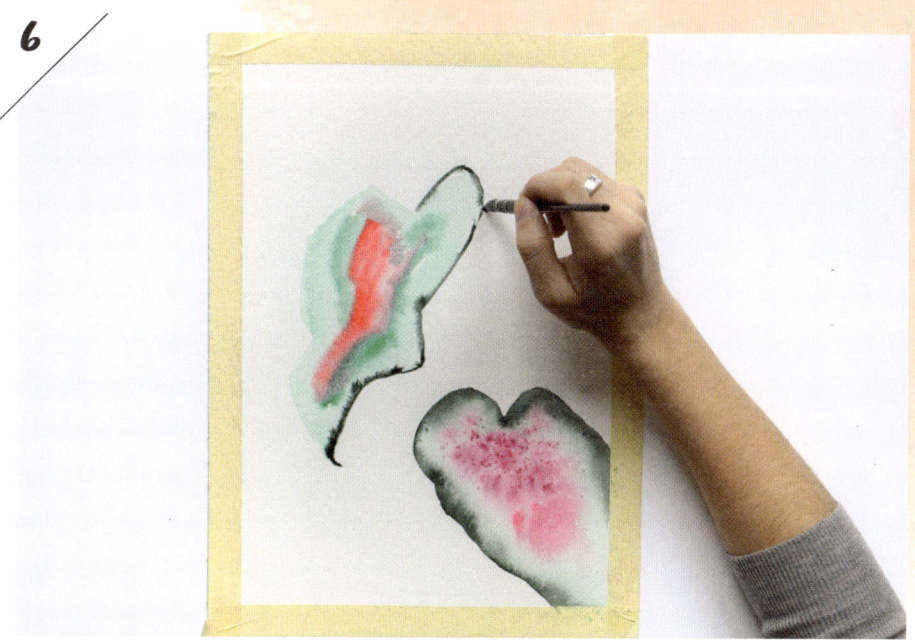

Paint the outlines with a dark green (Greenish Umber shown here) while everything is still wet to create a gradation effect. Add coarse salt crystals to this leaf too.

7 /

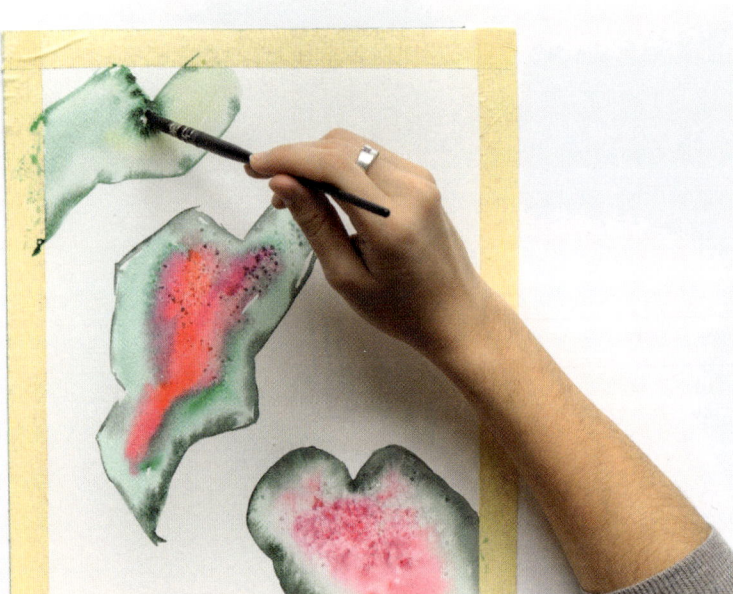

Paint a leaf in the same way in the top left corner. I didn't use pink this time but a light green mix (see page 23). Having added pigment to the edge, I did not add salt again, as this leaf is more in the background.

8 /

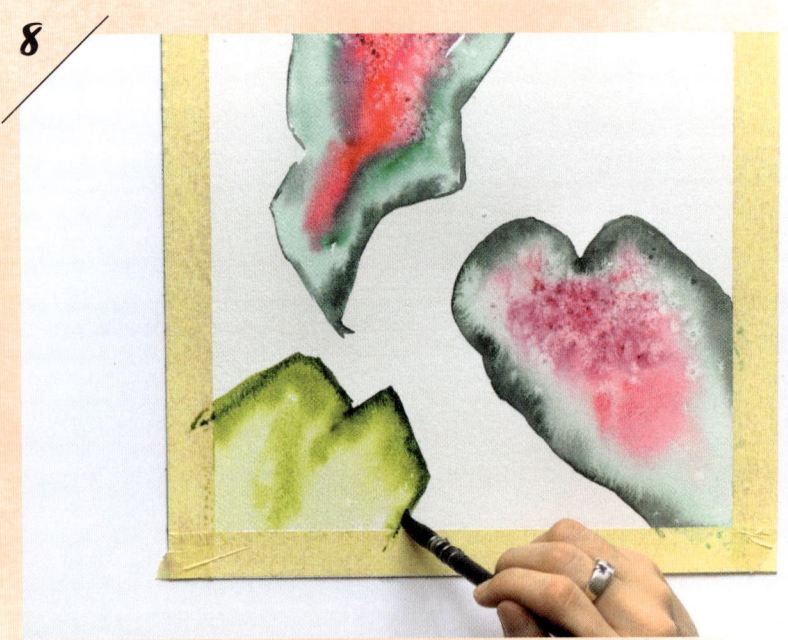

Paint a leaf in the bottom left foreground, half hidden by the frame. I used a yellowish green mix (Brown Green and Olive Green) and Greenish Umber for the edge of the leaf and I added coarse salt crystals.

9

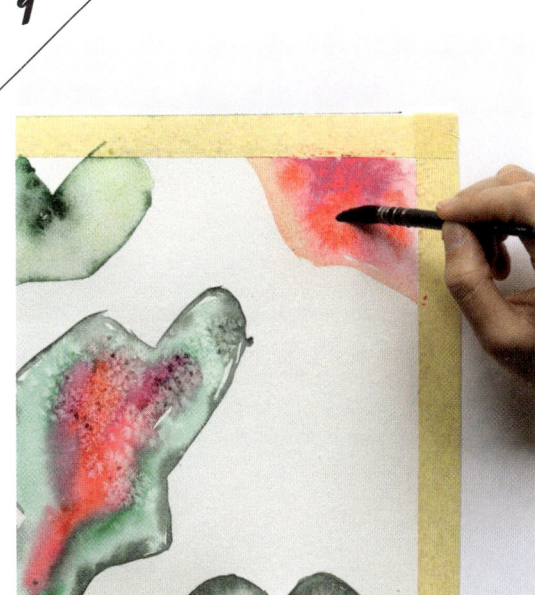

Paint the final leaf in the top right corner using a mix of deep Opera Rose, a little Carmine and an orangy shade (made here with Carmine and Brown Green). Do not do a dark green outline.

10

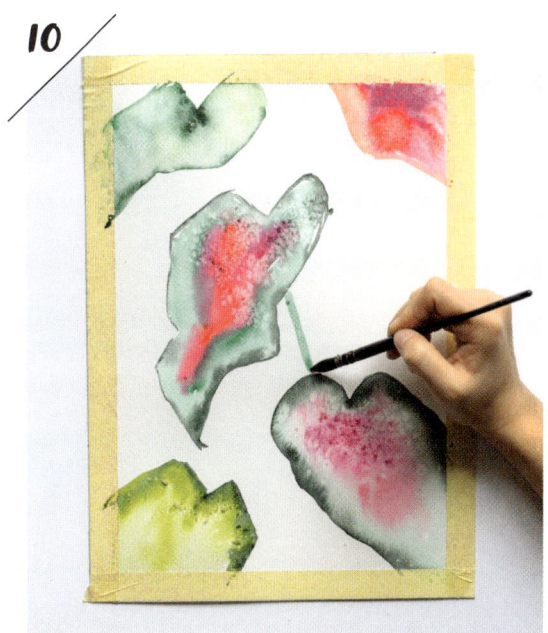

Start painting the stems. They are thick, straight and light, and they pick up the colors of the leaves.

11

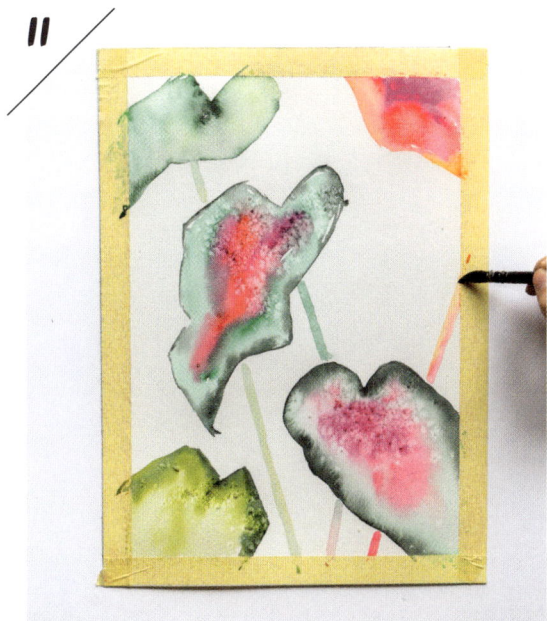

Make some of the stems longer, avoiding the leaves, and make them look as though they extend beyond the frame. Having checked that everything is dry, brush the salt off the paper.

12

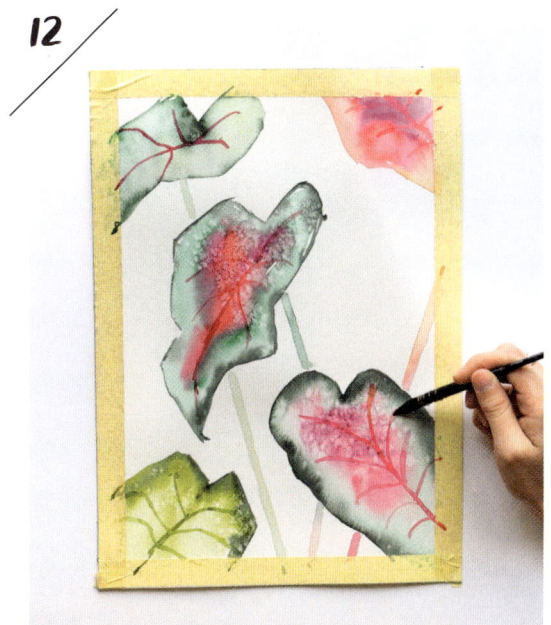

Using a deep Opera Rose, paint the veins. Curve them slightly to represent the undulations in the leaf. The leaf in the bottom left corner has yellowish green veins.

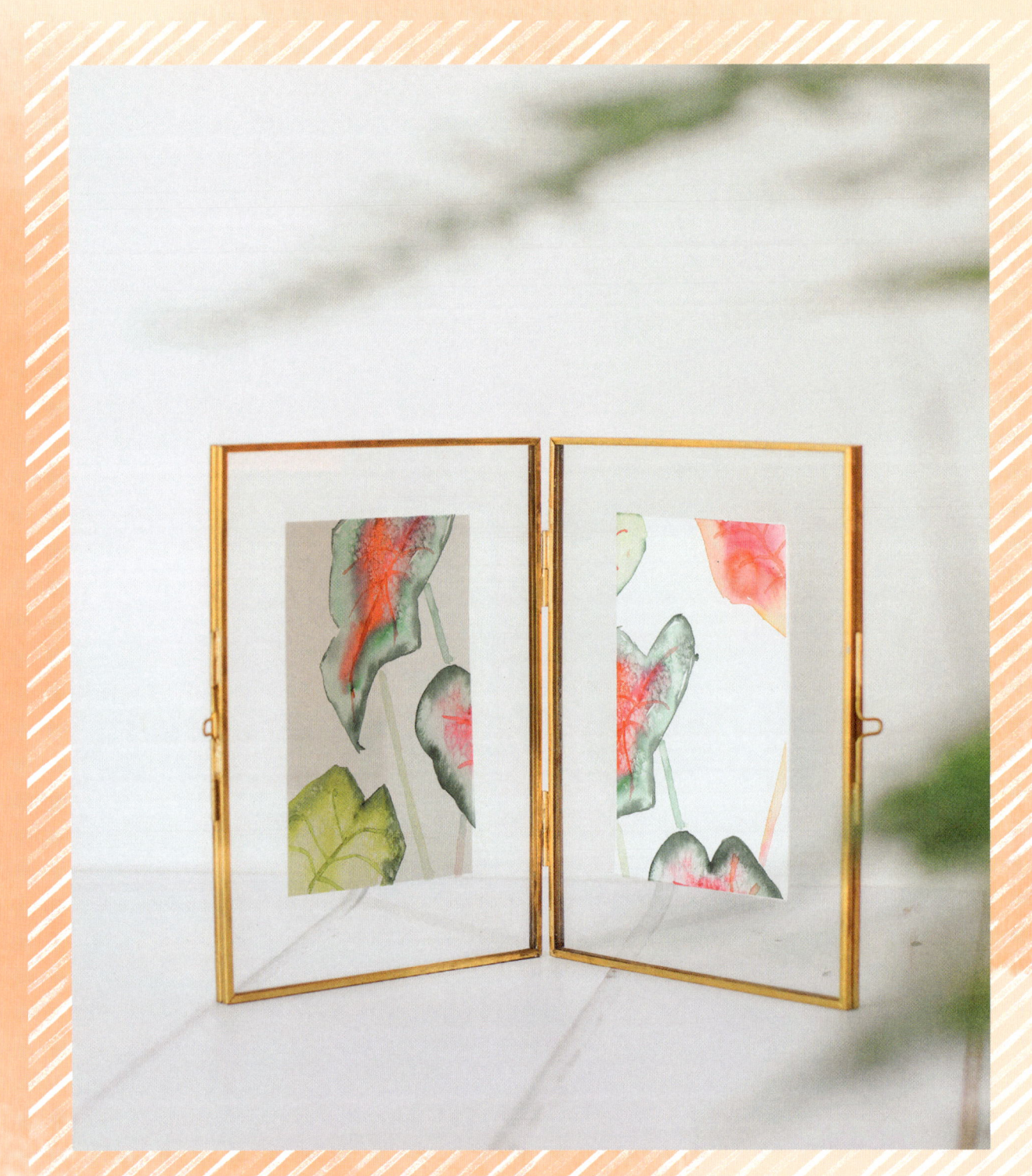

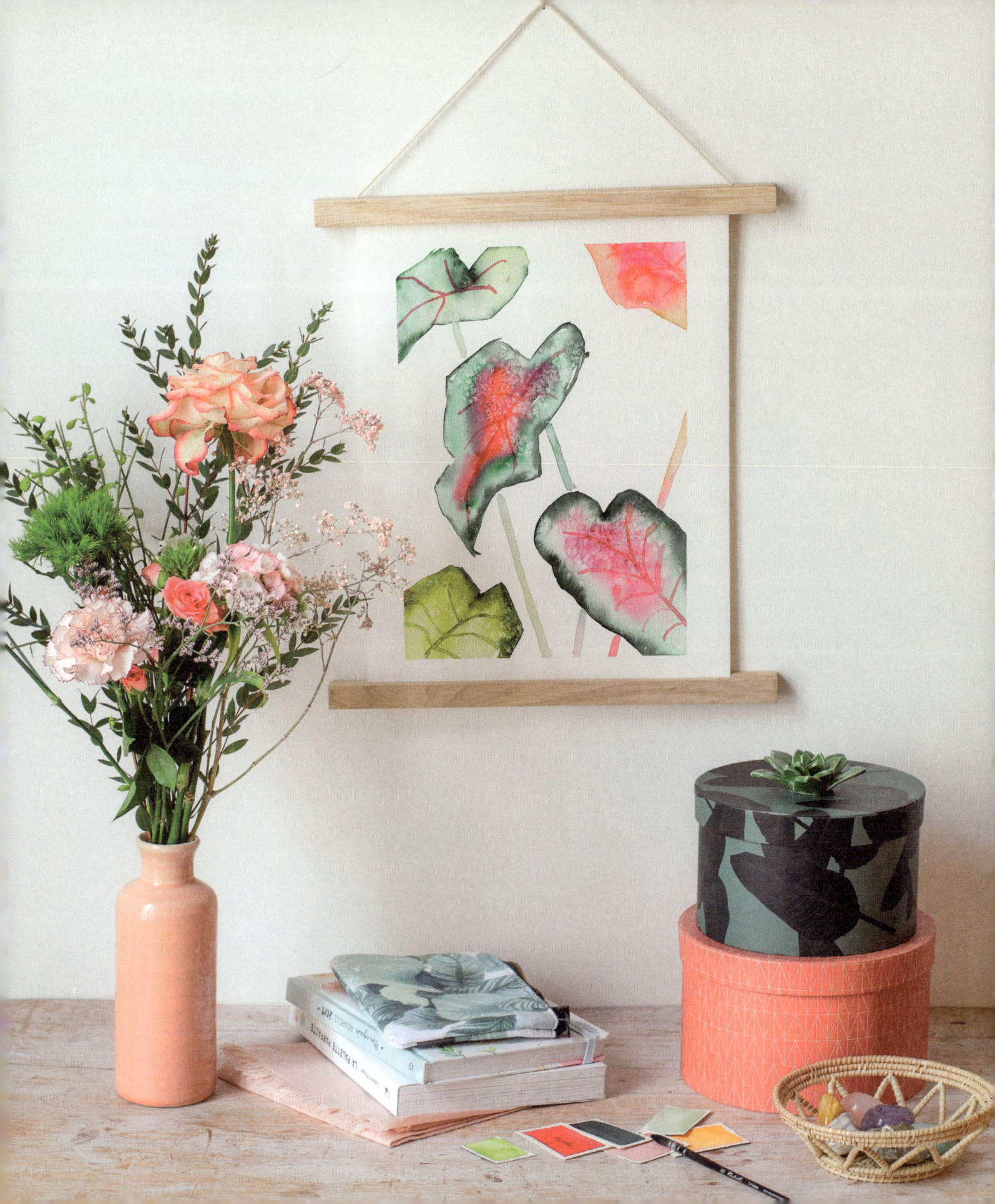

CALATHEA
orbifolia

THE WONDERFUL STRIPES ON THE CALATHEA , SEEN BOTTOM RIGHT
OPPOSITE, WERE MY INSPIRATION FOR THE FOLLOWING PAINTING.
USING THE NEGATIVE PAINTING TECHNIQUE, IT IS BY FAR THE MOST
COMPLEX IN THE BOOK, REQUIRING PATIENCE AND METHODICALNESS,
BUT YOU WILL ACHIEVE IT IF YOU FOLLOW THE SUGGESTED STEPS.
THE OVERLAPPING LAYERS GIVE A LOVELY EFFECT OF DEPTH.

THE MAIN COLORS

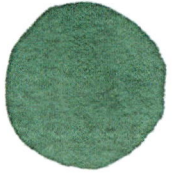

Dark blue-green
(see page 23)

Burnt Sienna

Remember

- The plant is divided into three sections: A, B and C.
- The leaves are numbered to avoid confusion. For your first attempt, I recommend you precisely replicate the same plant as me.

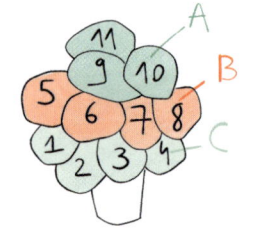

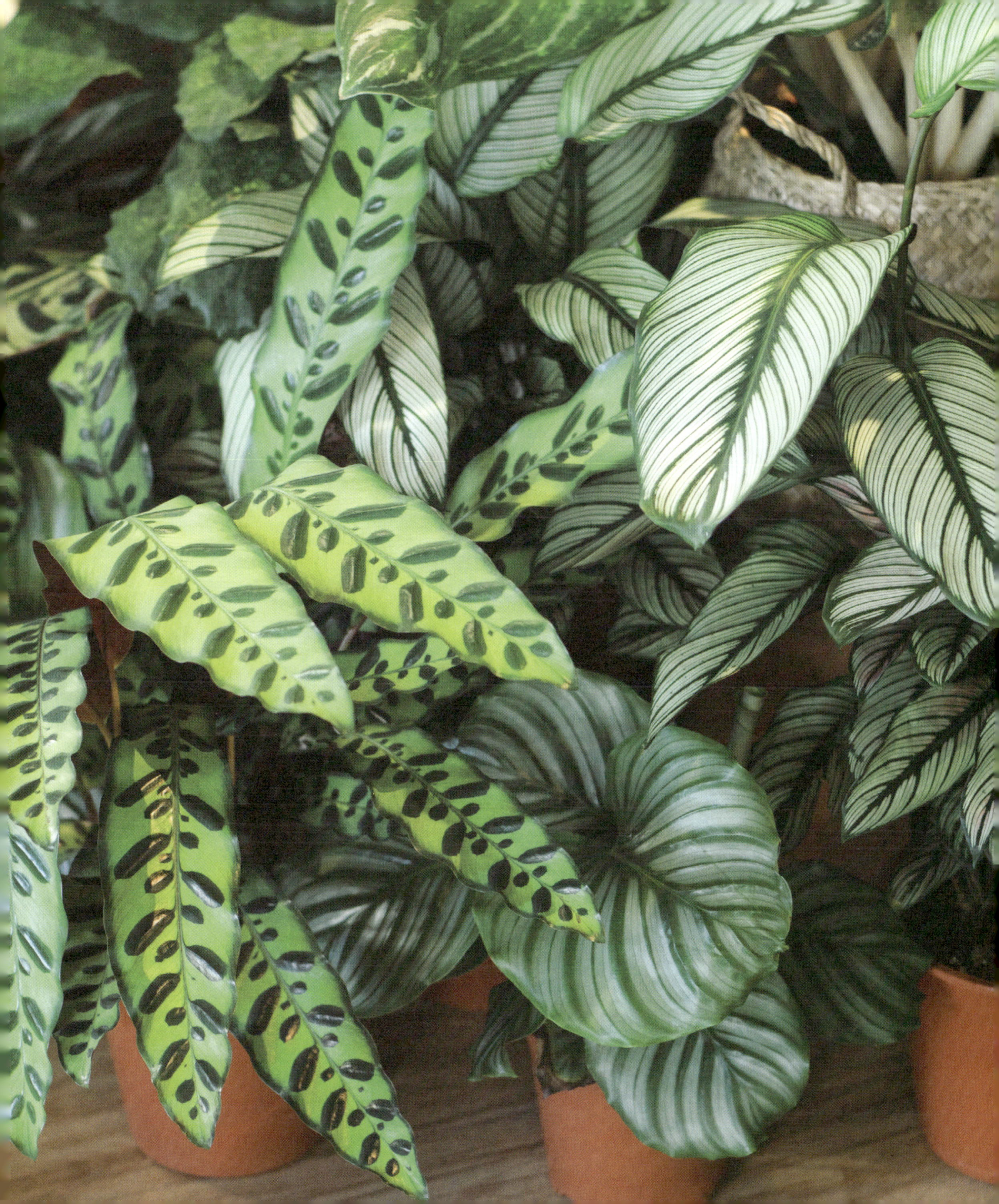

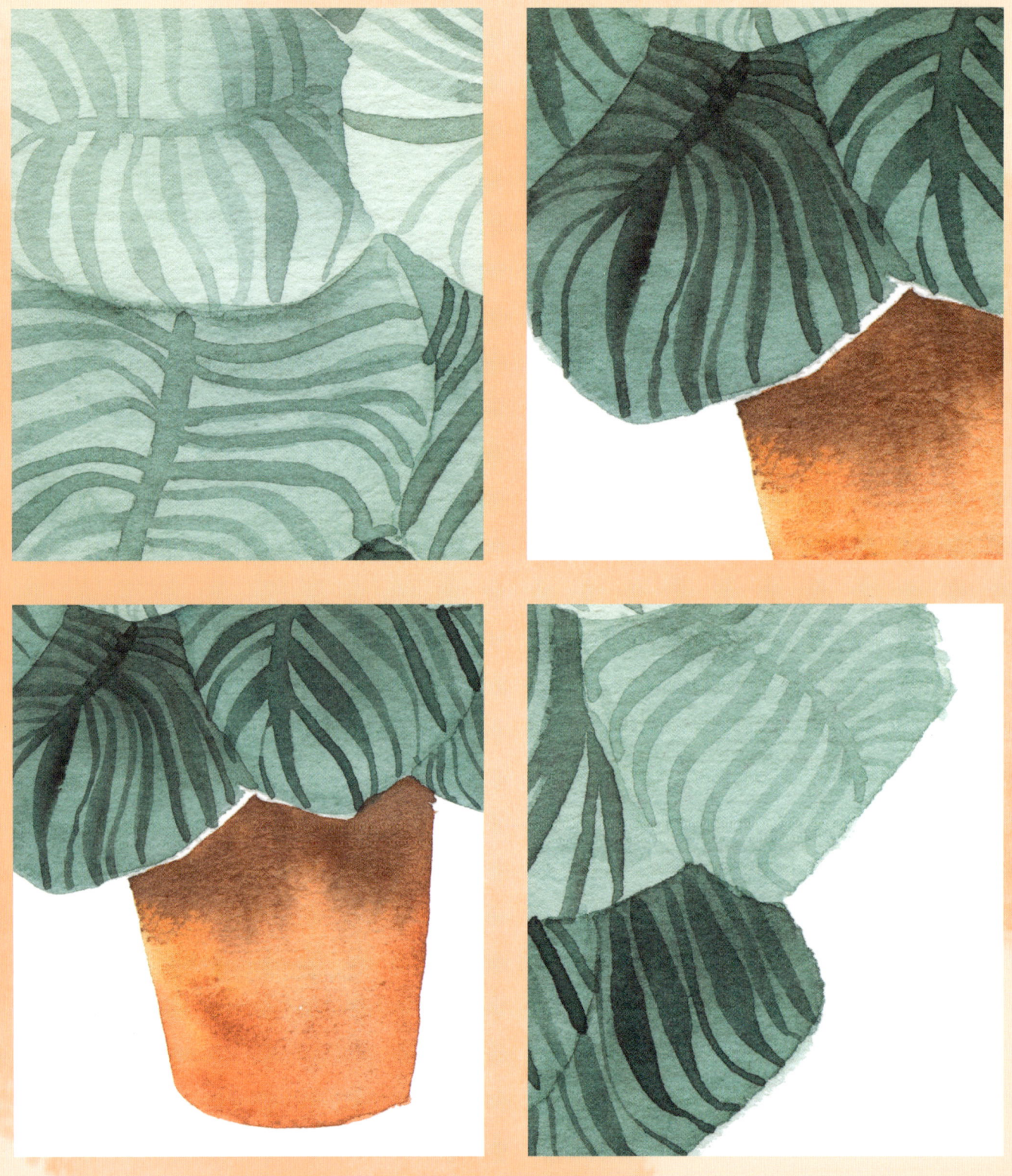

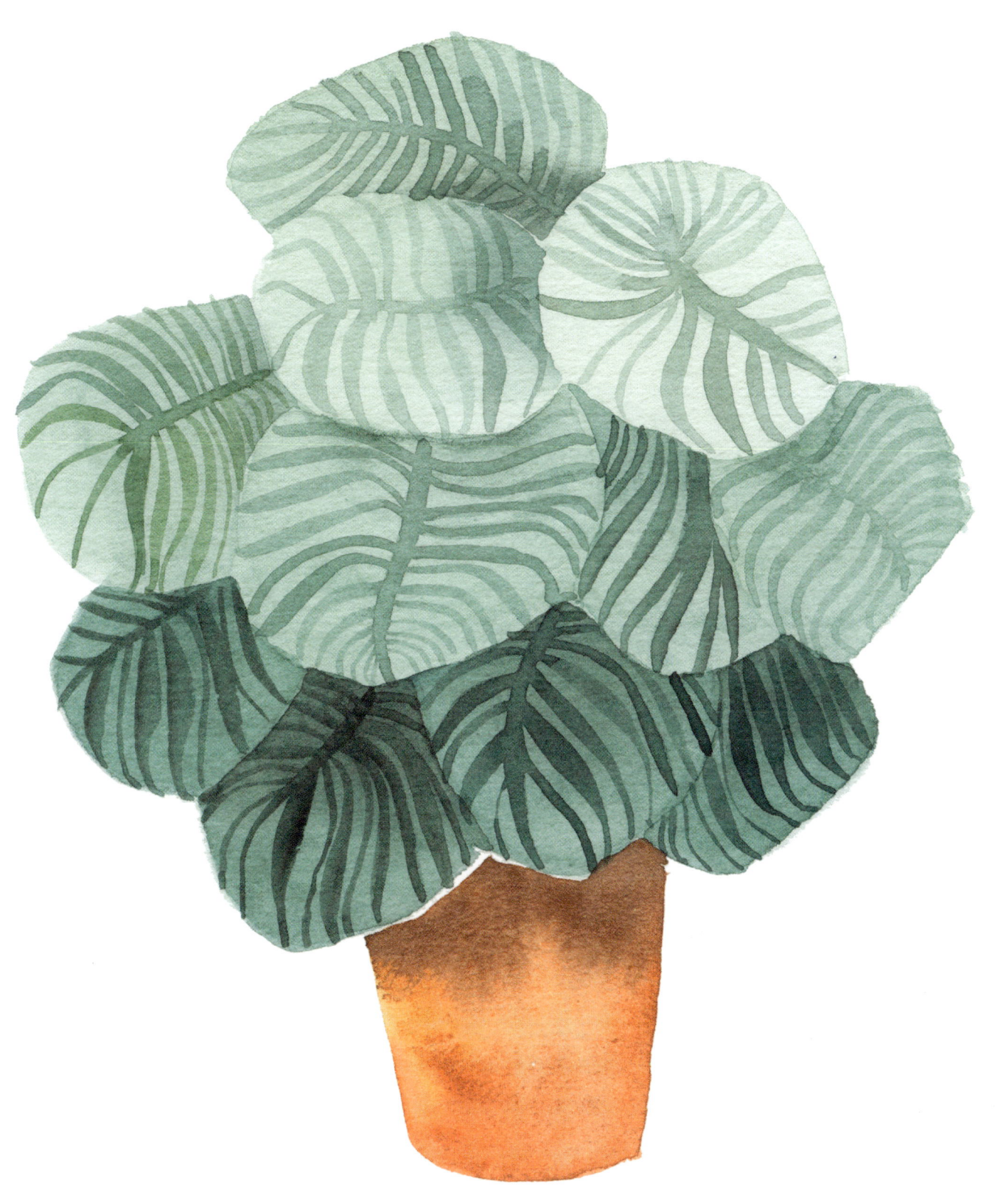

1 /

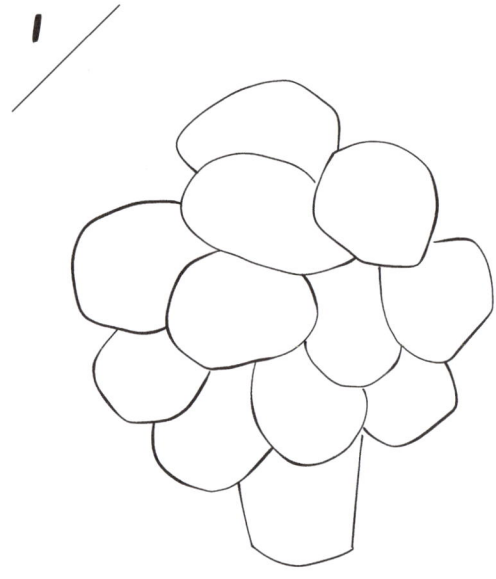

Start by lightly drawing the above sketch with a pencil or watercolor pencil. If you adapt it, take a photo of it on your phone as a reminder of what it looked like because it will disappear during the layering process.

2 /

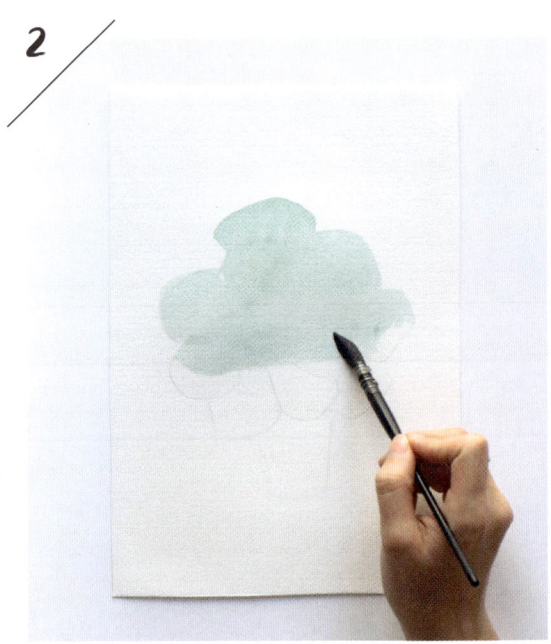

Fill in all the leaves evenly with a blue-green solution. Use the techniques shown in chapter 1 to avoid excess water (pages 19 and 29). Leave everything to dry (possibly assisted by a blow-dryer).

3 /

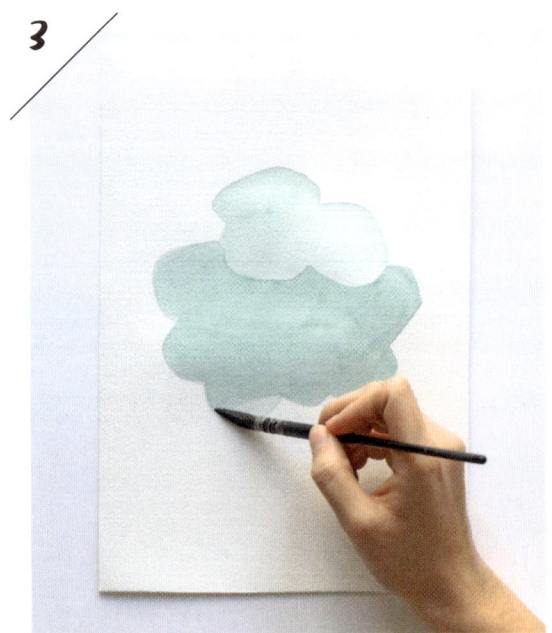

You are going to use the negative painting technique shown on page 34. Isolate the three leaves in section A and paint a blue-green layer on sections B and C.

4 /

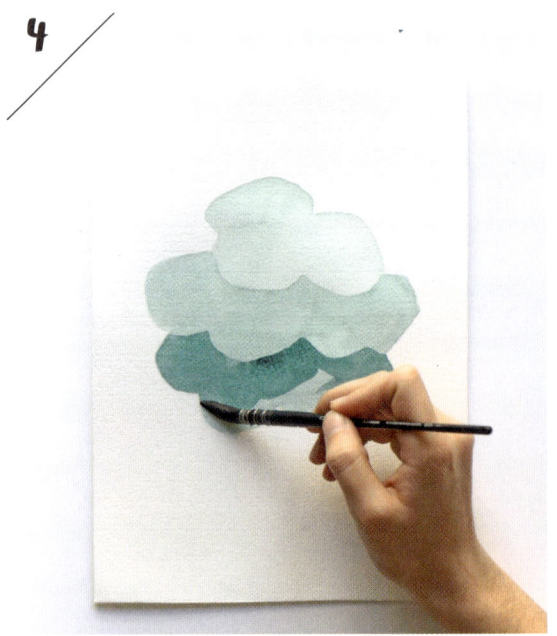

Once everything has dried, add another layer of more concentrated blue-green just to section C. This layering adds volume and depth to the plant.

5

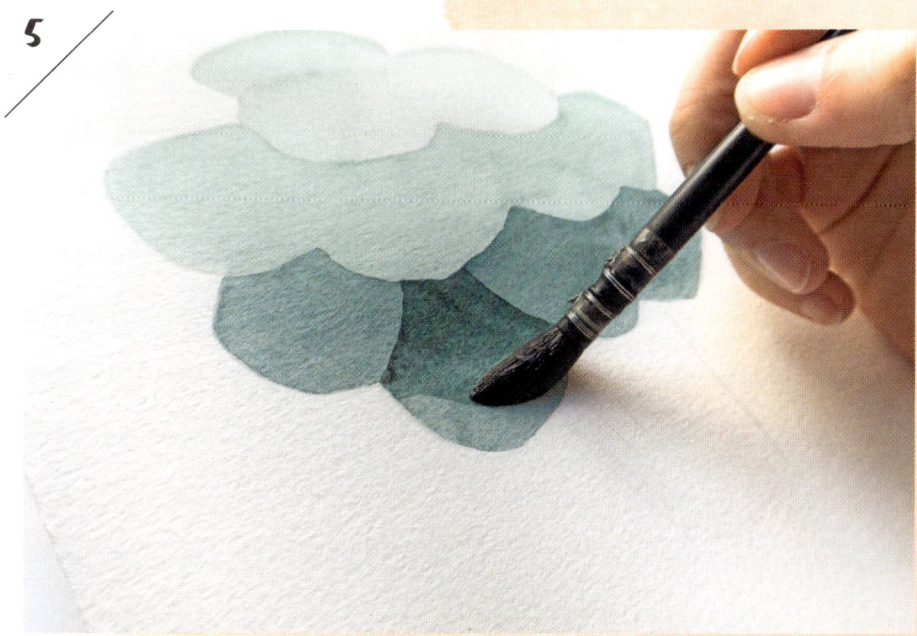

Once everything is dry, add the first shadow, starting with leaf 2. Without rushing, paint one leaf after the other by applying color to the border between section B and C, then creating a transparent gradation over the whole surface of the leaf (see pages 29 and 33).

6

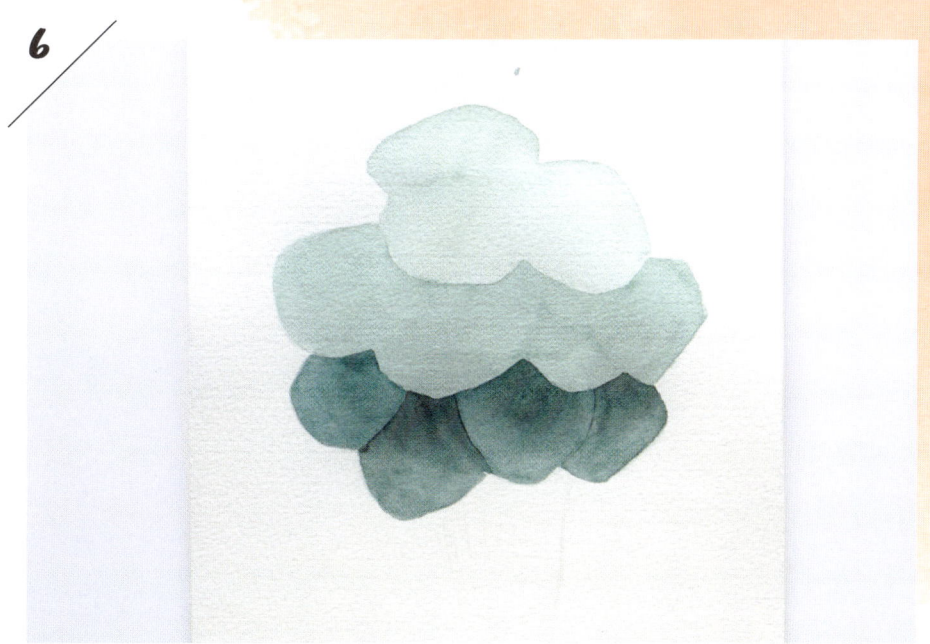

After leaf 2, paint the shadow on leaf 4. Wait for everything to dry before doing leaves 1 and 3. Wait for everything to dry again.

7

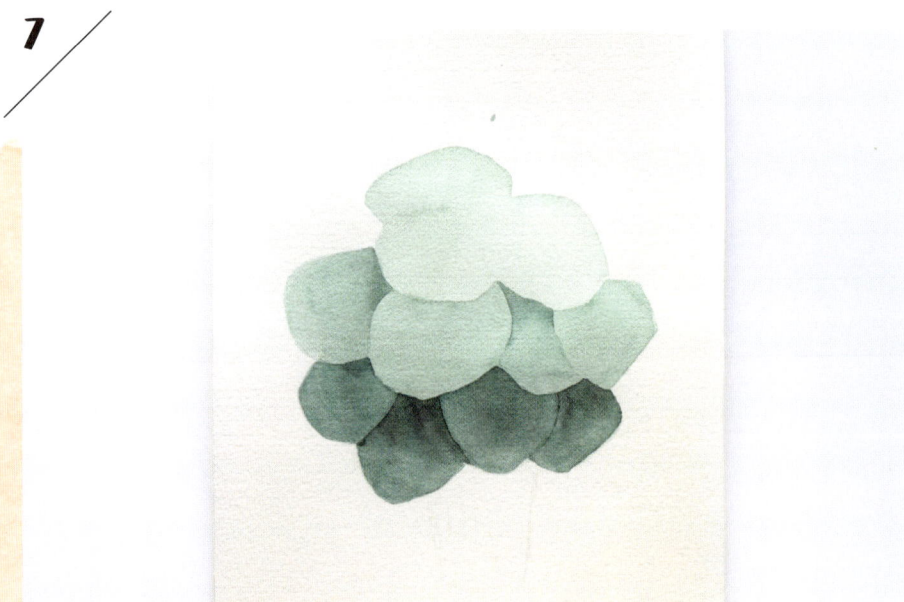

Continue painting shadows, leaf by leaf (5 and 7) working your way up with a blue-green solution.

8

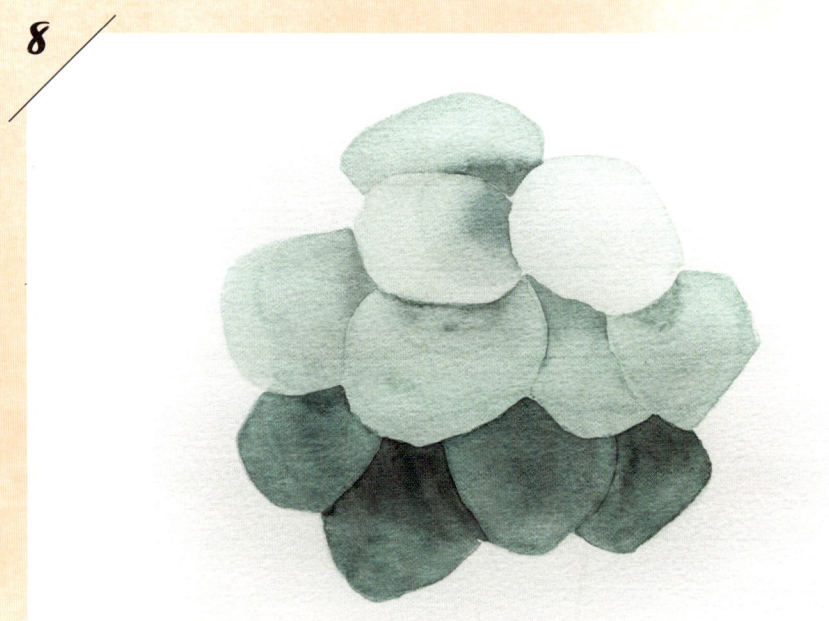

Finish the shadows on leaves 6, 8, 9 and 11 (leaf 10 has no shadow as it is the top one). I recommend you use a blow-dryer each time, to make sure everything is properly dry and doesn't smudge - this requires patience but the result is worth the wait.

9

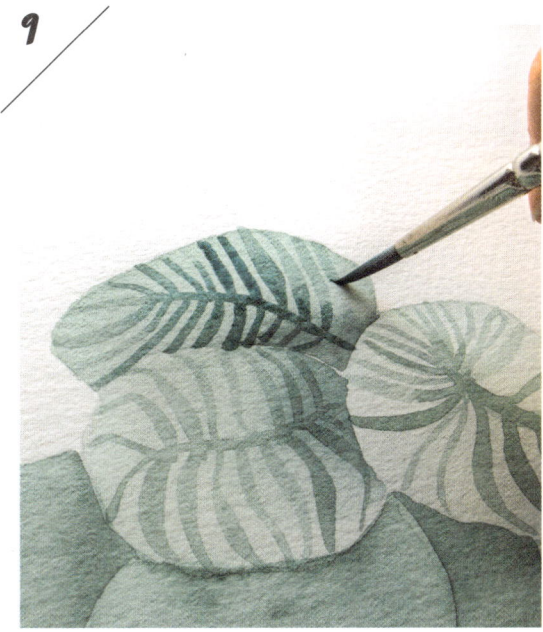

Now, for each leaf, paint the leaf vein and then the stripes. They are slightly curved, to give the impression of volume. Feel free to vary their thickness.

10

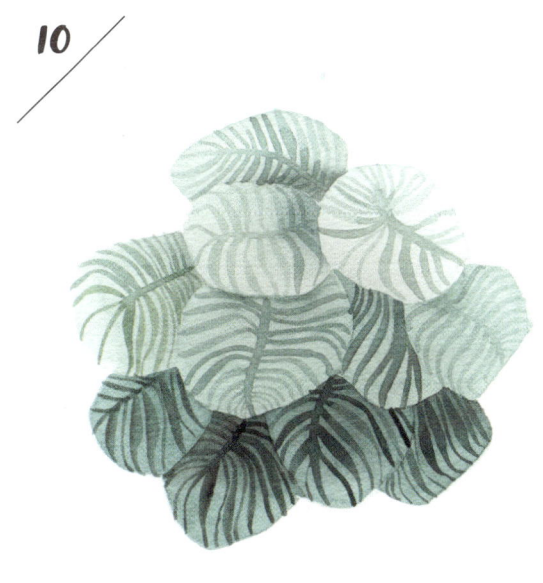

The stripes are painted using a solution with an increasingly high pigment concentration the nearer you get to section C. This accentuates the impression of volume.

11

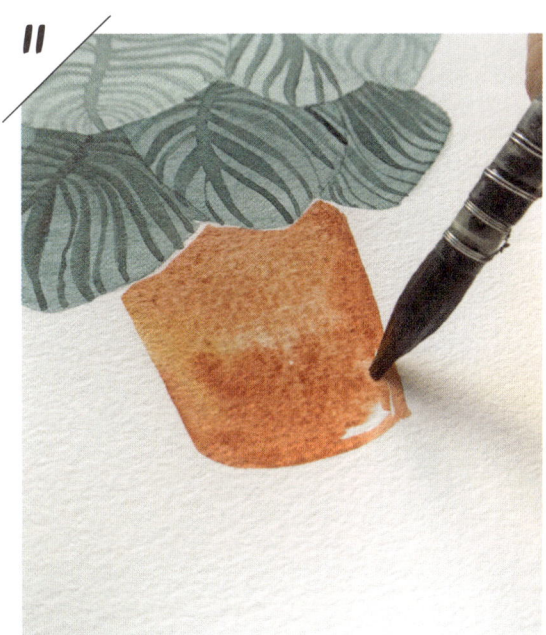

To finish off, paint the pot with an orangy mix. Use various shades of differing degrees of pink and brown to add more interest.

12

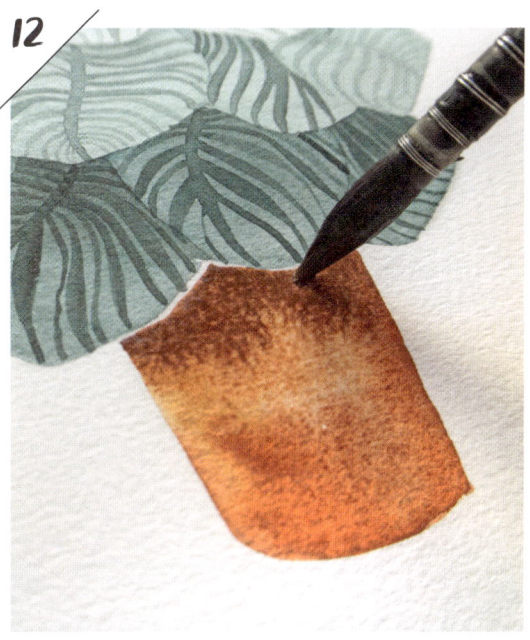

Finish the piece by adding dark brown pigment below the leaves to create a shadow.

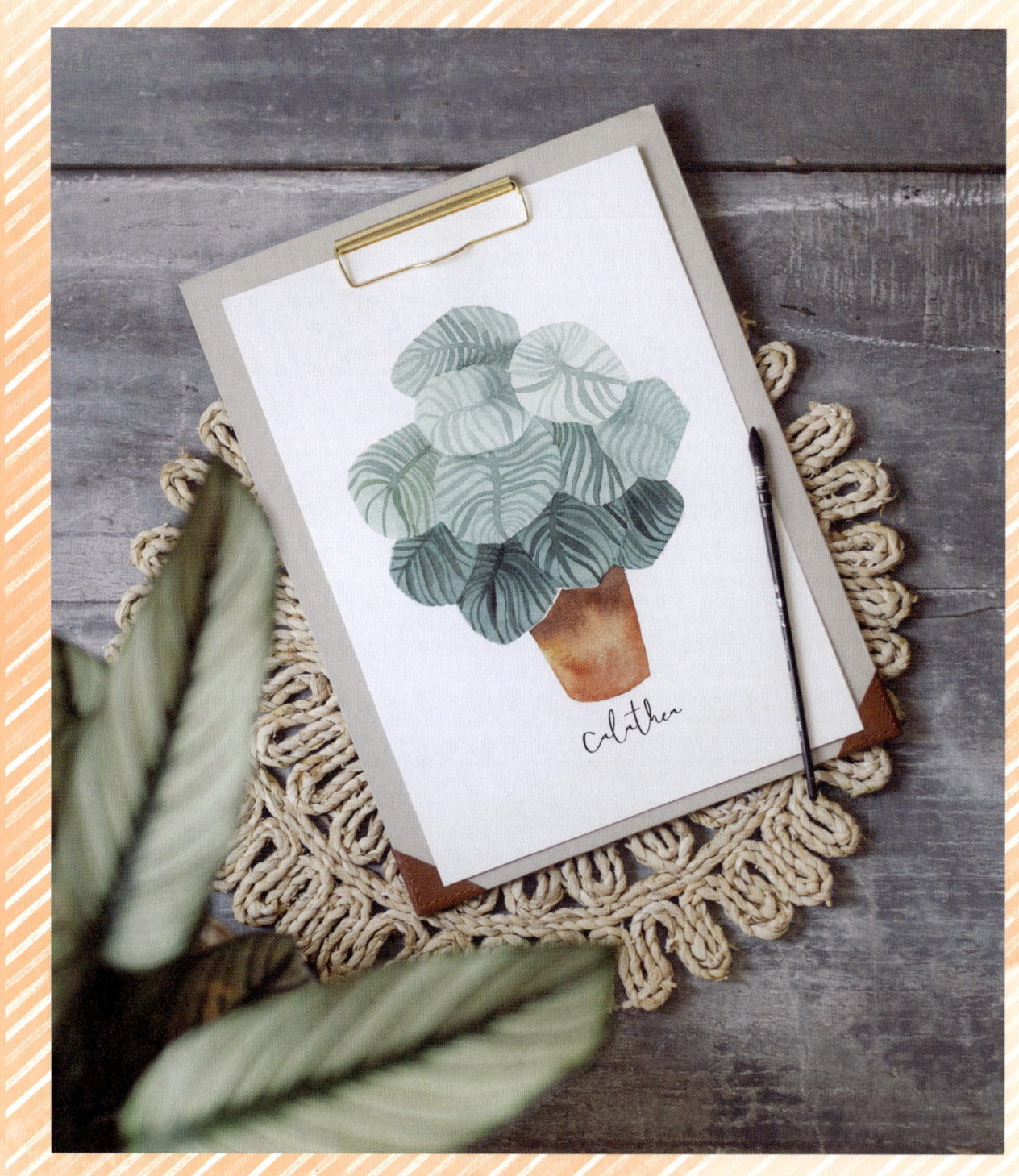

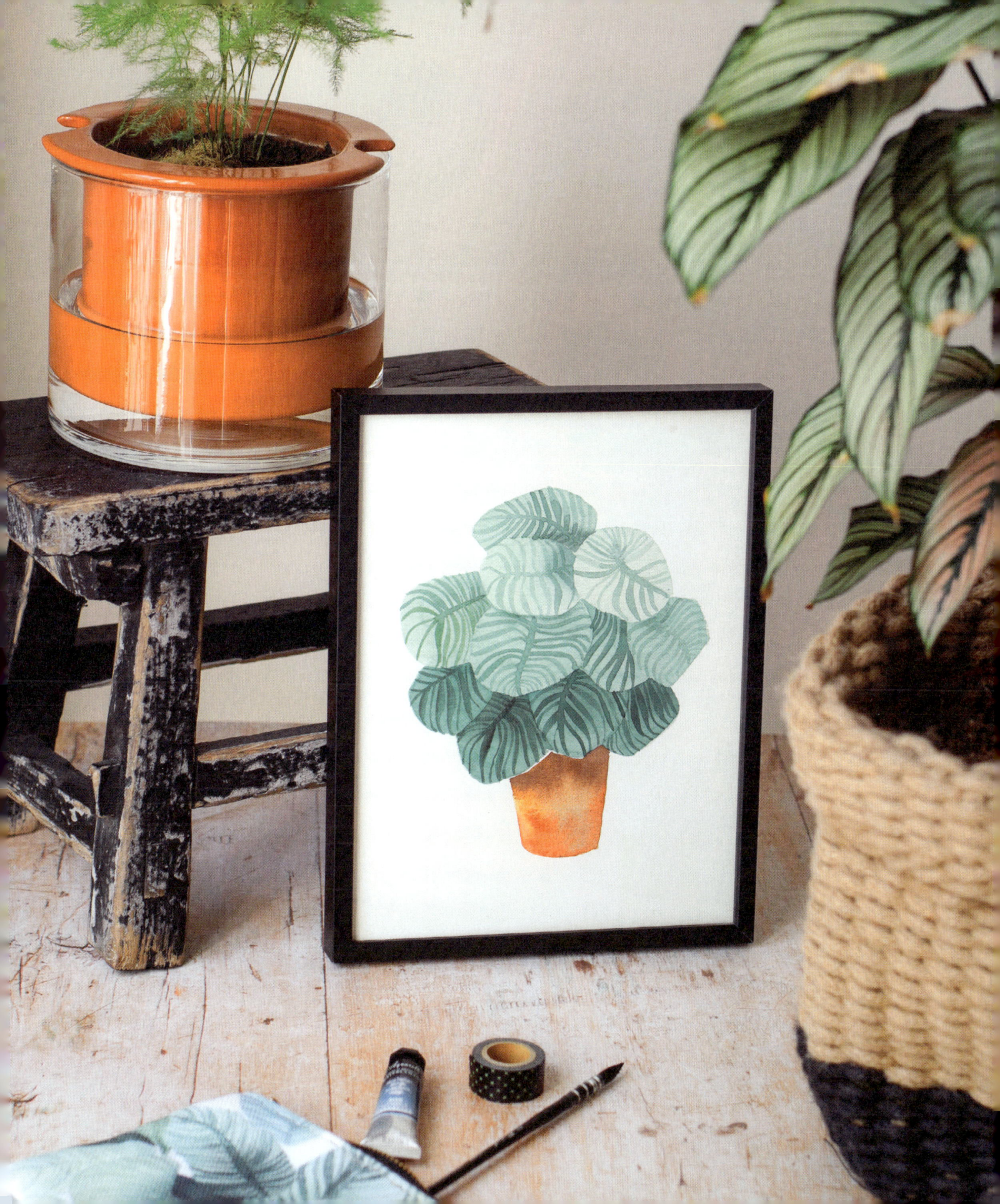

OTHER
ideas

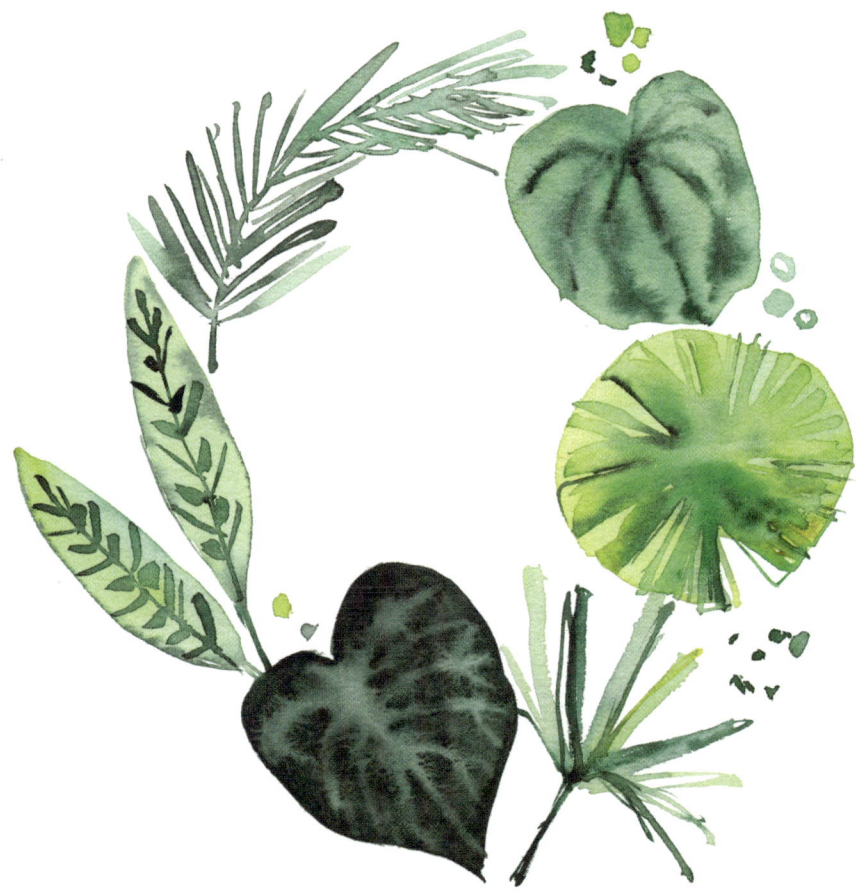

The tropical plants in this Urban Jungle Plants chapter lend themselves well to paintings in the form of a ring or a pattern, not just in a pot!

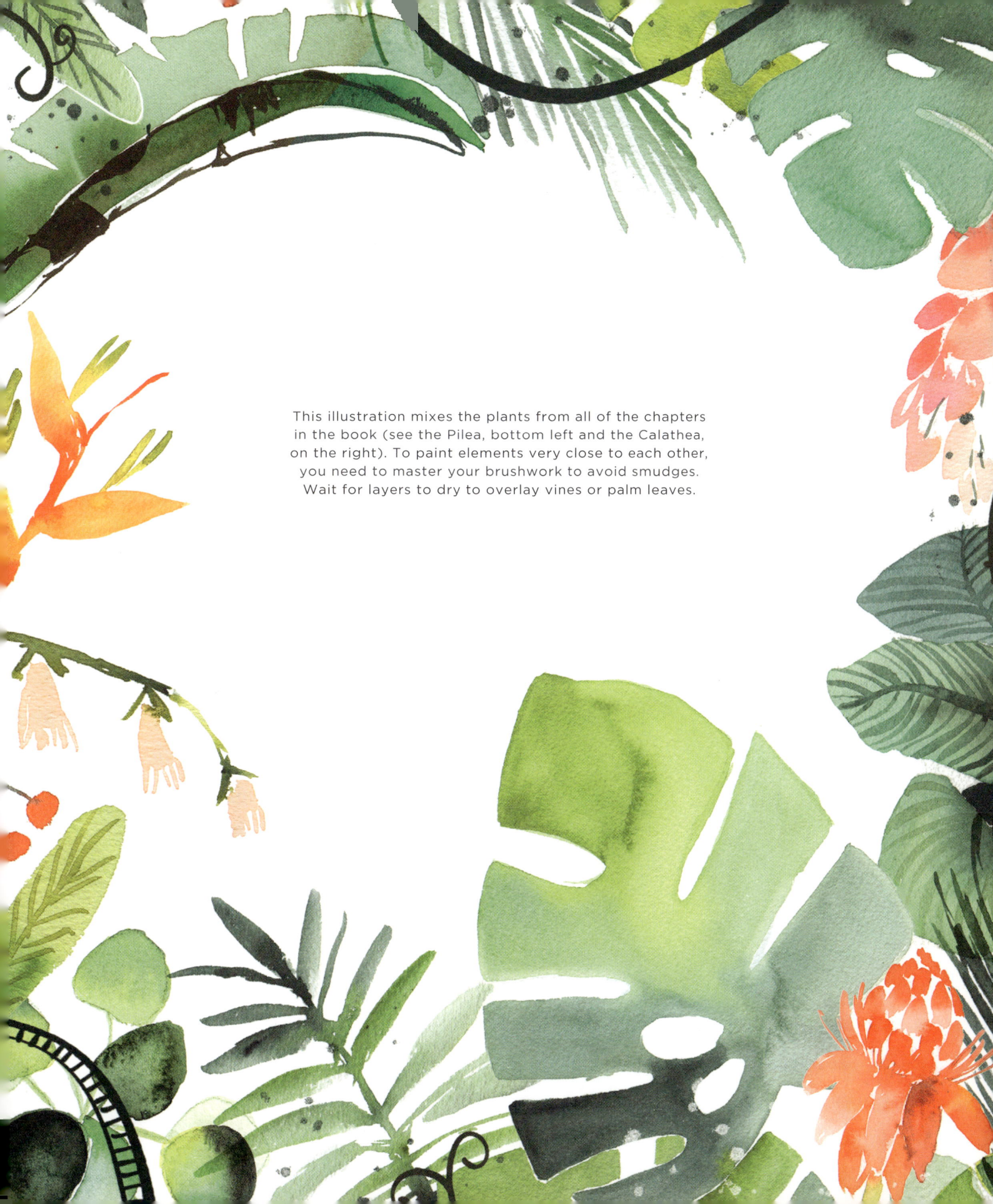

This illustration mixes the plants from all of the chapters in the book (see the Pilea, bottom left and the Calathea, on the right). To paint elements very close to each other, you need to master your brushwork to avoid smudges. Wait for layers to dry to overlay vines or palm leaves.

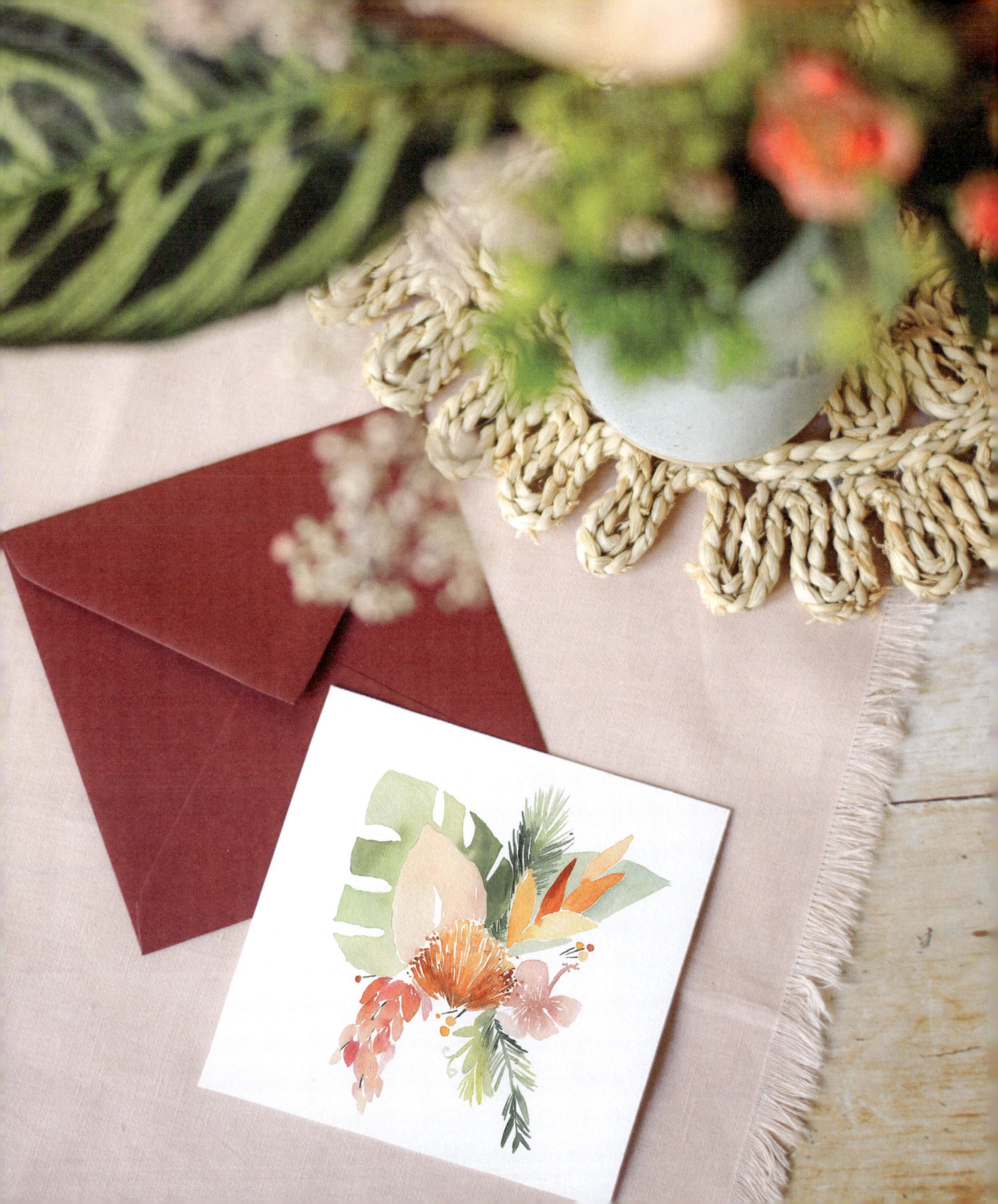

Index

A DAVID AND CHARLES BOOK
© Mango, Paris, France, 2019

Originally published in French as *Jungle à l'aquarelle* by Mango Editions
First published in the UK and USA in 2020 by David and Charles, Ltd

David and Charles is an imprint of David and Charles, Ltd
1 Emperor Way, Exeter Business Park, Exeter, EX1 3QS

A catalogue record for this book is available from the British Library.

ISBN-13: 978-1-4463-0813-4 paperback
ISBN-13: 978-1-4463-7965-3 EPUB

This book has been printed on paper from approved suppliers
and made from pulp from sustainable sources.

Printed in China by Asia Pacific Offset for:
David and Charles, Ltd
1 Emperor Way, Exeter Business Park, Exeter, EX1 3QS

10 9 8 7 6 5 4 3 2 1

David and Charles publishes high-quality books on a wide range of subjects.
For more information visit www.davidandcharles.com.

Layout of the digital edition of this book may vary depending on reader hardware and display settings.

UNDER THE SUPERVISION OF: Guillaume Pô
EDITORIAL DIRECTOR: Tatiana Delesalle
PUBLISHER: Hélène Raviart
ARTISTIC DIRECTOR: Chloé Ève
GRAPHICS AND LAYOUT: Caroline Soulères
PRODUCTION MANAGER: Thierry Dubus
PRODUCTION OFFICER: Audrey Bord
PHOTOENGRAVING: SNO

Thank you to Justine Jeannin and the team at the
wonderful plant shop (and hair salon!) What The
Flower in Paris, for allowing me to take photos.